D1447230

Socrates on Friendship and Community
Reflections on Plato's Symposium, Phaedrus, *and* Lysis

In *Socrates on Friendship and Community*, Mary P. Nichols addresses Kierkegaard's and Nietzsche's criticism of Socrates and recovers the place of friendship and community in Socratic philosophizing. This approach stands in contrast to the modern philosophical tradition, in which Plato's Socrates has been viewed as an alienating influence on Western thought and life.

Nichols' rich analysis of both dramatic details and philosophic themes in Plato's *Symposium, Phaedrus*, and *Lysis* shows how love finds its fulfillment in the reciprocal relation of friends. Nichols also shows how friends experience another as their own, and themselves as belonging to another. Their experience, she argues, both sheds light on the nature of philosophy and serves as a standard for a political life that does justice to human freedom and community.

Mary P. Nichols is professor of political science and department chair at Baylor University. She is the author of numerous books and articles in the history of political thought and in politics, literature, and film. Her main areas of research are classical political theory (for example, *Citizens and Statesmen: A Commentary on Aristotle's "Politics"*), Shakespeare, and film directors such as Woody Allen, John Ford, and Alfred Hitchcock. She is a senior Fellow at The Alexander Hamilton Institute for the Study of Western Civilization in Clinton, New York.

Socrates on Friendship and Community

Reflections on Plato's Symposium, Phaedrus, *and* Lysis

MARY P. NICHOLS

Baylor University

CAMBRIDGE
UNIVERSITY PRESS

CAMBRIDGE UNIVERSITY PRESS
Cambridge, New York, Melbourne, Madrid, Cape Town, Singapore,
São Paulo, Delhi, Dubai, Tokyo, Mexico City

Cambridge University Press
32 Avenue of the Americas, New York, NY 10013-2473, USA

www.cambridge.org
Information on this title: www.cambridge.org/9780521899734

First published 2009

A catalog record for this publication is available from the British Library

Library of Congress Cataloging in Publication data
Nichols, Mary P.
Socrates on friendship and community : reflections on Plato's Symposium, Phaedrus,
and Lysis / Mary P. Nichols.
p.   cm.
Includes bibliographical references and index.
ISBN 978-0-521-89973-4 (hardback)
1. Socrates.   2. Nietzsche, Friedrich Wilhelm, 1844–1900.   3. Kierkegaard, Søren,
1813–1855.   4. Love.   5. Friendship.   6. Plato. Lysis.   7. Plato. Phaedrus.
8. Plato. Symposium.   1. Title.
B317.N53 2009
177ʹ.62–dc22   2008018058

ISBN 978-0-521-89973-4 Hardback
ISBN 978-0-521-14883-2 Paperback

Contents

Acknowledgments   *page* VII

Introduction   1

1. The Problem of Socrates: Kierkegaard and Nietzsche   7
    Kierkegaard: Socrates vs. the God   8
    Nietzsche: Call for an Artistic Socrates   15
    Plato's Socrates   23

2. Love, Generation, and Political Community
    (The *Symposium)*   25
    The Prologue   31
    Phaedrus' Praise of Nobility   36
    Pausanias' Praise of Law   39
    Eryximachus' Praise of Art   44
    Aristophanic Comedy   47
    Tragic Victory   52
    Socrates' Turn   57
    Socrates' Prophetess and the Daemonic   59
    Love as Generative   64
    Alcibiades' Dramatic Entrance   70
    Alcibiades' Images of Socrates   72
    Alcibiades' Praise of Socrates' Virtues   79
    Aftermath   82
    The Incompleteness of the Symposium   86

3. Self-Knowledge, Love, and Rhetoric (Plato's *Phaedrus*)   90
    The Setting   95
    Non-Lovers (Lysias' Speech and Socrates' First Speech)   98

Souls and Their Fall   105
Lovers and Their Ascent   113
Prayer to Love   120
Contemporary Rhetoric and Politics   122
A Genuine Art of Rhetoric   136
Writing   142
Prayer to Pan   149

4. Who Is a Friend? (*The Lysis*)   152
Joining the Group   155
Getting Acquainted   162
Seeking a Friend   167
Are Friends the Ones Loving, the Ones Loved, or Both?   169
Are Likes Friends?   170
Are Unlikes Friends?   174
*Are Those Who Are Neither Good Nor Bad Friends
to the Good?*   177
Are the Kindred Friends?   183
Who Might Friends Be?   185
Friendly Communities   190

5. Socratic Philosophizing   195
Socrates' Youthful Search for Cause   197
Socrates' Second Sailing and the Ideas   202
Piety, Poetry, and Friendship   207

Works Cited   217
Index   223

Acknowledgments

I was first introduced to Socrates by my teacher, Joseph Cropsey, at the University of Chicago. Plato's *Gorgias* and *Phaedrus* were among the first dialogues I studied with him. The questions he raised about Socrates' relation to Plato, and the relation of both of them to poetry and philosophy, have guided my work throughout my career – in classical political thought and in politics, literature, and film. In his last class on the *Phaedrus*, after summarizing the dialogue's complex treatment of love and philosophy, rhetoric and speech, and Socrates and Plato, Mr. Cropsey acknowledged that it might be difficult for us to explain to our friends what we had learned in our course. I often thought of his words as I passed out student evaluations over the years. For some classes, the typical praise, "students learned a lot," is less appropriate than "students learned what they do not know." This is surely one of the ways in which I learned a lot from Joseph Cropsey, and how to me he became a model teacher. I hope that my interpretations of Socrates on friendship and community are true to this core of his teaching.

My work on the classical concept of friendship was first supported by a grant from the National Endowment for the Humanities in the mid-1990s, and more recently by the Earhart Foundation in 2004–05. My book is the fruit of this work. I am grateful to both foundations for their generosity, which gave me the opportunity to pursue this topic.

I thank the following publishers and publications that kindly gave me permission to use material from previously published articles of mine, and which I have expanded and incorporated into Chapters 2 and 4 of this book: *Political Theory* (SAGE Publications), *Polity* (Palgrave Macmillan), and *The Review of Politics* (Cambridge University Press). The original sources are cited in full in the chapter footnotes.

I am grateful to many friends who have discussed the questions of political thought with me for many years and who have taken the time to comment on all or part of this book in manuscript. Among them are Susan Benfield, Ronna Burger, Michael Davis, Carly Riisager, Denise Schaeffer, Natalie Taylor, and Catherine Zuckert. Zuckert's monumental work *Plato's Philosophers* (forthcoming from University of Chicago Press, 2009), and in particular her insights into the development of Socrates' thought, have been immensely helpful. Ronna Burger's detailed and thoughtful criticism of my entire manuscript, even (or especially) when she disagreed with me, has given me much food for thought and has improved the book in many ways. Harvey C. Mansfield made it possible for me to teach at Harvard University on several occasions, and to explore "The Problem of Socrates" with students there. I am grateful to both him and Harvard for this opportunity. I have been blessed with patient and persistent graduate students at Fordham and now at Baylor with whom I have developed many of the arguments in this book. Jenice Langston helped me with the index and assisted me in countless ways in my position of department chair at Baylor. Without her help it would have been impossible for me to do any other work during the last four years. I am grateful to all of these colleagues and friends for their efforts on behalf of my book.

Beatrice Rehl, my editor at Cambridge University Press, recognized the potential of my work from the beginning. Her keen judgment and steady hand supported this project at every stage. Ronald Cohen edited the manuscript with a deft hand and a light touch and helped polish the presentation. I thank both of them profoundly.

My husband, David Nichols, encouraged me to write this book, commented on and criticized the entire manuscript during the writing, and acted generously as my chief interlocutor throughout. It is my close relationship with him that has given me great confidence that the most important statements I make in this book are true.

Introduction

This book is about Socrates and the place that friends play in his life of philosophy. Through friendship we experience both our own as not wholly our own and another as not wholly other. It is such an experience, I argue, that characterizes philosophy. Only by experiencing our own as other do we become aware of our need or incompleteness that leads us to pursue wisdom; only by experiencing another as our own do we have any reason to suppose that learning is possible. This twofold character of friendship not only connects it to philosophy for Plato, but means that friendship can serve as a model for a political community where there is both a common bond among citizens and recognition of their separate identities. This view of Socrates and friends, with its implications for philosophy and political life, emerges from my analyses of Plato's *Symposium*, *Phaedrus*, and *Lysis*.

Since at least Hegel, however, Socrates has been presented less as a proponent of friendship than as an alienated and alienating figure, even when his freedom has been a source of admiration. This is true of the interpretations of both Kierkegaard and Nietzsche. Kierkegaard's *Philosophical Fragments* contrasts the universality of the truth to which Socrates led his interlocutors with the Christian demand for faith in a God who enters time or history.[1] Whereas Socrates presents philosophy as drawing us away from temporal life, the god redeems human life by becoming man himself.[2] Even more forceful in his criticism of Socrates, Nietzsche identifies the problem of Western civilization and its enthronement of

---

[1] Søren Kierkegaard, *Philosophical Fragments* (*PF*), ed. and trans. Howard V. and Edna H. Hong (Princeton: Princeton University Press, 1985).

[2] It is not until almost the end of the *Fragments* that it is stated that the "thought-project" is about Christianity, which "is the only historical phenomenon that . . . has wanted to base [the individual's] happiness on something historical," 109.

reason as "the problem of Socrates." In *Twilight of the Idols*, he claims that Socrates' "rationality at any price" means a denial of the instincts and ultimately a denial of life.[3] Just as Kierkegaard insists that the monastery is a medieval idea and that faith, in contrast, is "for this life,"[4] Nietzsche urges us "to remain faithful to the earth, and not [to] believe those who speak of other worldly hopes." The "way of the creator," in contrast to the otherworldly asceticism of Socrates, reveals "the meaning of the earth."[5]

In spite of Kierkegaard's and Nietzsche's attempts to present alternatives to the otherworldly alienation that they trace to Socrates, however, their influence on Western thought has not been in the direction of community. Because the highest appears in Kierkegaard's works as an incommunicable relation between the individual and the god, for example, it does not become manifest in communal life (see, e.g., *FT* 71 and 76–80). And Nietzsche's Zarathustra proclaims that "in the end one experiences only oneself" (*TSZ* 264). Under the influence of Kierkegaard and Nietzsche, the twentieth century to a large extent reduced religion to a leap into the absurd, on the one hand, and philosophy to arbitrary or willful creativity, on the other. Such turns to subjectivity, whether they be to an individual's private relation to God or to his own self-creations, undermine communal and hence political life as it has long been understood in Western thought. When reason no longer serves as a bond among human beings or as a means of discovering and implementing common purposes, alienation is as likely the result as the life-affirming challenges that Kierkegaard and Nietzsche intended to offer humankind.

My purpose in this book is to revisit their view of an "alienated" Socrates and to recover the place of friendship and community in Socratic philosophizing as an antidote to the alienating aspects of modern thought. We must look beyond the visions bequeathed to us by Kierkegaard and Nietzsche, I argue, to Plato's understanding of community as essential to human fulfillment.

[3] Friedrich Nietzsche, *Twilight of the Idols* (*TI*) in *The Portable Nietzsche*, ed. and trans. Walter Kaufmann (New York: Viking Penguin, 1954), 473–79.

[4] This is the way in which Kierkegaard's pseudonym Johannes de Silentio (John the Silent) describes Abraham's faith in *Fear and Trembling*(*FT*), ed. and trans. Howard V. and Edna H. Hong (Princeton: Princeton University Press, 1983), 20. According to Johannes, entering the monastery belongs to the Middle Ages rather than to faith, 98. While he expresses admiration for the "deep and earnest souls who found rest in the monastery," he claims that "to enter a monastery is not the highest," 100.

[5] This is the advice of Nietzsche's character Zarathustra in *Thus Spoke Zarathustra* (*TSZ*), in *The Portable Nietzsche*, 125 and 176–77.

At the same time, my study of friendship in the philosophic life of Plato's Socrates contributes to the contemporary scholarship on Plato. In *Love and Friendship*, for example, Allan Bloom argues that love and friendship "are distinctively human and inseparable from man's spirituality."[6] But while he gives the two equal place in his title, his work gives short shrift to friendship. Friendship differs from love in being necessarily reciprocal: one can love without being loved in return, whereas one can be a friend with another only if that other is one's friend. But according to Bloom, reciprocity is "missing from the Platonic understanding of love and friendship."[7] More generally in the scholarly literature on Plato, there is relatively little discussion of friendship as compared with love. Those interested in classical friendship are more likely to turn to Aristotle. My focus on friendship in my study of Plato's Socrates fills this lacuna. It is in part because of the place of friendship in his philosophic life, I argue, that Plato's Socrates offers an alternative to both Kierkegaard and Nietzsche.

As a point of departure for my study of Socrates and friends in Plato's dialogues, Chapter 1 begins with a brief examination of Kierkegaard's and Nietzsche's portrayals of Socrates. In the course of Kierkegaard's *Fragments*, Socrates becomes an example of someone whose understanding collides with the unknown, and in doing so encounters a gap between the temporal and the eternal that only the god – and faith – can bridge (*PF* 37–48). Socrates thus comes closer to Kierkegaard than it appears at the outset. In *The Birth of Tragedy*, Nietzsche, although seeking an artistic rather than a moral justification of the world, calls not for a rebirth of tragedy but for a new "artistic Socrates."[8] He hopes that the discipline required by Socratic rationalism will lead to the emergence of a new art or poetry whose need, he thinks, even the dying Socrates came to recognize (*BT* 93). Kierkegaard and Nietzsche thus find more in Socrates, their paradigmatic representative of Western rationalism, than the self-denying universalism or otherworldly asceticism than appears at first sight. Taking them as guides in Chapter 1, I examine Socrates' understanding of knowledge in Plato's *Meno*, to which Kierkegaard points us in *Philosophical Fragments*, and Socrates'

---

[6] Allan Bloom, *Love and Friendship* (New York: Simon and Schuster, 1993), 548.

[7] Bloom, *Love and Friendship*, 34.

[8] Friedrich Nietzsche, *The Birth of Tragedy* (*BT*), in *The Birth of Tragedy* and *The Case of Wagner*, trans. and commentary by Walter Kaufmann (New York: Random House, 1976), 92.

recourse to art or poetry in Plato's *Phaedo*, to which Nietzsche points us in *Twilight of the Idols*.[9] Kierkegaard and Nietzsche are correct to connect Socratic philosophizing with piety and poetry, even though their interpretations do leave Socrates alienated from friendship and political community.[10]

In Chapter 2, I turn to Plato's *Symposium*, where Socrates encounters the leading poets of Athens at the time, as well as its great political figure, Alcibiades, a man whom Socrates claims to have loved and whom he was accused of corrupting. Scholarly discussion of that dialogue emphasizes either Socrates' philosophic ascent along a "ladder of love" away from ordinary human life to beauty itself, or the tension between Socratic philosophy and political life, as Plato captures it in Socrates' relationship with Alcibiades. While not ignoring the difficulties in Socrates' relationship with Alcibiades and ultimately with the city of Athens, my reading of the *Symposium* focuses on Socrates' understanding of the human condition as both needy and resourceful. It is this position between lack and possession that is the basis of generation at all levels of human life. Love connects human beings to others through their desire to generate and nurture their offspring in political communities (*Symposium* 209a). As for Nietzsche, philosophic pursuit culminates in generation, but for Plato it is born from and strengthens our connections to others and to our political communities. The *Symposium* thus prepares for Socrates' connecting love to friendship and both to an art of rhetoric in the *Phaedrus*, which is the subject of Chapter 3.

Plato's *Phaedrus* examines love in the context of self-knowledge, including the extent to which self-knowledge is possible through our relations to others, and the role of "a true art of speaking" in generation and immortality (*Phaedrus* 260e and 276e–277a). Whereas for Kierkegaard the divine itself must descend to human beings if they are to learn the truth, Love serves to connect human and divine in the *Symposium*, and in the *Phaedrus* not only love but the individual beloved

---

[9] For a fuller examination of Kierkegaard's relation to Socrates, see Jacob Howland, *Kierkegaard and Socrates: A Study in Faith and Philosophy* (Cambridge, UK: Cambridge University Press, 2006). For a fuller examination of Nietzsche's relation to Socrates (and to Plato), see Catherine H. Zuckert, *Postmodern Platos* (University of Chicago Press, 1996), 10–32.

[10] See Howland's telling observation: "Both Kierkegaard and Climacus [Kierkegaard's pseudonym in *Philosophical Fragments*] tend to represent Socratic philosophizing as the heroically independent endeavor of a solitary individual," *Kierkegaard and Socrates*, 216.

plays this role.[11] If the beloved were reduced or subordinated either to the lover or to divinity, he could no longer do so. So too do our political communities, where we encounter a heterogeneity of human types, both like and unlike ourselves, reflect and thereby make accessible the truth about the whole.

Our relation to the truth, for Socrates, is a mediated one, whether he describes it in terms of loving another, as in his speech about love in the *Phaedrus*, or in terms of his conversing with different human beings and discovering the speeches appropriate to them, as he describes later in that dialogue. From Plato's *Lysis*, which is the subject of Chapter 4, we learn that love must be transformed into friendship to fulfill this promise. This dialogue begins with Socrates' encounter with the lover Hippothales, who asks for the philosopher's help in winning his beloved Lysis. Socrates offers to give him a demonstration of how to do so, while turning his discussion with Lysis to the question of what or who is the friend. Instead of demonstrating how to woo a beloved for Hippothales, Socrates demonstrates for a larger group listening in the palaestra how one becomes the friend of another. The *Lysis* shows that philosophy must be grounded in an experience analogous to friendship. In experiencing our own as other, as we do in friendship, we experience the strange in the familiar; in experiencing the other as our own, we experience the familiar in the strange. As Socrates says, philosophy begins in wonder (*Theaetetus* 155d): we have reason to think that we do not know; and we also have reason to trust that we might do so. Whereas the experience of alienation is only that of a distance between self and other, friendship offers an experience of a connection as well. That is why it can serve as the standard for a political life that does justice to both freedom and community.

Finally, in Chapter 5, I return to the *Phaedo*, where Socrates before his death gives an account of his philosophic development – his famous "second sailing," his own way of pursuing the truth when natural science fails to understand the place of human life within the whole, including the pursuit of the good. Socrates' new approach, he explains, involves "taking refuge in speeches," a way of inquiry that distinguishes him from pre-Socratic philosophy, and that entails his examination of opinions about what is good that underlie and are articulated in political life. In this context, Socrates gives an account of the ideas as causes that raises the question of how something that is separate can also be related

---

[11] I have capitalized Love whenever he is personified.

to something else (*Phaedo* 78b ff.). The problem of the ideas is the problem that comes to light in friendship itself, and underlies both the conflict and community found in political life. Socrates' search for a friend, which he announces in the *Lysis*, and his questioning how one becomes the friend of another, are expressions of his new approach to philosophy, which we understand as political philosophy. Because that approach understands difference or diversity as a condition for community rather than simply as a threat to it, Socrates can offer a remedy for modern alienation while preserving a fundamental place for the individualism central to modern thought and politics. It is for this reason that we can find a friend in Socrates.

1

The Problem of Socrates

Kierkegaard and Nietzsche

Kierkegaard gave his dissertation, *The Concept of Irony*, the subtitle, *With Continual Reference to Socrates*. In a way, this subtitle might characterize Kierkegaard's thought as a whole. *Stages on Life's Way*, for example, includes an imitation of Plato's *Symposium*, in which Socrates encounters representatives of Athens' intellectual and political life, and presents what he has learned about love.[1] *Fear and Trembling* presents Socrates as an intellectual tragic hero, in contrast to a knight of faith, while *Philosophical Fragments* explores faith as an alternative to the Socratic understanding of knowledge and truth. Kierkegaard's journals and papers have numerous and profound references to Socrates.[2] Nietzsche as well used Socrates as a point of departure for his own work. His first book, *The Birth of Tragedy*, presents Socrates as the turning point of world history.[3] And *Twilight of the Idols*, one of the last works that Nietzsche wrote, takes Socrates as an idol requiring a tuning fork to reveal his hollowness. He explains how Socrates "fascinated" the youth of Athens, but Nietzsche would be the first to admit that Socrates fascinated him as well, even if he regarded his own work "as a great declaration of war" against idols.[4]

One does not take as one's primary interlocutor someone for whom one has no affinity.[5] In this chapter, we shall explore the ways in which

---

[1] Søren Kierkegaard, "In Vino Veritas," in *Stages on Life's Way*, ed. and trans. Howard V. Hong and Edna H. Hong (Princeton: Princeton University Press, 1988), 7–86.

[2] Howland, *Kierkegaard and Socrates*, 209.

[3] Nietzsche, *Birth of Tragedy*, 96.

[4] Nietzsche, *Twilight of the Idols*, 465–66 and 478.

[5] According to Howland, Kierkegaard "felt himself to be the soulmate of [this] pagan Athenian who lived and died for philosophy," *Kierkegaard and Socrates*, 2. There is a substantial literature on Nietzsche's admiration for Socrates. See, for example, Walter Kaufmann's classic work on Nietzsche, in *Nietzsche: Philosopher, Psychiatrist, Antichrist*, 3d. ed. (Princeton: Princeton University Press, 1968), esp. ch. 13. As Nietzsche wrote,

Kierkegaard and Nietzsche point to a much more complex Socrates than their more obvious criticisms of his self-denying universalism and otherworldly asceticism suggest. Following Kierkegaard's lead in *Philosophical Fragments*, I discuss Socrates' understanding of knowledge in Plato's *Meno*. Then following Nietzsche's lead in *Twilight of the Idols*, I discuss Socrates' turn to art or poetry in Plato's *Phaedo*. Finally, I suggest that a more complete examination of Plato's Socrates, as I undertake through my analyses of the *Symposium*, the *Phaedrus*, and the *Lysis*, will reveal an understanding of the relation between philosophy and community that takes us beyond even Kierkegaard and Nietzsche.

KIERKEGAARD: SOCRATES VS. THE GOD

Kierkegaard is famous for criticizing the Hegelians of his day for their presumption of final and absolute knowledge made possible by the progressive development of mind or spirit in history. In *Fear and Trembling*, for example, Kierkegaard's pseudonym John the Silent attempts to cast doubt on the modern wisdom of those "unwilling to stop with faith," who presume that they have gone further. In "ancient days" it was different, for "faith was then a task for a whole lifetime." Ancient wisdom also understood doubting to be such a task, and "after all [the ancient Greeks] did know a little about philosophy." *Fear and Trembling* thus begins by pointing out that there are two alternatives to Hegelianism – faith and philosophical doubt. The work, however, turns its attention away from that "veteran disputant" of antiquity who "maintained the equilibrium of doubt," to Abraham, the Biblical father of faith (*FT* 6–7).[6]

Socrates, however, comes into his own in another of Kierkegaard's works, *Philosophical Fragments*, in which Kierkegaard adopts the pseudonym Johannes Climacus to explore a "Socratic question": "Can the truth be learned?" (*PF* 9). Socrates appears in that work not as the consummate doubter but as the advocate of the doctrine of recollection, the teaching that every human being has the truth within himself, but has forgotten what he once knew. Only if the truth is within each of us,

---

"Socrates, simply to confess it, stands so near to me, that I almost always fight a battle with him," quoted in Werner Dannhauser, *Nietzsche's View of Socrates* (Ithaca, NY: Cornell University Press, 1974), 15.

[6] Socrates returns briefly toward the end of *Fear and Trembling*, when its author presents him as an ironic figure whose elasticity toward his own life allows him to banter with his jury when he hears his death sentence (*FT* 117).

Socrates argues, could we come to know anything, for if we did not in some way already possess it, we would not even know what to seek, or whether we had found it (*PF* 9). The "teacher" in this view gives the learner nothing and his questions provide a mere occasion for the learner's recollection. Socrates therefore presents himself merely as a midwife, who draws out by his questioning what the learner has within himself, rather than as a teacher. To defend the possibility of philosophic inquiry, Socrates thus describes learning as recollection, and teaching as reminding. The latter is "the highest relation a human being can have to another" (*PF* 10). Plato's "enthusiasm" for Socrates, from which his dialogues were born, is from this perspective only an illusion, for the truth was in Plato and emerged from Plato: "The person who understands Socrates best understands specifically that he owes Socrates nothing" (*PF* 61). That Socrates or anyone else prompted his recollection of the truth is a historical accident, and can be of no concern with regard to eternal happiness (*PF* 12). The moment of recollection has no decisive significance, and should disappear in light of the eternal truth.

Consequently, Climacus concludes that for Socrates "every human is himself the midpoint" (that is, no intermediary is strictly speaking necessary between the learner and the truth) and "self-knowledge is God-knowledge" (for to know oneself is to know the truth, which every human soul possesses) (*PF* 11). From this Socratic perspective, as Climacus presents it, we all live with a view to eternity; our temporal lives are but the outer casings of our eternal selves, which it is our task to recover. Socrates is thus the advocate of reason, which grasps the truth latent in the human soul.

After presenting this Socratic understanding, Climacus turns to the alternative possibility that teaching rather than reminding occurs. In such a case, the truth is not previously possessed by the learner, but he acquires it from another. The teacher does not simply serve as an occasion for learning, as does the midwife Socrates, but gives to the learner what no human being possesses or can possess on his own. Someone who does this cannot be a human being. The teacher must be the god. That human beings lack the condition for understanding the truth, which they receive from the god in the moment of teaching, cannot be an accident, for the condition for the truth is an essential condition, nor could our lack be due to the god, for this would be a contradiction in the god. Human beings must be deprived of the condition for understanding the truth because of themselves. This state of untruth Climacus calls sin (*PF* 15).

"Consciousness of sin," which is a condition for understanding the truth, "only the god can teach," otherwise we would ourselves possess the condition or be able to obtain it from another (*PF* 47).

In the act of teaching, the eternal, the truth, comes to the learner at a moment in time, a moment that is of decisive significance for his eternal happiness, and in which he undergoes a radical change, a second birth. In this moment, there occurs "the eternalization of the historical and the historicizing of the eternal" (*PF* 61). This does not mean that in this moment the learner grasps an eternal truth. Doing so would be nothing more than the Socratic position, which holds that the truth is always accessible if the occasion is right. An eternal truth, by virtue of its being eternal, is *always* accessible to human understanding, at least in principle, even if it is forgotten and must be discovered. For the understanding to grasp an eternal truth, there can be no teacher, only a midwife. What is taught, in contrast, is not the eternal, but the paradox that the eternal becomes historical. Truth undergoes as radical a change as the learner. The god becomes man. The object of teaching and the act of teaching are therefore identical. The medium is the message, but only in this para-doxical case. This paradox must come from the god inasmuch as the understanding on its own could have never originated such a thought. We cannot be led to it by being questioned, for example, or understand it by reason. In fact, the paradox seems to be the downfall of the under-standing, which will therefore have objections to it (*PF* 47). If the understanding takes offense at the paradox, the encounter between the paradox and the understanding will become an unhappy one (*PF* 48). Only when the paradox is accepted by the learner in faith is the encounter happy (*PF* 59). Nor is there any way for a believer to give or teach the truth he has received from the god to another, for the truth is that the god has become the teacher (*PF* 99–101). Only when the god teaches the learner does he encounter the paradox, and is faith possible.

Socrates' position thus serves as the foil in the *Fragments* for the position that the truth is paradoxical, or beyond reason. A radical dichotomy between understanding and faith emerges from these alternative answers to the question of whether the truth can be learned (*PF* 9–22). This dichotomy between Socrates and the god, with which *Philosophical Fragments* begins, however, is qualified as the work pro-ceeds.[7] In the third of the book's five chapters Climacus tells us that

---

[7] See Howland's *Kierkegaard and Socrates* for an excellent discussion of this aspect of *Philosophical Fragments*.

Socrates himself, the "connoisseur of human nature" who made the pursuit of self-knowledge his calling, becomes bewildered about himself when he "came up against the different": he no longer knows, as he admits in Plato's *Phaedrus*, whether he is a more furious monster than the dragon-headed Typhon or a gentler and simpler animal sharing a divine lot (*Phaedrus* 229e; *PF* 37). Although Socrates still lacks the consciousness of sin (*PF* 47), he has too much intellectual honesty to delude himself that he can be simply at home in the eternal. There is no simple equation, then, for Socrates of self-knowledge with God-knowledge, and the doubter of *Fear and Trembling* makes an appearance in the *Fragments*. In the sequel he wrote to the *Fragments*, Climacus confirms this when he admits that Socrates "continually parts with [the thesis of recollection], because he wants to exist."[8] It is "in relation to an existing person," he explains, that "truth becomes a paradox" (*CUP* 199).[9] This must be why doubt for Socrates is "a task for a lifetime."

The author of the *Fragments* himself moves back and forth as he investigates the different alternatives he presents, and so does not speak simply from either perspective. His work, moreover, is a "thought-project," and appears as a work of reason rather than of faith. On the other hand, Climacus questions how he could be the source of his own thought-project, when he imagines an interlocutor who engages him in good-natured banter, who accuses him of plagiarizing and of claiming as his own what belongs only to the deity (*PF* 35–36). His self-questioning and his engaging in dialogue remind us of Socrates.

Climacus' exchanges with his interlocutor discuss not only the possibility that he is robbing the deity, but the possibility that he is plagiarizing "the whole human race" – and thus claiming as his own what belongs to humanity as such (*PF* 35). Curiously, there is yet a third possible source of Climacus' plagiarism – the single individual or, indeed, a number of individuals whom the interlocutor mentions – from Luther, to Shakespeare, to Tertullian (*PF* 35 and 53). And although he states at the outset of the *Fragments* that he does not know what served as the occasion for his questioning as to whether the truth can be learned, as soon as he starts discussing it he claims it is "a Socratic question" and refers us to the *Meno* in particular.

---

[8] Kierkegaard, *Concluding Unscientific Postscript* (*CUP*), ed. and trans. Howard V. Hong and Edna H. Hong (Princeton: Princeton University Press, 1982), 201n.

[9] Howland discusses the *Concluding Unscientific Postscript*'s treatment of Socrates, *Kierkegaard and Socrates*, 188–208.

The *Meno*, however, begins not with the question of whether the truth can be taught (or learned), but whether virtue can be taught (*Meno* 70a). Only later does the discussion arrive at the issue of knowledge and how it comes to be (*Meno* 80d ff.). Climacus slides the question of virtue into that of knowledge, inasmuch as Socrates defines virtue as knowledge (*PF* 9), but the *Meno*, at least structurally, does not collapse the two questions. Moreover, readers of the *Meno* will remember that while the dialogue begins with the question of whether virtue can be taught, it is one raised by Meno, and rejected by Socrates, who insists that one must first investigate what virtue is before inquiring how it is acquired (*Meno* 70a–71b). How virtue comes to be – its beginning – is not the proper beginning for an inquiry into virtue (see also *Laches* 190c–e).

When Meno tries to define virtue as ruling others, Socrates points out that Meno has given only one example, and not what all the instances of virtue have in common, or what defines virtue (*Meno* 71e–73d). Frustrated by the discussion, Meno presents what Climacus calls the "pugnacious proposition" that inquiry is not possible – we cannot seek what we do not know, for we would not know either what to seek or when we had found it (*Meno* 80d). Presumably unaware (see *Meno* 81e–82a), Meno has turned the discussion away from Socrates' "what is" question to another "how it comes to be" question, this time about knowledge. In order to defend inquiry, Socrates turns to the sayings of "wise men and women," priests and priestesses, and poets such as Pindar, who say that the human soul is immortal, comes to an end and is reborn, has seen all things here and in Hades, and thus can recollect what it knew before about virtue and other things. Socrates attributes to priests, priestesses, and poets the view that, in Climacus' language, the god is not necessary for human beings to acquire the truth. Their teaching undergirds our search for truth, and Socrates can answer Meno: because "all nature is akin," by recollecting one thing we can recollect the rest, if we do not tire in our search (*Meno* 81b–c). Since we "always" knew (and have forgotten), there is no coming into being of knowledge, and Socrates has dismissed another of Meno's questions about genesis.

Socrates demonstrates this theory of recollection by questioning Meno's slave boy about how one might derive a square that is double the size of another one (*Meno* 82b–86b). Inasmuch as Socrates' successful attempt to elicit the diagonal of a square from the slave boy follows his unsuccessful attempt to elicit an answer about virtue from Meno, the action of the dialogue does not bear out the proposition that "the truth about things that are is always in our soul," as Socrates concludes

(*Meno* 86b). Far from demonstrating that "every human being [is] universal man," as Climacus says (*PF* 38), or that the questioner is not, theoretically speaking, necessary to another's coming to possess the truth, the *Meno* indicates that everything depends on the questioner's choice of questions and the character of his interlocutor. Meno asked his question about virtue without any sense that he lacked it, as indicated by his "fearless and magnificent" answers characteristic of his associate Gorgias (*Meno* 70b–c). And his question about inquiry, should it stand unanswered, would put an end to inquiry. Because Meno is as indifferent to the truth as he is to virtue, Socrates' choice of a mathematical proposition to answer his objection to learning is an appropriate one. As Climacus says in another context, "in a mathematical proposition, the objectivity is given, but therefore its truth is also an indifferent truth" (*CUP* 294). Meno asked about virtue, but might just as well have asked about math. Whether virtue can be recollected in the same way as mathematical propositions is another matter.

When Meno insists on returning to his original question – how virtue comes to be for human beings – Socrates yields (*Meno* 86c–d). The question about knowledge does not determine the question about virtue, at least in the *Meno*.[10] Even if we possess the truth for all eternity, our coming to possess virtue remains an open question. The possession of knowledge does not imply our possession of virtue. Moreover, in agreeing to pursue Meno's question about how virtue comes to be, rather than the question of what virtue is, Socrates acknowledges his limits – if he ruled Meno as he does himself, Socrates says, their inquiry would concern the question that he, Socrates, proposes (*Meno* 86d). Far from leading Meno to agreement between the two of them, or reminding Meno of what he once knew and has forgotten (see also *Meno* 71d and 76b), Socrates cannot even produce agreement with his interlocutor on the question to be asked.

Socrates and Meno do draw a conclusion from their discussion, one that looks surprisingly like a position that Climacus presents in the *Fragments* – namely, that virtue (or, in Climacus' formulation, the truth) cannot be taught precisely because those who possess it are incapable of giving it to others. Virtue when it comes to human beings therefore comes from the god (*Meno* 99b–100a). Consideration of the *Meno* does not only provide the occasion for Climacus' question, but even for the

---

[10] See also Kierkegaard, *Soren Kierkegaard's Journal and Papers*, ed. and trans. Howard V. Hong and Edna H. Hong (Bloomington: Indiana University Press, 1967–68), I, 463.

alternatives that his "thought-project" explores. Socrates thus plays a larger role in Climacus' thought-project than Climacus indicates. And inasmuch as Socrates acknowledges his limits in ruling Meno, and therefore pursues Meno's question, he acknowledges the inadequacy of his "what is" questions to human life. Meno's name means literally "what remains." The *Meno* is about what remains after one answers the "what is" questions. Meno's question of how one acquires virtue rather than what virtue is turns out to be Socrates' question as well, even if Socrates insists that one must begin with the "what is" question in order to arrive at the more personal one. Although Climacus seems to confuse Socrates and Meno at the outset of the *Fragments* by attributing Meno's question to Socrates, in this deeper sense Climacus is correct when he claims that the question of coming into being is a Socratic one. The *Meno* is about the inadequacy of the theory of recollection, understood in the sense of "universal man."

When Climacus first refers to the meeting of the understanding and the paradox as a "happy" one rather than an "unhappy" relation of offense (*PF* 49), he does not immediately give the happy encounter a name. In fact, he admits that he "must simply try to find a name for it" (*PF* 48; see also 54). Only later does he assign to this "happy passion" the name of "faith" (*PF* 59). As Climacus discusses, Socrates discovers that he does not understand himself when he confronts the difference between himself and the truth. Yet Socrates does not take offense at the unknown. Plato, in fact, implicitly contrasts Socrates with the guardians of the *Republic*'s city, who treat those whom they know as friends and those whom they do not know as enemies (*Republic* 376a–b). Socrates' love of wisdom is a happy (i.e., non-offensive) encounter with the unknown.

As the preface to *Fear and Trembling* suggests, we are left with a dichotomy not so much between philosophy and faith as between a presumption of reason's finality and an awareness of human incompleteness. That awareness emerges for both Socrates and Kierkegaard from reflection on the attempt to know the truth. For the Hegelians, in contrast, there is no essential incommensurability in human life. Inasmuch as spirit fully realizes itself in history, there is no interiority that must or can remain hidden, whereas "faith is the paradox that interiority is higher than exteriority," according to the pseudonymous author of *Fear and Trembling* (*FT* 68–69, 82). In fact, faith can never become manifest in the external world. John the Silent knows that if he could find a "knight of faith" he would look "just like a tax collector!" There is "not a crack through which the infinite would peek," nothing that "betrays the infinite in its heterogeneity with the finite" (*FT* 38). Knowledge of the world does not yield knowledge of ourselves, just as Meno's question about virtue is not decided by Socrates' answer about learning. When Socrates becomes aware that he does not know whether he is a monster more furious than Typhon or a gentler, simpler animal sharing a divine lot, something essential to who or what he is remains unknown.

NIETZSCHE: CALL FOR AN ARTISTIC SOCRATES

Kierkegaard discloses a hiddenness not only in the knight of faith and in Plato's Socrates, but also in the poet. At the outset of *Either/Or*, the poet is described as "an unhappy person who conceals profound anguish in his heart but whose lips are so formed that as sighs and cries pass over them they sound like beautiful music." The poet's inner tortures can never be communicated to others, for his sufferings are heard only as sounds of joy. Others, hearing only the music on the poet's lips and not seeing the anguish in his heart, ask him to continue his singing.[11] For Kierkegaard, however, there is an alternative to this suffering poet, as we have seen. Whatever terrors faith holds insofar as it is invisible and incommunicable to the outside world (e.g., *PF* 70 and *FT* 74–79), faith is a *happy* encounter with the unknown. The true joy of faith serves for Kierkegaard as an alternative response to the only apparent joy of poetry.

In his *The Birth of Tragedy*, Nietzsche too presents poetry as born out of the transformation of inner suffering into an outer form that hides the suffering (*BT* 21). Indeed, the world itself is the poetry of a god in pain, made bearable by his creation of a world of appearance that distracts him from his pain. His inner torment appears even to himself as sounds of joy. In Nietzsche's words, the god "finds salvation in appearance" (*BT* 22). The thought appears in *Zarathustra* as well, when Zarathustra explains that he used to suppose that the world was created by a suffering god who wanted to look away from his suffering. Now Zarathustra recognizes that it is humanity itself that creates gods in order to look away from its suffering. It is thus that the "otherworldly" create "other worlds" (*TSZ* 143). And in *The Birth of*

---

[11] Kierkegaard, *Either/Or*, ed. and trans., with introduction and notes, Howard V. Hong and Edna H. Hong (Princeton: Princeton University Press, 1987), 19.

Tragedy, Nietzsche claims that the Greeks had to create the Olympian gods from a most profound need in order to endure "the terror and horror of existence" (*BT* 42).

Inasmuch as the outer appearance serves as a distraction from inner suffering, Nietzsche denies in *The Birth of Tragedy* the Hegelian view that inwardness can become fully expressed in the external world, as did Kierkegaard. Moreover, Nietzsche also presents Socrates, at least initially, as the paradigmatic expression of the Western rationalism that culminates in Hegel – the hostility to life expressed in the superficial equation of virtue, knowledge, and happiness (*BT* 91 and *TI* 478; see *FT* 55). Like Kierkegaard, Nietzsche tries to find a way to recover an inwardness or depth that he thinks contemporary philosophy has obscured. He also understands the effects of Hegel on the human soul: the "last men" Zarathustra describes, beings without love or longing who "know everything that has ever happened" (*TSZ* 129–30), resemble the children of the epilogue of *Fear and Trembling*, who play all the games before the day is over, and can find nothing else to do with themselves (*FT* 122). Both Kierkegaard and Nietzsche undertake the challenge of finding a way to save human life from decadence by presenting challenging tasks yet to be accomplished (e.g., *FT* 122–23 and *TSZ* 128 and 136–37). For Kierkegaard, as we have seen, faith is a task "for a lifetime," not something to be completed before the clock strikes twelve. And Nietzsche, in *The Birth of Tragedy*, seeks a "purely artistic" evaluation of life, which justifies "the existence of the world . . . only as an aesthetic phenomenon," which takes art, not morality as "the truly *metaphysical* activity of man" (*BT* 22 and 24, emphasis Nietzsche's). Where Kierkegaard turns to faith, Nietzsche, at least in *The Birth of Tragedy*, turns to art.

Nietzsche begins *The Birth of Tragedy* by contrasting the Greek gods Apollo and Dionysus. Apollo is the Greek god of light, or, as Nietzsche says referring to the etymology of his name, "the shining one." Apollo is the god of things that can be seen, and hence of appearances, and shapes, boundaries, or forms. Nietzsche refers to Apollo as "the god of individuation and of just boundaries" (*BT* 72). Appearance is absolutely necessary for life, but it is still appearance. And so Apollo is the god of "beautiful illusions," the god of dreams (*BT* 34). Underlying this dream world is the Dionysian, which represents the undifferentiated being that the appearances hide or conceal. Contact with the Dionysian involves the breakdown of form and individuality and thus provokes fear and terror, and even that sense of the divine that we might call awe (*BT* 40). While the Dionysian is hidden by the appearances, it does not remain hidden, for "it is as if [nature] were heaving a sigh at its dismemberment into individuals" (*BT* 40). In contrast to faith as John the Silent describes it, we glimpse the infinite.

One way in which the Dionysian heaves a sigh and thus reveals itself is in Greek tragedy, for the tragic hero becomes a representation on stage of Dionysus himself. Nietzsche offers the example of Oedipus as a revelation of Dionysus in Greek tragedy, for Oedipus tries to become one with his origins through patricide and incest, at the same time as his answer to the riddle of the Sphinx reveals the sameness underlying different manifestations of human life in time. "Oedipus, the murderer of his father, the husband of his mother, and the solver of the riddle of the Sphinx! What does the mysterious triad of these fateful deeds tell us?" Nietzsche exclaims (*BT* 68). Nietzsche also mentions Euripides' last play, the *Bacchae*, which brings the god Dionysus on stage and pits him against Pentheus, the ruler of Thebes. Pentheus is the Apollonian man who defends the boundaries of the city against the worship that Dionysus demands. But his secret attraction toward Dionysus leads him to spy on the bacchants in the woods outside the city, and as a result leads to his own destruction (*BT* 81–82).

Dionysus, however, meets his match when he encounters Socrates, "an opponent of tragic art" and "the prototype of the theoretical optimist" (*BT* 67, 87, and 97). "The Socratism of morality, the dialectics, frugality, and cheerfulness of the theoretical man" is "that of which tragedy died" (*BT* 18). Nietzsche's exploration of the relation between Dionysus and Apollo sets the stage for the deeper opposition he presents in *The Birth of Tragedy* between Dionysus and Socrates. With Socrates, we find "the unshakeable faith that thought, using the thread of causality, can penetrate the deepest recesses of being, and that thought is capable not only of knowing being, but even of *correcting* it" (*BT* 95, emphasis Nietzsche's; cf. *Republic* 500d–501a). With Socrates, according to Nietzsche, the daylight of reason obscures gruesome night, the answer to the riddle of the Sphinx does not bode doom, and no horror awaits in the woods outside Thebes. Human beings are in control. Tragedy is no more. To be sure, like the Greek tragedians, Socrates seeks what underlies the appearance of things, but instead of discovering "primordial contradiction and primordial pain in the heart of the primal unity" (*BT* 55), Socrates discovers the Ideas or Forms. From Nietzsche's perspective, Socrates moves from one Apollonian world to an even more Apollonian world, from visible forms to pure forms, almost as if he had moved in the opposite direction to the one Nietzsche is suggesting. Socrates penetrates existence, and understands its inner intelligibility. Hence science's correction of nature to improve the human condition becomes possible.

This Socratic world view, in Nietzsche's analysis, undermines Greek tragedy when it makes its way to the Athenian stage in the plays of Euripides. Although the *Bacchae*, Euripides' last play, serves as a recantation, a testimony to Dionysus' terrifying power, Nietzsche argues, the damage has already been done, for Euripides "reconstruct[ed] tragedy purely on the basis of an un-Dionysian art, morality and world view" (*BT* 81). The Euripidean hero, for example, like Socrates' interlocutor, "defends his actions by arguments and counter-arguments," and risks sacrificing our tragic pity in the process. The optimism of Socratic dialectic, which "celebrates a triumph with every conclusion," sounds the death knoll of Greek tragedy. In the face of reason's cool clarity, Greek tragedy takes a "death-leap into bourgeois drama" (*BT* 91). And there is the "notorious *deus ex machina*," with its "superficial and insolent principle of poetic justice," whereby Euripides enacts the Socratic equation of virtue, knowledge, and happiness (*BT* 91; see also 85). A counterpart to Socrates' "virtue is knowledge," Euripides' "aesthetic Socratism" holds that "to be beautiful everything must be intelligible" (*BT* 83–84).

Nietzsche's Socrates has a remarkable similarity to the Socrates whom Climacus contrasts with the god in *Philosophical Fragments*. The Socrates that Climacus presents there is also the theoretical man, the optimist, characterized by the belief that reason can penetrate being, precisely because each man has the truth within himself, and so can be reminded of it. The truth does not come from outside, and thus there is no question of its inaccessibility. If self-knowledge is God-knowledge in the way that Climacus attributes to Socrates, the innermost nature of things is accessible through reason.

However, just as there are indications in Kierkegaard's work that Socrates understood the limits of reason, so too does Nietzsche suggest that the Socratic pursuit of truth leads to the very alternative Nietzsche seeks to the theoretical optimism of Socratism. Although Nietzsche traces the decline of Greek tragedy to Socrates, he also says that Socrates' "faith that the nature of things can be fathomed" was the means by which Western humanity saved itself. On the basis of that faith, human beings turned their energies to science and its progress. It is only when the pursuit of truth is "spurred by its powerful illusion" in the power of reason that science "speeds irresistibly toward its limits, where its optimism, concealed in the essence of logic, suffers shipwreck." At the "periphery of the circle of science . . . from which one gazes at what defies illumination," tragic insight emerges which merely to be endured requires art "as a protection and remedy." This in fact is *really the aim of this mechanism* [the attempt to penetrate being]" (emphasis Nietzsche's). Only Socratism, with its impulse toward "infinite knowledge," "guarantees the infinity of art" (*BT* 83–98), Nietzsche writes, just as Kierkegaard's Climacus recognizes that "it is the paradox of thought to want to discover something that thought itself cannot think" (*PF* 37). For both Nietzsche and Kierkegaard, reason seeks its own downfall, for the one opening a way for art, for the other for faith.

Not surprisingly, if science serves art by leading its advocates to the edge of the abyss, as Nietzsche says, Socrates as the great pursuer of knowledge would understand this. In Plato's *Phaedo*, in Nietzsche's analysis, this becomes apparent. That dialogue, to be sure, leaves us with a "new ideal" of the dying Socrates, able to face death with calm, and presents an argument that the soul cannot fully grasp truth until it becomes free of the body (*Phaedo* 66d–67b). Here, Plato's Socrates comes close to what Kierkegaard describes as the Medieval ideal – the ascetic life of the monastery. Thus in *Twilight of the Idols*, Nietzsche refers to the *Phaedo* for evidence of Socrates' hostility to life. As he lies dying, Socrates acknowledges that he owes a cock to Asclepius, the Greek god of medicine, for the cure for life that death brings. "To live – that means to be sick a long time" (*TI* 473). Nietzsche points out, however, that the *Phaedo* also shows us that "that despotic logician occasionally had the feeling of a gap, a void, half a reproach, a possibly neglected duty" (*BT* 89 and 92–93). Here Nietzsche refers to the dream vision Socrates reports in that dialogue, which came to him often and urged him to "practice music." Although Socrates had understood that apparition to be encouraging him in the practice of philosophy, he now questions whether the apparition speaks of music in the ordinary sense, and so composes a hymn to Apollo and puts one of Aesop's fables to verse (*BT* 92–93; *Phaedo* 60e–61b). In other words, Socrates discovers and admits on his dying day that the life of reason for which he is famous may be insufficient and in need of art, or in Nietzsche's words, that unless he "practice music" he is "in danger of sinning against a deity" (*BT* 93).

Had Nietzsche given a fuller analysis of the *Phaedo*, he would have found even more indications of Socrates' awareness of "the limits of logic" (*BT* 93). Because the *Phaedo* is set on the day that Socrates is slated by the city to be executed, his companions' fear of death looms large in that dialogue. Early in the dialogue, Socrates offers to tell tales or myths (*muthologein*) about the afterlife inasmuch as he will soon be journeying there, and it is not clear where his tales (*muthoi*) end and his arguments (*logoi*) begin. Socrates even suggests near the end that his arguments about the immortality of the soul might seem to be "comforting tales" for both his interlocutors and himself (*Phaedo* 115d). Like the tragic poet whom Nietzsche discusses in *The Birth of Tragedy*, Socrates appears to confront the fears and terrors of human existence (see, e.g., *Phaedo* 77e), and to turn to an Apollonian vision in order to deal with them. The hymn to Apollo that Socrates admits composing at the beginning of the *Phaedo* and that Nietzsche singles out in importance, by this reading, is actually the key to the *Phaedo* as a whole.

The doctrine of recollection, which figures so centrally in the *Fragments'* presentation of Socrates' rationalism, comes up in the *Phaedo*, as it does in the *Meno* and other dialogues. But in the *Phaedo*, Socrates and his interlocutors discuss recollection not simply to account for learning but to buttress the argument for the immortality of the soul (*Phaedo* 77a). Its discussion thus has an ulterior purpose, a rather pressing one in that Socrates and his companions face his death at the end of the day. Theirs is a discussion, Socrates observes, that disproves all suspicion that he is babbling idly about things of no concern to himself, as Aristophanes accused him of doing (*Phaedo* 70b–c). The discussion of recollection in the *Phaedo*, time after time, demonstrates not how our ability to know (i.e., recollect) is a sign of our universality, but rather how it manifests our particular experience of life in this world.

In the first place, Cebes reminds Socrates of the argument for recollection by claiming that it is one Socrates "is accustomed to make" (*Phaedo* 72e–73a). The argument is thus introduced when another reminds Socrates of himself and his customary speeches. So too Cebes' friend Simmias wants to be reminded of the argument itself, and even makes a joke about his need to be reminded of reminding, the very thing the argument is about (*Phaedo* 73a–b; see *Meno* 81e–82a). He wants to be reminded, in other words, not of the objects he knew before birth but of the argument about them that he once knew. He does not now recollect the argument, but he does remember that he once knew it. So too when he recollects the argument he once knew, with Socrates' help, he will remember not only what he knew but that he knew it. In the *Phaedo*, being reminded implies remembering oneself.[12] Then, when

[12] See Michael Davis, "Socrates' Pre-Socratism: Some Remarks on the Structure of Plato's *Phaedo*," *Ancient Philosophy* (1980): 69–80.

Cebes reminds Simmias of Socrates' theory of recollection, Cebes gives a clear statement of the all-importance of the questioner: "when human beings are questioned, *if someone questions them well*," he explains, "they themselves tell everything as it is," indicating that knowledge was already in them (*Phaedo* 73b; emphasis mine). Cebes knows that recollection requires someone who questions well. It is also something that Simmias himself does not forget: after Socrates' account of recollection, Simmias admits that he is "terrified" that once Socrates dies, there will no longer be anyone among human beings worthy of the task of giving such an account (*Phaedo* 76b). Yet when Socrates starts questioning them about the theory, he says little about his own role, the role of the questioner, and traces being reminded to images rather than to the questions asked by another (*Phaedo* 74a–76a). He seems to be preparing for his disappearance. His self-forgetting is due to his remembering that he is going to die.

Among the examples with which Socrates illustrates the theory of recollection in the *Phaedo* are these: A lover will be reminded of his beloved when he sees his cloak or lyre; acquaintances will be reminded of Cebes when they see Simmias; a sketch of a lyre will remind of a person, just as one of Simmias will remind of Cebes; a sketch of Simmias will remind one of Simmias; and sticks that are more or less equal to each other will remind one of equality itself (*Phaedo* 73d ff.). In all the examples that Socrates gives, except that of the sticks, recollection requires not prior knowledge of ideas but prior knowledge or experience of particular relationships. As Ronna Burger points out, "in all cases but the last, the link between the present perception and the thought it awakens depends on the subjective association in the observer."[13]

Consistently, the *Phaedo* indicates the extent to which Socrates is bound to the earth, even though the prison guard releases Socrates from his chains at the outset of the dialogue (*Phaedo* 59e). Plato

[13] Ronna Burger, *The Phaedo: A Platonic Labyrinth* (New Haven: Yale University Press, 1984), 72. Even the lone example of the recollection of an "idea," that of "equality," requires a comparison of two sticks, an ability to understand relationships between two things that are alike but are not identical. As the editors of a 1998 translation of the *Phaedo* ask in their introduction, "Why does Socrates use, as his example of a form, a mathematical relation rather than a mathematical property of an individual thing (for example, an object's circularity)?" *Plato's Phaedo*, with trans., introduction, and glossary, by Eva Brann, Peter Kalkavage, and Eric Salem (Newburyport, MA: Focus Classical Library, 1998), 8. See the discussion of this question by Burger, *The Phaedo*, 74 ff.

dramatizes his connection to the earth when he has Phaedo relate how in the morning Socrates "put his feet down on the earth and for the rest of the time conversed this way" (61d). Far from enjoying the unmixed pleasures that are often associated with philosophy (e.g., *Phaedrus* 258e; Aristotle, *Politics* 1267a5–12, and *NE* 1173b16–19), Socrates begins his last conversation with reflections on the inseparability of pleasure and pain as he experiences it in prison. He even imagines a fable about how the god yoked the two together (*Phaedo* 60b–c). As to the cock Socrates wants to offer to Asclepius, which Nietzsche highlights, this healing god was rumored to have been bribed to heal someone at the point of death. Thus Burger observes that Socrates may have found an opportunity for "one last affirmation of the goodness of life."[14]

Plato calls our attention to the limits of Socrates' arguments through the action of the dialogue. When Cebes and Simmias question the conclusions the group has drawn about the survival of the soul, Socrates' companions are deeply disturbed. Not only do they doubt the arguments they previously accepted, but they also hesitate to accept any arguments whatsoever, of which they suppose themselves to be equally poor judges (*Phaedo* 88c). Sensing that "misology," or "hatred of argument," threatens to take hold of his companions, Socrates explains that there is greater cause for mourning "if our argument meets an end and we cannot bring it back to life" than if he, Socrates, dies (*Phaedo* 89b). When Phaedo, the dialogue's narrator, meets Echecrates in his later travels, however, he does not simply carry on a discussion with him about the soul, and in this way keep the argument alive, but he recounts the story of Socrates' last day, as Echecrates requests. Echecrates wants to hear not simply Socrates' arguments, but "what was said and done," and Phaedo himself admits that "to remember Socrates is the most pleasant of all things for him," even if it is not without the pain of loss (*Phaedo* 58d and 59a). The arguments must be understood along with the "deeds," and it is Socrates, not simply his arguments, whom Phaedo remembers with pleasure. And it is Socrates' conversing, not simply the conversation, that Plato captures in the *Phaedo*. At the end of that dialogue, when Crito asks Socrates how they should bury him after his death, Socrates laughs gently at the thought that they may not be able to catch him, for he is not the one whom they will soon see as a corpse but "the one who is now conversing" with them (*Phaedo* 115c). In asserting who he is to Crito, Socrates in effect tells Plato what or whom to save. The arguments that come from Plato

[14] Burger, *The Phaedo*, 216.

come only embedded in stories, and Plato has learned from Socrates of the need for art (see also *Phaedo* 61d–e).

When criticizing Socratic dialectic in *Twilight of the Idols* – Socrates' insistence that his interlocutors justify themselves with reasons – Nietzsche enigmatically observes, "Socrates was also the great erotic" (*TI*, 477). Again, Nietzsche implies that there is more to Socrates than the rationalism with which he associates him. Presumably Nietzsche is referring to the passage in Plato's *Symposium* where Socrates claims "to know nothing but erotic matters" (*Symposium* 177d). Nietzsche's aphoristic form allows him to leave undeveloped the connection between Socrates' eroticism and his dialectic approach to philosophy. Socrates' eroticism may seem consistent with his rationalism if love directs us to knowledge, to the unchanging and pure form of beauty, for example, as Socrates claims in the *Symposium* (210d and 211b). Socrates nevertheless denies that love itself is beautiful and good, and insists that love is itself a sign of our lack or deficiency (e.g., *Symposium* 202e–203a). Love may connect us to heaven, but it also reveals our connection to the earth. Socrates also acquiesces in that dialogue to the proposal that he be judged not by Apollo but by Dionysus, the god of the poets and the god of intoxication (*Symposium* 175e). By the end of the *Symposium*, Alcibiades, dressed like the god Dionysus, grants victory to Socrates. The dialogue ends with Socrates' persuading the poets present, the comic poet Aristophanes and tragic poet Agathon, of a connection between comedy and tragedy (*Symposium* 212d–e and 223d). Far from presenting an optimistic world view, Socrates corrects Agathon when the poet does so (*Symposium* 199c). It is Socrates who reveals the illusions underlying such poetry.

So too in the *Phaedrus*, which further explores the erotic character of philosophy, does Socrates present a world torn by suffering and conflict between, for example, lover and beloved, whose relationship Socrates compares to that between a wolf and a lamb (*Phaedrus* 241d). Although Socrates offers a recantation of this view of love, his recantation takes the form of poetry, or "a palinode," in which he claims to imitate a poet (Stesichorus) (*Phaedrus* 243b). Moreover, his recantation praises not reason but madness (*Phaedrus* 244a). He concludes the dialogue with a prayer to Pan (*Phaedrus* 279b), who in Greek mythology is a monster, half-goat and half-human. His name in Greek also means "the whole."

This is the dialogue, we remember, that Climacus cites, in which Socrates claims not to know whether he is more monstrous than Typhon or a gentler simpler being. Socrates' prayer acknowledges that his perplexity about himself has implications for his understanding the whole itself. When Socrates prays to Pan at the end of the *Phaedrus*, he recognizes that he is not the whole, and therefore that self-knowledge could not be God-knowledge. He suggests in effect the unintelligibility of the whole insofar he is a part, and connects that unintelligibility with his own piety.

   Building on these insights of Kierkegaard and Nietzsche concerning Plato's Socrates, I shall explore the *Symposium* (Chapter 2) and the *Phaedrus* (Chapter 3), especially Socrates' awareness of the limits of reason, and the place of poetry and piety in human life. Nevertheless, there is a fundamental difference between Socrates and these later thinkers that makes his approach to philosophy relevant today. That difference can be captured in his understanding of friendship and political community, how the latter is a reflection of the former, and how both are fundamental to a good human life. In the *Symposium*, Socrates' understanding of both our need and our resourcefulness allows him to join self-love to love of the beautiful, connecting human beings, even the philosopher, with others in communities that make generating and nurturing possible. In the *Phaedrus*, Socrates' perplexity about himself does not isolate him, but leads him to a true art of speaking and to conversations with others. In my exploration of the *Lysis* (Chapter 4), we shall see how love transformed into friendship both supports Socrates' pursuit of wisdom and serves as a standard for political community. I find confirmation of this understanding of Socrates even in the *Phaedo* (Chapter 5), one of Plato's most "otherworldly" dialogues, where Socrates tries to preserve through his friends his understanding of philosophy as "political philosophy." Plato's Socrates thus responds to both Kierkegaard and Nietzsche, offering them – and us – a remedy for alienation.

2

Love, Generation, and Political Community
(The *Symposium*)

Any argument that the philosophic pursuits of Plato's Socrates exemplify an understanding of love and friendship supportive of political life, as I make in this book, must confront the charges against Socrates made by his own political community, the city of Athens. Socrates was accused and found guilty of doing injustice "by corrupting the young, and by not believing in the gods of the city but in new daemonic things" (*Apology* 24b). Whereas in his *Apology of Socrates* Plato presents Socrates giving his defense in an Athenian court, his *Symposium* serves as his own consideration of those charges against Socrates, and I shall argue his own "apology for Socrates." As Allan Bloom observes, "the accusation of philosophy's destructiveness was made on behalf of the political men and the poets. [The *Symposium*] is the only place where we see [Socrates] with the poets."[1] Indeed, one of those poets at the symposium was Aristophanes, whose portrayal of Socrates in the *Clouds* in 423 BCE fueled the charges against him in 399 (*Apology* 18c–d). In the *Symposium*, Socrates accepts a contest with the poets, including Aristophanes (175e, 205e, and 212c).[2] At issue is

---

[1] Allan Bloom, "The Ladder of Love," in *Plato's "Symposium,"* trans. by Seth Benardete, with commentaries by Allan Bloom and Seth Benardete (Chicago: University of Chicago Press, 2001), 73.

[2] References in parentheses in this chapter unless otherwise noted, are to Plato's *Symposium*. Translations from the Greek are my own, although I have relied on Seth Benardete's translation in *Plato's "Symposium."* The Greek texts for Plato's works are *Platonis Opera*, ed. J. Burnet, Vols. I–IV (Oxford: Oxford University Press, 1901). The argument of this chapter is adapted from my "Socrates' Contest with the Poets in Plato's *Symposium*," *Political Theory* 32, no. 2 (April 2004): 186–206 (SAGE Publications); and my "Philosophy and Empire: On Socrates and Alcibiades in Plato's *Symposium*," *Polity* 39, no. 4 (October 2007): 502–21. Sections from the latter article (copyright © 2007, Palgrave Macmillan) are used here with the kind permission of Palgrave Macmillan, Houndmills, Basingstoke, Hampshire, UK. I thank Palgrave Macmillan for its courtesy.

their respective piety, along with their wisdom. We also see Socrates there with Alcibiades, one of Athens' leading politicians, one who was thought to have been corrupted by Socrates. His was one of the names, according to Xenophon, most frequently mentioned in connection with the accusation that Socrates did "the greatest evils to the city" (*Memorabilia* I.ii.12). The charges that led to Socrates' trial and execution lie close to the *Symposium's* surface.

The *Symposium* is the only Platonic dialogue that takes a god as its theme. At least according to Phaedrus, with whom the proposal to praise Love at the symposium originates, Love is "a great god," indeed "the most honorable and sovereign of the gods" (178a; 180b). The symposiasts may be praising a god, but there seems from the outset something impious about what they are doing. In the first place, is Love a Greek "god," of the status of other Olympian gods, such as Zeus, Athena, Hermes, or Ares? Unlike these gods, Love's proper name has a common meaning, and in many of their speeches the symposiasts present love as a kind of psychic, or even cosmic, force (e.g., 179a, 183a–b, and 186a). At the very least, Love's being "most sovereign of the gods" seems to fly in the face of Zeus's designation as "father of gods and men" (e.g., Homer, *Iliad* I. 544; see also *Symposium* 197b). At the symposium, Eryximachus reports Phaedrus' complaint that "it is a terrible thing that there are hymns and paeans composed for the other gods, but no poet has yet composed an encomium for so [great] and so old a god as Love" (177a–b). Reproaching the Greeks on behalf of Love, Phaedrus reminds us of Aristophanes' Clouds – the "new deities" introduced and worshiped by Socrates in the play of that name – who blame the audience: "although we benefit the city most of all the gods, we are the only daemons to whom you neither sacrifice nor pour a libation, we who watch over you" (*Clouds* 877–79). By the end of Phaedrus' own encomium, it is Love who, as "most sovereign over happiness for both the living and the dead" (180d), appears to most benefit human beings. One could easily see in the gathering at Agathon's house a deposing of the Olympian gods in favor of a new ruler, whom the symposiasts worship through their encomia (see e.g., 197b).

If the guests at the *Symposium* are proposing a new god, or at least a new ruler of gods and humans, Plato is portraying them as doing the very thing Socrates was accused of doing – introducing new divinities. The religious character of the *Symposium* is highlighted by the aura of mystery in which Plato clothes the event in the dialogue's opening frame and by the frequent references throughout the discussion to the revelation of mysteries (e.g., 209e–210a and 218b). But revealing mysteries often suggests desecration, as when the Athenian political leader Alcibiades was accused of impiety for revealing secret mystery rites. This crime, and that of mutilating statues of Hermes of which he was also accused, were understood as signs of his aspirations to tyranny and as an attack on the Athenian democracy (Thucydides 6.28.2). Plato sets the symposium not long before Alcibiades was supposed to have committed these impious deeds, and has Alcibiades himself break in on the party before the evening is over.

By introducing Alcibiades into the *Symposium*, Plato highlights the charges against Socrates of impiety and of corrupting the young. Within a year of the dramatic date of the *Symposium*, Alcibiades led the Athenian forces in an attempt to conquer Sicily, was recalled to stand trial in Athens on the charge of impiety, escaped to join Athens' enemy, Sparta, and later engaged in further intrigues with the king of Persia, the traditional enemy of the Greeks, against both Athens and Sparta (Thucydides 6.6.2; 6.88.9; 6.93.1–2; 8.46.1–47). The Sicilian expedition, once Alcibiades had been relieved of his command, ended in disaster for Athens, and signaled the end of its ascendancy in the Greek world. Seth Benardete speculates that had Alcibiades not led Athens to disaster in Sicily, which led ultimately to the city's defeat in the war with Sparta, Socrates might not have been executed for corrupting the young.[3] Plato shows us the popular interest in Socrates' relationship with Alcibiades that leads Apollodorus to narrate the events of the *Symposium* on more than one occasion, even a long time after they occurred, and not long before the charges were brought against Socrates (172a–c).[4] In Plato's *Apology*,

---

[3] Seth Benardete, "On Plato's *Symposium*," in *Plato's "Symposium,"* 192.

[4] Even though Alcibiades does not arrive at the symposium until the end of the evening, it is his presence there with Socrates that is remembered when inquiries are made about the event (172b). In comparison to the date of the dinner party, which is precise due to our knowledge of the year of Agathon's first victory in the dramatic contests, the date of the narration is unclear. When Glaucon supposes that the dinner party was held recently, Apollodorus points out that Agathon has been away from Athens for many years (172e). R. G. Bury suggests 401–400 BCE as a possible date for the narration, looking for a date as far removed as he can find from Agathon's departure from Athens around 408 BCE, but while Socrates is still alive. *The Symposium of Plato*, ed. with introduction, critical notes, and commentary, 2nd ed. (Cambridge: W. Heffer and Sons, Ltd., 1969), lxvi. Alcibiades, however, was assassinated, in 404 BCE. Glaucon could have hardly supposed the event to have been recent if Alcibiades had been long dead. Thus it seems we need a date as far as possible from 408 BCE, but not long after 404 BCE. Martha Nussbaum speculates that the narration occurs in 404, immediately after Alcibiades' assassination, an event that prompts interest in this past drinking party. *The Fragility of Goodness* (Cambridge: Cambridge University Press, 1986), 168–71.

Socrates asks why his accusers do not bring forward as witnesses against him any of those he had corrupted (*Apology* 33c ff.), but by the time of Socrates' trial, Alcibiades has been assassinated.

While in the *Apology* Socrates avoids mentioning any association he may have had with this enemy of Athens, elsewhere in his corpus Plato is not so silent. Plato dramatizes a number of encounters between Socrates and Alcibiades in addition to the *Symposium*. Alcibiades supports Socrates in the *Protagoras*, set in 433 BCE (*Protagoras* 348b–c), for example, and in the *Alcibiades I*, set around that same time, we see Socrates seeking the young man out to question him about his way of life.[5] Plato singles out Alcibiades as especially loved by Socrates in the *Gorgias*, where Socrates volunteers that he has two beloveds – Alcibiades, son of Cleinias, and philosophy. He even contrasts himself with his interlocutor Callicles, who loves Demus and Demus, the one the son of Pyrilampes, and the other the Athenian people (*Gorgias* 481d). Alcibiades is a silent figure hovering over Socrates' trial.

The most dramatic meeting of Socrates and Alcibiades in the Platonic corpus, however, is the *Symposium*, set roughly sixteen years after their meeting in the *Alcibiades I*. Scholarly treatments of the *Symposium* often focus on Socrates' encomium to Love, and its relationship to Alcibiades and his speech about Socrates. Since Alcibiades' speech follows Socrates' encomium to Love, most famous for its "ladder of love" on which lovers transcend their love for bodies, and perhaps even for particular human beings, it has been suggested that Plato brings Alcibiades into the *Symposium* to tell his story about Socrates in order to illustrate how Socrates lives his understanding of Love: Socrates is indifferent to Alcibiades' attempt to seduce him, and his higher love leads him to a vision of the eternal.[6] As to Alcibiades himself, he serves as a foil, in the words of G. K. Plochmann, a "clarification of what philosophy is *not*."[7] Others sympathetic to Alcibiades' plight have

---

[5] In that dialogue, Socrates describes himself as "the first of [Alcibiades'] lovers, [who] alone persists when the others have left off" (*Alcibiades I* 103a). Also extant is an *Alcibiades II*, although its authenticity is disputed. Like the *Alcibiades I*, it begins with Socrates' speaking to Alcibiades.

[6] For example, Paul Friedlander, *Plato: The Dialogues, Second and Third Periods*, vol. 3, trans. Hans Meyerhoff (Princeton: Princeton University Press, 1969), 30–31.

[7] George Kimball Plochmann, "Hiccups and Hangovers in *The Symposium*," *Bucknell Review* 11, no. 3 (May 1963): 16, see also 14. For more recent defenses of Socrates through interpretations of Alcibiades' role in the *Symposium*, see Mark J. Lutz, *Socrates' Education to Virtue: Learning the Love of the Noble* (Albany: State University of New York Press, 1998), 136–47; Gary Alan Scott, "Irony and Inebriation in Plato's *Symposium*:

understood Plato's inclusion of Alcibiades in the *Symposium* as an implicit critique of Socrates. Martha Nussbaum, for example, in her provocative and influential essay on the *Symposium*, argues that in Alcibiades' passionate love for the unique individual Socrates, Plato presents a counterexample to Socrates' love of the ideas or forms, a love for the whole person and not simply for the good qualities that he shares with others.[8] One set of scholars thus defends the erotic ascent Socrates describes, and understands Alcibiades as a foil to Socrates and philosophy, whereas the other explains Alcibiades' presence in the *Symposium* as Plato's implicit criticism of Socrates. In spite of their differences, however, both views emphasize the gulf between the two, and therewith between philosophy and politics.[9]

Scholars raise the question of whether Socrates may have contributed to Alcibiades' betrayal of his city by attenuating his attachment to its laws and conventions. Allan Bloom, for example, suggests that Socrates' questions "liberate[d] Alcibiades from loyalty to his own city," and that "[Alcibiades'] political activities were probably informed by what he learned from Socrates."[10] Lutz similarly raises the question of whether Socrates undermines Alcibiades' law-abidingness[11] (see also *Republic*

The Disagreement Between Socrates and Alcibiades over Truth-telling," *Journal of Neoplatonic Studies* 3, no. 2 (Spring 1995): 30 n. 5; and Gary Alan Scott and William A. Welton, "An Overlooked Motive in Alcibiades' *Symposium* Speech," *Interpretation* 24, no. 1 (Fall 1996): 67–84. See also Steven Forde, *The Ambition to Rule: Alcibiades and the Politics of Imperialism in Thucydides* (Ithaca, NY: Cornell University Press, 1989), 235–36.

[8] Nussbaum, *The Fragility of Goodness*, 190. Thus she objects to Vlastos – not to his characterization of Socrates as missing something fundamental in our experience of love – but to his assumption that Socrates speaks for Plato, 166. See Gregory Vlastos, "The Individual as Object of Love in Plato's Dialogues," *Platonic Studies* (Princeton: Princeton University Press, 1973), 1–34. Stanley Rosen sees a similar relation between Socrates' speech on Love and Alcibiades' role in the dialogue, in *Plato's* Symposium, 2nd ed. (New Haven: Yale University Press, 1968), 279. See also Michael Gagarin, "Socrates' *Hybris* and Alcibiades' Failure," *Phoenix* 31 (1977): 22–37, esp. 35–36 and Arlene Saxonhouse, *Fear of Diversity: The Birth of Political Science in Ancient Greek Thought* (Chicago: University of Chicago Press, 1992), especially 159–60, 183–84. For a perceptive argument against Nussbaum on the relation between Socrates and Alcibiades, see Joseph P. Lawrence, "Socrates and Alcibiades," *Southern Humanities Review* 37 (Fall 2003): 301–27.

[9] According to Nussbaum, Plato gives us "a harsh and alarming" tale of conflict between "two kinds of value," between goodness and love, between reason and humanity, between philosophy and poetry, starkly confronting us with a choice in a way that makes it impossible for us to choose. This is "our tragedy," *The Fragility of Goodness*, 198. Bloom makes a similar point in relation to Socrates' and Aristophanes' accounts of love, "The Ladder of Love," 138.

[10] Bloom, "The Ladder of Love," 166.

[11] Lutz, *Socrates' Education to Virtue*, 127.

538d–539a; Xenophon, *Memorabilia* I.ii.40–46; and *Apology* 24d–25c). The freedom from accepted opinions and conventions of the day produced by philosophical questioning might free an individual from political restraints. Alcibiades' lack of good citizenship, from this perspective, is a reflection of Socrates' independence from the city. Transcending the political has political consequences.

Moreover, one might connect Alcibiades' "universal ambitions" with the universal ambitions of philosophy in its pursuit of the truth. Not simply the liberating character of philosophy but its goals and aspirations might find tyrannical expression in a politics of empire. Bloom points us to this possibility when he observes that the "Alcibiadean vision of politics seems like a political version" of the "vision of the Ideas and the beautiful" that Socrates presents in the *Symposium*.[12] This argument points to the universality of outlook that the two have in common, whether it be the imperialistic drive that ignores the laws and customs of particular peoples or the love of the truth that leads a philosopher to look toward "all time and all being" (see *Republic* 486a) rather than the opinions of particular times or places.

I shall argue, in contrast, that whereas Plato uses the *Symposium* as an occasion to revisit the issues surrounding Socrates' indictment, trial, and execution, he shows not the corrupting influence of Socrates on Athens but rather the mutual dependence of Socratic philosophizing and political life. It is Socrates' understanding of love, as we shall see, rooted in both human need and resourcefulness, that explains Socrates' piety, his philosophic life, and his connection to and even his love for other human beings. That same understanding limits imperialism while encouraging noble political action.

We shall first explore the dialogue's setting, the drinking party at Agathon's house, and what the first three speakers who praise Love reveal about the state of Athenian life. Phaedrus and Pausanias, from their different perspectives, offer advice to the city in the course of praising Love. Their self-serving political advice and implicit reforms of the city's poetry and laws indicate the moral and political corruption of Athenian intellectual and cultural life. This is true as well of the doctor Eryximachus, who speaks for the arts or sciences in the *Symposium*. Like the artisans Socrates recounts examining in the *Apology*, Eryximachus supposes that his knowledge of his own art gives him

---

[12] Bloom, "The Ladder of Love," 155.

knowledge of the whole, as he draws an understanding of the cosmos from his knowledge of medicine (186a–b; cf. *Apology* 22d).

I shall then turn to the speeches of two of Athens' leading poets, the comic poet Aristophanes and the tragedian Agathon. Their inadequate understandings of love and indeed of their own poetry, I argue, are indicative of Athenian decline. Socrates' speech, which I treat in the next section, addresses those of the two poets by presenting a more comprehensive understanding of love that offers a foundation for both comic and tragic poetry as well as a view of human striving that can explain and inform political life. Poets might say many beautiful things without understanding (*Apology* 22c), but with understanding they might say what is both beautiful and true (see 198d). Socrates' recourse to the foreign prophetess Diotima, whom he claims taught him about Love, like Chaerophon's to the oracle at Delphi (*Apology* 21a), attests to Socrates' human wisdom, a wisdom that connects philosophy to both political life and the divine, and by doing so responds to major charges against him. The guests may praise Love as if he were a new divinity, but Socrates objects – Love is not a god, but rather our link to the divine (202d and ff.). The intellectual leaders of Athens are the impious ones, and not Socrates, Plato shows, and Plato even has his character Aristophanes mock them for their impiety. Although Socrates is present, it is not his party. On several occasions, Plato presents his actions as attempts to intervene in the night's events (e.g., 194a–e, 198b–199b, and 222c–e). Plato suggests that far from contributing to the Athenian corruption, he tries to stem its tide.

Moreover, insofar as Socrates knows his own ignorance, and thus the imperfection of his knowledge, he also recognizes his affinity with his fellow humanity. In his "in-between" state, between knowledge and ignorance, Socrates depends on others for sustenance, and nurtures them in turn. Plato's poetic defense of Socratic philosophy in the *Symposium* therefore provides an alternative to the hubristic images of philosophy that we shall see Alcibiades present in the culminating speech of that dialogue, an alternative that indicates a mutually beneficial relation between philosophy and political life.

THE PROLOGUE

The *Symposium* is narrated many years after the event by Apollodorus, who heard the story from Aristodemus, who was present there. Apollodorus is described as "always raging against [himself] and everyone else except

Socrates" and thought by others to be mad (173d–e). He is a man who thinks he is as capable of making philosophic speeches as any other; at least he claims "immense delight" in such speeches "whether I make them myself or hear them from another" (173c). Aristodemus imitates Socrates in going about barefoot (173b). The somewhat fanatical disciples of Socrates appear eager to narrate the story to others (e.g., 173d). It is an exciting story about a time when heroes contested – when Agathon celebrated his victory in the dramatic contests, when Aristophanes and Socrates presented speeches about Love, and when an intoxicated Alcibiades had his say about Socrates and their relationship. Whether intentional or not, and whether for good or ill, these disciples of Socrates, as Plato presents them, are contributing to a legend.[13] Plato cautions us about their account when he presents their eccentricities, and emphasizes that they do not have the whole story, when he has Apollodorus relate that Aristodemus does not remember everything, and that he does not remember everything that Aristodemus told him (178a). And although Apollodorus did check with Socrates "some points" that he had heard from Aristodemus (173b), he apparently did not ask him about any of the speeches about Love that Aristodemus could not remember (180c), or about the conversation Socrates had with Aristophanes and Agathon that Aristodemus missed because he was dozing (223b–c). Thus, when Apollodorus offers to relate what he deems "most worthy of memory" (178a), we know that we are receiving an incomplete account.

Aristodemus begins his story of the evening, Apollodorus reports, with his meeting Socrates, who is dressed for a party. In fact, Socrates comes from the baths, is wearing fancy slippers, and claims that he "made himself beautiful, so that as a beauty he might go to another beauty," as he refers to his host of the evening (174a). In the *Apology*, Socrates claims that he will not follow the practice in court of using "words adorned and made beautiful," but will speak only the

---

[13] The other two narrated dialogues that are not narrated by Socrates similarly convey the sense that Socrates is an epic hero of sorts from the past, whose "labors" deserve recounting. The *Parmenides* is narrated when men come to Athens from Clazomenae seeking an account of "a conversation that Socrates and Zeno and Parmenides once had" (*Parmenides* 126b–c). The *Phaedo* is narrated in Phlius when a Phliasian, who has already heard an account of Socrates' trial, asks Phaedo for the story of Socrates' death (57a). Tales of memorable events in Socrates' life in these two cases, as Plato presents them, are spreading beyond Athens and throughout the Greek world.

truth (*Apology* 17b–c). At the symposium, in contrast, Socrates makes concessions to common practice, and even adorns himself for the occasion. In the same spirit, later that evening, he agrees to praise Love, intending "to select the most beautiful [aspects] of Love and put them in their most splendid [form]" (198d). And yet one might question how "beautiful" any fancy slippers can make an ugly man. They are more likely to accentuate his ugliness by acting as a foil and by making their wearer ridiculous.[14] And when he claims that encomia present the most beautiful aspects of their subjects, he also calls attention to their incompleteness and to the partiality of beauty. The selection of "on the good" for the subtitle, rather than the more obvious "on the beautiful" (see, e.g., 197b as well as 174a and 198d), may point to this as well.[15]

The question of the relation between the beautiful and the good underlies Socrates' pun on the beautiful Agathon's name, which literally means "good" in Greek. While Socrates has made himself beautiful to visit the beautiful Agathon, he urges the uninvited Aristodemus to accompany him there because, according to the proverb, "the good go of their own accord (*automatoi*) to the feast of the good" (174b–c). Socrates nevertheless claims that they will "change and corrupt" the proverb.[16] Aristodemus humbly assumes that Socrates means that he is unworthy of such a host as Agathon, especially since Socrates claims that Homer likewise corrupts the proverb by having the unworthy Menelaus show up on his own at the worthy Agamemnon's feast (174c). But since we have no reason to suppose that Socrates insults the companion whose company he seeks, perhaps it is the worthiness of the host that Socrates questions rather than that of the uninvited guest, and the beautiful Agathon is good in name only. Aristodemus of course does not go entirely uninvited to Agathon's, for Socrates insists that he go. This in fact Aristodemus claims will be his defense when he arrives at the party (174d). Perhaps Socrates corrupts the proverb by refusing to leave matters alone. Regardless of the reason, it seems important to Socrates that his comrade attend, and he

---

[14] Socrates, as it were, has dressed himself for the comic stage in which he is the comic figure, as Aristophanes did to him earlier in the *Clouds*. See also Alfred Geier, *Plato's Erotic Thought: The Tree of the Unknown* (Rochester, NY: The University of Rochester Press, 2002), 25.

[15] It is not clear whether Plato wrote the subtitles of the dialogues, or whether they were added later. See Robert G. Hoerber, "Thrasylus' Platonic Canon and the Double Titles," *Phronesis* 2 (1957): 19–20.

[16] Scholars are uncertain how Socrates "corrupts" the proverb. See Bury, *The Symposium of Plato*, 7–8, note on 174b.

quotes Homer when Aristodemus hesitates to accompany him: if "two go together" (*Iliad* x. 224), they will better deliberate about what to say.

The words are spoken by Diomedes, when he chooses Odysseus to sneak in with him under the cover of night to the Trojan camp, in order to make a covert attack – certainly an ominous reference on Socrates' part, almost as if he sensed that he is going into enemy territory.[17] He will in fact spend the evening with the leading men of Athens – such as those most reputed to be wise whom he recounts questioning in his *Apology* – the statesmen, poets, and craftsmen. Unlike many Platonic dialogues in which foreigners are often present, those named as guests at the party are all Athenians. Socrates is going into the heart of the city. But if, like Diomedes, he chooses not to go alone, his entrance is anything but covert. Aristodemus, in fact, announces his coming, for Socrates lags behind, "turning his mind to himself," and Aristodemus precedes him to the party (174d). When Socrates finally arrives, as a result of his own maneuvering he faces a gathering with one of his own disciples there. If Plato is reenacting the *Iliad*'s night foray into enemy territory, Socrates' antagonists the poets, unlike the slaughtered Trojans, end up only falling asleep, and their only "compulsion" is that of the argument (223d).

When Socrates arrives "in the middle of dinner," Agathon offers him a seat beside himself "so that I may touch you and hence enjoy the piece of wisdom that occurred to you" along the way (175c–d). If wisdom flows from the fuller to the emptier, Socrates responds, then he would be the gainer by sitting next to Agathon, for "your wisdom is brilliant and expansive," and "yesterday became conspicuous among more than thirty thousand Greeks witnessing it" (175c–e). Suspecting Socrates' disdain, Agathon accuses him of hubris, claims that he and Socrates will go to court later, and insists that Dionysus act as judge (175e). In Aristophanes' *Frogs*, Dionysus, the god of the theater as well as of wine, judges a contest in Hades between tragic poets.[18] Agathon is now

---

[17] Rosen draws the same inference from Socrates' quotation of Diomedes, but understands the enemy Socrates faces as sophistry, and refers us to the overlap between the group at the party and the group listening to Protagoras in the *Protagoras*. *Plato's Symposium*, 24. While no one could deny the influence of sophistry on Athens' intellectual and political life, Socrates in the *Symposium* more directly faces the leaders of the city. Rosen's point applies more obviously to the *Protagoras*, where Socrates also quotes these lines from Homer, *Protagoras* 316a.

[18] For ways in which Plato uses Aristophanes' *Frogs* as a model for his *Symposium* and thus responds to it, see Leo Strauss, *Plato's Symposium* (Chicago: University of Chicago Press, 2001), 26–27.

suggesting one between poetry and philosophy itself. But Dionysus would be an appropriate judge only if all wisdom were poetic wisdom. It is Agathon who might be accused of hubris.

The pastime of the evening is decided when Eryximachus proposes that instead of drinking after dinner they give encomia to Love. As Phaedrus pointed out to him, he recounts, Love is a great god, but his praises are unsung. Friedlander argues that Phaedrus' claim is "not altogether justified," for "both in [Sophocles'] *Antigone* and [Euripides'] *Hippolytus*, the chorus addresses a passionate song to Eros."[19] These "passionate" choral odes to which Friedlander refers, however, are hardly "encomia," for the odes sing of the dangers of Love, and rather than of his benefit to humanity. The chorus in the *Hippolytus*, for example, speaks of Love as "tyrant over men," who leads them to disaster (*Hippolytus* 538–41). In the *Antigone*, the chorus addresses Love, noting that "who has you within is mad," and "you twist the minds of the just" and destroy them (*Antigone* 790–93). Perhaps it was this very choral ode in Sophocles' play that provides the backdrop for Cephalus' report at the beginning of the *Republic* that Sophocles told him that Love is "a frenzied and savage master," of which he is pleased that old age has rid him (*Republic* 329b–c). Phaedrus, the young man who has been with his lover Eryximachus for at least sixteen years, may want something more upbeat on Love, something that justifies his long-standing relationship.[20] Perhaps Phaedrus' own experience has taught him a goodness of love that the poets do not present. When he himself quotes the poet Hesiod at the beginning of his own speech on Love, he stops just before the lines that Love "conquers the mind and wise counsel" of gods and humans (178b; *Theogeny* 116–22).

Apart from Phaedrus' observation that Love is a great but unsung god, Eryximachus has a reason of his own for delivering speeches instead of drinking, for drunkenness is "a hard thing for human beings," and the group is somewhat hung over from yesterday's celebration of

---

[19] Friedlander, *Plato: The Dialogues, Second and Third Periods*, 9–10.

[20] The Greek custom of pederasty, between an older man and a youth, has been much discussed; see K. J. Dover, *Greek Homosexuality, Updated and With a New Postscript* (Cambridge: Harvard University Press, 1989); and, more recently, S. Sara Monoson, *Plato's Democratic Entanglements: Athenian Politics and the Practice of Philosophy* (Princeton: Princeton University Press, 2000), 68–80. In the *Symposium*, there are two such lover–beloved relationships, Eryximachus and Phaedrus, and Pausanias and Agathon, whom we meet in the *Protagoras*, set approximately sixteen years before Agathon's dinner party (*Protagoras* 315c).

Agathon's victory (176b–177d). Eryximachus includes himself and Phaedrus among the weaker drinkers of the group, who could profit from some other entertainment for the evening. Whether it is a devotion to love or to health, for that most explains the evening's pastime, Phaedrus is knowledgeable about health issues, for he reads the ancient Greek equivalent of our dietary guides – "a book that praises the benefits of salt and many other such things"(177b).[21] Not surprisingly, Phaedrus claims he is "accustomed to obeying [his lover Eryximachus], especially in medical matters" (176d). Whether his health concerns are the cause or effect of his long relationship with a doctor, Phaedrus is aware of the advantages of their relationship.

Other reasons as well move others present to participate. Socrates at any rate proclaims that he could not refuse to praise Love, "inasmuch as [he] claims to know nothing but erotic matters," nor could Agathon and Pausanias, to whose relationship Socrates alludes, nor Aristophanes, who "spends all his time in matters concerning Dionysus and Aphrodite" (177e). They all assent. Since Phaedrus has the head couch and is also the one who originally proposed encomia to Love and is therefore "the father of the *logos*" (177d), he speaks first.

PHAEDRUS' PRAISE OF NOBILITY

Phaedrus begins, "Love is a great god, and among humans and gods a wonder in many ways and not in the least in his birth." The wonder of Love's birth is that he has no parents, and thus "receives the honor of the oldest god" (178a–b). Parents, to whom one owes one's existence, are a sign of dependency (see Aristotle, *NE* 1161a). Phaedrus' initial praise of Love therefore reveals his own admiration for self-sufficiency. As Rosen explains, Love in this view "has a genesis but not a generation," for "if Eros is the god of sexual love, then he cannot be the cause of his own origin."[22] Even if Phaedrus frees Love from generation

---

[21] When we meet him again in the *Phaedrus*, we see him going for a walk outside the city, for the sake of his health, following the advice of a doctor (*Phaedrus* 227a-b).

[22] Rosen observes that since Phaedrus presents Love as having come into being, he "does not elevate him to the status of an eternal or unchanging principle." He must, then, have some sort of intermediate status. *Plato's Symposium*, 45. Implied from the very beginning of the speeches in the *Symposium*, then, is the question of the link between the changing and the eternal, which Socrates' speech addresses later in the dialogue.

and the dependence it implies, however, what is the cause of Love's genesis? Dependence hides under the wonder of self-sufficiency.

Phaedrus moves quickly over any conundrums, and focuses instead on the goods that Love brings human beings. In fact, when he quotes Hesiod as an authority for Love's birth, he leaves out the divine: he takes from the poet natural principles, chaos, earth, and love, while omitting his lines referring to the birth of the Olympian gods, "the immortals who hold the peaks of snowy Olympus" (178b; *Theogony* 116–22).[23] Presumably his tendency to demythologize, or to rationalize the Greek tales of the gods that he later expresses in the *Phaedrus* (*Phaedrus* 229c), comes into play here. The lines he omits refer not only to the Olympian gods but to "murky Tartarus, in the deepest nook of the wide-wayed earth." Phaedrus severs human life from what is both above and below it. In a world with neither heaven nor hell, with neither "snowy Olympus" nor "murky Tartarus," limits to human action are hard to discern. Goals for human aspiration become problematic as well.

As the oldest god, Phaedrus continues, Love causes the greatest goods for humans. Indeed, Phaedrus "can speak of no greater good for anyone from youth onward than a worthy lover, or for a lover than a beloved" (178c). The word translated as "worthy" is *chrēstos*, which means "useful" as well as "good" and is related etymologically to the word for money, *chrēmata*. *Chrēstos* appears to be Phaedrus' favorite word of praise.[24] Love produces "shame in the face of shameful things and ambition for noble or beautiful ones," especially in the sight of those one loves. Cities should therefore arrange lovers next to their beloveds in battle, for a lover would rather die than be seen by his beloved acting cowardly; nor would he desert his beloved or hesitate to come to his aid when he is in danger (178c–179a). Phaedrus emphasizes the lover's self-sacrifice rather than that of the beloved. After all, it is only the lover who by definition loves, and who therefore has the ambition for the noble that love inspires. Phaedrus' halfhearted attempt

---

[23] Whereas editors of the Greek text generally assume that these lines are spurious on the basis of Phaedrus' omission of them here, Rosen argues that Phaedrus' omission of them is explicable by an intention to demote the Olympian gods. *Plato's Symposium*, 48.

[24] As Rosen observes of one of Phaedrus' usages of the word, *chrēstos* "is not the only word meaning 'good' which Plato could have written in this passage," 36 n. 100. For a discussion of Phaedrus' "utilitarianism," see also Bloom, "The Ladder of Love," 82 and Strauss, *On Plato's Symposium*, 53.

to point to the utility of beloveds as well as that of lovers finally fails.[25] At best, beloveds are useful to cities because they keep lovers in their place and directed to the noble deeds the city needs. But there seems to be very little, other than their own interest, that keeps beloveds in place. If they run from battle, would not their courageous lovers run with them, in order to protect them? Unlike lovers, the beloveds that Phaedrus describes are free agents. It is for this reason, as we soon see, that Phaedrus concludes that the highest virtue belongs to them.

Phaedrus illustrates the connection between Love and noble deeds with three examples – Alcestis, Orpheus, and Achilles. Alcestis was so much the lover of her husband that she gave up her life in his place so he would not have to die. She alone was willing to do so, Phaedrus remarks, even though Admetus had both father and mother, so far did her love exalt her over them in affection or friendship (*philia*) (179b–c). Like Love itself, in Phaedrus' analysis, Admetus in effect had no parents. The only source of affection or friendship that means anything is love. Without his lover, who serves him, Admetus is fundamentally alone. Phaedrus includes not only men but also women among those lovers who willingly die for those they love (179b), but women are no more tied to their offspring than men, and play no role in binding together the family. Not families, but cities, as we have seen, are the beneficiaries of the ties between lovers and beloveds.

Pleased at Alcestis' noble sacrifice of herself for her beloved, the gods send her back from Hades. Orpheus, in contrast, did not sacrifice himself for his beloved, contriving to rescue his beloved from Hades without giving his own life for hers. Just as Phaedrus denigrates him as "soft, inasmuch as he was a minstrel" (179d), the gods punish him as a result of his defective love. Phaedrus' gods share his predilections for the absolute service of the lover, as he revises the old tale that has Orpheus punished because he challenged the gods. Phaedrus sees less problem with human arrogance toward the gods than with a lover's independence from his beloved.

Phaedrus' example of Achilles, however, does not fit his previous pattern – of lovers who do (Alcestis) or do not (Orpheus) sacrifice themselves for their beloveds. Achilles, who revenges his lover Patroclus' death even though he knows it will mean his own, is the beloved in Phaedrus' interpretation. Phaedrus emphasizes the novelty of his position on this

[25] Note how Phaedrus drops the beloved from his considerations of utility as his speech progresses. Cf. 178c and 178e with 179a.

point by citing Aeschylus' view to the contrary. Phaedrus' revision accords to the beloved the highest award for nobility – for the gods "honor Achilles more than Alcestis and sent him to the Isles of the Blessed." The condition of Achilles' superiority, surprisingly, is his not loving, although Phaedrus leaves this inference unspoken. Whereas the noble deeds of the lover are "god-inspired," those of the beloved are his own (179e–180b).

Phaedrus' revision of poetry depreciates love and praises self-sufficient virtue. The lover, whom the gods deprive of the opportunity for virtue through the compulsion of love, is at best an occasion for the beloved's triumphant nobility. Achilles' lover Patroclus, who goes into battle wearing Achilles' armor, and dies in his place, plays the role that Alcestis plays in Phaedrus' first story. But no honor accrues to him in Phaedrus' account. Indeed, Phaedrus does not even mention Patroclus' deed of valor. He says that Achilles "dared *to choose* to rescue his lover Patroclus" (emphasis mine) without saying that it is his corpse that he dares to rescue, or that Achilles himself is in part responsible for his death. Achilles, Phaedrus does mention, dies "after him who has died" (180a),[26] but if Achilles is trying to join his lover in the Isles of the Blessed, Phaedrus neglects to tell us. He appears to have forgotten about the lover. One wonders what Phaedrus' lover Eryximachus hears in his speech.

Phaedrus' selfish use of others takes its most beautiful appearance as an admiration for self-sufficient nobility, an admiration that Phaedrus attributes to the gods themselves (180a). In Phaedrus' speech, gods honor human beings, rather than the contrary.[27] Phaedrus wants to be a denizen of the healthy city of pigs, but he also wants relishes (see *Republic* 372c). He does not fully understand himself, insofar as he lauds salt simply for its utility. Nor does he recognize how important in his own account Patroclus remains to Achilles' noble deed. Phaedrus should pay more attention to his relationship with his own lover, for it is Phaedrus who "is accustomed to obeying [Eryximachus]" (176d), and not vice versa.

PAUSANIAS' PRAISE OF LAW

Phaedrus speaks from the perspective of a beloved, and speaks of the benefits Love brings not to lovers but to those whom they love. Every

---

[26] W. R. M. Lamb mistranslates "to die after" (*epapothanei*), as "sought death . . . to be joined with." Plato, *The Lysis, Symposium,* and *Gorgias* (Cambridge, MA: Harvard University Press, 1925), 105. His mistranslation indicates what one might expect Phaedrus to say.

[27] Rosen, *Plato's Symposium,* 55.

lover whom Phaedrus mentions dies as a result of his love. He seems to
have no concern that his lover will desert him, except by sacrificing his
life for his. After all, he and Eryximachus have been together for at
least sixteen years. Pausanias, however, whose speech we hear next,
focuses throughout on the tenuous position of the lover. One might
suppose that Phaedrus had done more than enough to establish that
being loved is a good thing, but Phaedrus had blithely ignored the
force of conventions and opinion, the laws (*nomoi*) in the broadest
sense.[28] Because those conventions disapprove of young men and boys
accepting lovers (see 183d–e), the lover's position is insecure. Pausanias' speech is an attempt to explain to a beloved that his accepting a
noble lover is a good at which Athenian law itself aims. Agathon, after
all, has just reached the height of public acclaim with the victory of one
of his tragedies, a position Socrates observed earlier in the evening
that much delights him (175e). While we are told of nothing new in the
relationship between Phaedrus and Eryximachus, we can speculate
what effect Agathon's recent success is having on his relationship with
Pausanias.

Pausanias exploits an ambiguity in Athenian law or custom concerning lovers. Conventions adverse to lovers are promoted especially
by fathers, who try to keep lovers away from their sons, believing that
lovers are the corrupters of youth. In fact, when lovers appear, fathers
instruct their sons' attendants to prevent their speaking with them.
Should they yield to lovers, they are reproached by their companions,
and the elders of the city concur. From this one might infer that for
boys to gratify their lovers is held in Athens to be shameful (183d–e).
But Athens, Pausanias notes, encourages lovers, and holds capturing
one's beloved to be noble, and failing to do so shameful. In fact, the
custom allows those in love to do without reproach what would
otherwise be considered most disgraceful behavior. It is even held that
gods pardon the lover when he forsakes an oath he swore to his beloved,
for there can be no oaths where sex is concerned (182d–183b). The gods
too encourage lovers.

Pausanias, however, turns what might have been a criticism of the
contradictions in Athenian law or custom into the greatest praise, and
the unsatisfactory position that lovers occupy within those customs into
a satisfactory one, at least for "noble" lovers like himself. Neither those

---

[28] Phaedrus had not once used the word *nomos* in his speech. Pausanias, in contrast, uses
     it twelve times.

who praise lovers, nor those who blame them, according to Pausanias, have adequately understood the complexity of the situation. Like Phaedrus before him, Pausanias revises Greek theology and poetry to serve his purposes. There are two Aphrodites, Pausanias claims, an elder, daughter of Heaven (Ouranos), whom we name Heavenly, and a younger, born of Zeus and Dione, we call Pandemic. And if there are two Aphrodites, he continues, there must be two Loves, for there is no Aphrodite without Love (180d–e).[29]

By duplicating gods of traditional Greek theology, Pausanias creates purified versions of gods, standards by which human beings and even Olympian gods – since Zeus fathers the pandemic Aphrodite – can be judged. Those devoted to the Heavenly Aphrodite and Love, according to Pausanias, will devote themselves to education, the good of their souls, and to philosophy. The noble lover, he says, loves the soul rather than the body, and "assists in making [his beloved] wise and good . . . contributing to prudence and the rest of virtue" (184c–e). Through the Heavenly Aphrodite – and the Love who accompanies her – humans gain access to a higher life than made possible by the Olympian gods worshiped by the city.

Although Pausanias describes a way of life beyond the city and its conventions, including its gods, he also recognizes the extent to which noble love requires the support of the city and its laws. Pausanias in fact presents a clever interpretation of what appears to be a double standard for lovers and beloveds as the attempt of Athenian law to move lovers in the direction of a nobler love. When "exhorting lovers to pursue and beloveds to flee," the law intends that the capture be made difficult but not impossible, thereby giving the lover and beloved time to test each others' characters (184a).

---

[29] The evidence for "two" Aphrodites seems questionable, although there are at least two accounts of Aphrodite's birth. In Hesiod, Aphrodite is born out of the white foam that formed around Ouranos's genitals, which Cronos severed and threw into the sea (*Theogony* 188–200). In the *Iliad*, Aphrodite is the daughter of Dione (Homer, *Iliad* 370 ff. See also Euripides, *Helen* 1098). Pausanias creates separate divinities on the basis of these two accounts of Aphrodite's birth. Bury cites evidence of a temple to Aphrodite Urania and to Aphrodite Pandemos. *The Symposium of Plato*, 31, note on 180d. This does not mean, however, that there are "two" Aphrodites, as Pausanias claims, rather than two names under which Aphrodite was worshiped. Moreover, the title "Pandemic" seems to refer to Aphrodite as a common deity of a deme (Bury, 31) with no sense of "popular" or "vulgar" which Pausanias gives it. In any case, Pausanias uses a complex tradition for his own purposes. And there is no evidence, other than Pausanias' speech, for two Loves.

Thus it is not that Athenian law is contradictory, according to Pausanias, but that it is complex, and that complexity is a sign of Athens' superiority to other cities. Athenian customs can be seen as a mean between the unqualified praise of pederasty, as in Elis or Boeotia, and its simple prohibition, as in Ionia and other places ruled by barbarians. In the former, "the gratification of lovers has been unqualifiedly legalized as noble . . . in order that they might have no trouble in trying to persuade the young, because they are incapable of speaking." Tyrannies, on the other hand, prohibit all activities that engender the pride and strong friendships that threaten their authority, including the relation between lovers and beloveds, but also philosophy and gymnastics (182a–d).

Whereas Phaedrus' praise of love turns into a praise of virtue, Pausanias' praise of love adds a praise of Athenian law. In cities of license, there is no care for the development of virtue; tyrannies even go so far as to prevent its acquisition. It is only a city like Athens, with its complex law on love, that fosters the development of its citizens' minds and characters. The obstacles placed on love by the law combined with the praise of successful lovers encourages intellectual and moral virtues to emerge. Lovers as well as those they love benefit from Athens' care: the abuse of lovers that Athenian law heaps upon them makes their cultivating a capacity to speak necessary for success. To win his beloved, the lover must persuade him, he must come to express his love in terms of his beloved's good. He must rise above the immediate gratification of body. A lover in Athens, who is subject to the city's complex laws, is therefore educated in virtue, and it is his own education by the laws that presumably makes possible in turn his education of his beloved in "prudence and the rest of virtue."

Or does it? As Pausanias presents the two Aphrodites and the two Loves, they are worlds apart, with different origins, and different purposes. If there is a middle ground, it is the law, whose double standard aims to separate the high from the low, souls from bodies, education from bodily pleasures. The middle ground does not bring together but disjoins. Pausanias' use of the dual, a Greek form that indicates a pair, rather than singular or plural, for the two Aphrodites and the two Loves is deceptive: there is nothing but the name that unites them. And yet even the noble lover desires the same physical pleasures as his shameful counterpart (cf. *Laws* 837c–d). His purpose is not education, even if he can provide it, and even if this alone makes his love justifiable; his purpose is sex. If his relationship with his beloved were not a sexual one, there would be no need to revise the law and public opinion to make it acceptable. As Pausanias reinterprets the law, its appearance of contradiction hides its noble purpose, but his own noble rhetoric veils the purpose he shares with the pandemic lover.

The education and concern for souls that Pausanias attributes to the higher Love is only a means to satisfy the desire that he attributes to the lower one. A young man approached by a lover faces a dilemma: it is noble to gratify only noble lovers, inasmuch as it is these who will educate them, but how will he distinguish noble from base ones, especially since they both want sex? Pausanias dismisses the concern: if the youth is deceived about his lover's character, it is no disgrace, for he has "granted his favors for the sake of virtue alone," and that is noble (184e–185b). The effect of Pausanias' reinterpretation of Athenian law is to make it easier for clever speakers – who talk of such things as "prudence and the rest of virtue," education, souls, philosophy, and noble love – to seduce those whom they love than for others less skilled in speech to do so. Pausanias' unscrupulousness can be seen in his argument that it is only tyrannies that reproach all sorts of lovers, and that they do so simply to maintain their power. Those fathers who try to protect their sons against lovers, he implies, resemble tyrants whose authority is threatened.

Pausanias has nevertheless been moved by Athens' blame of young men for accepting lovers to distinguish between a noble and base love, to present the former in terms of an education in virtue, and to explain Athenian law in similar terms. He is not simply shameless in his revision of Athenian law in his own interests, for were he shameless the law would not matter to him. He wants to gratify his desire while retaining the good opinion of others. To this extent, those who understand Pausanias as conventional are correct.[30] Although he reinterprets convention, his reinterpretation makes his satisfaction of his desires conventional, even honorable. He knows that he needs the city, and that he must find a way to justify his passion to his beloved and to the public. When he speaks of the faithless lover who loves only the body, and so reneges his promises of fidelity when his beloved loses his youth (183d–e), we should

---

[30] Plochmann sees in Pausanias "a willingness to abide by local customs." "Hiccups and Hangovers in the *Symposium*," 17. And Rosen objects. *Plato's Symposium*, 48 n. 17. Pausanias, in fact, is more than willing to abide by local customs; he is so conventional that he tries to transform local custom so that it allows him to satisfy his desire. See Paul W. Ludwig, *Eros and Polis: Desire and Community in Greek Political Theory* (Cambridge, UK: Cambridge University Press, 2002), 44.

remember that he has been with Agathon for many years. He himself has not reneged. And Agathon has matured into a publicly acclaimed poet.

It is Aristophanes' turn to speak next, but he is so overcome by hiccups that he must pass. He asks the doctor Eryximachus who is next in line either to stop his hiccups or to speak in his place until they stop. Eryximachus offers to do both, and gives his speech while the comic poet employs the cures he suggests (185c–e). While his art of medicine brings order to the comic poet's body (189a), his speech describes the power of art to give order to the cosmos.

ERYXIMACHUS' PRAISE OF ART

Since Eryximachus is present at the symposium with his beloved Phaedrus, as Pausanias is with Agathon, we might expect him to follow Pausanias' lead in justifying the nobility of a lover's love. But Eryximachus says nothing in his speech about human lovers and their beloveds. Although he acknowledges that Pausanias did well to describe two Loves, he objects to limiting love to the souls of human beings. His "own art of medicine has shown that love presides over many other things as well, including the bodies of animals and those things that grow on the earth, and so to speak over all things that are" (186a–b).

Eryximachus reproaches Pausanias for taking a human perspective on love, rather than speaking of all living beings, or even of all things. But when he does so, the beautiful or the noble disappears from sight. Other than in his references to Pausanias' speech, Eryximachus associates *kalon*, the noble or beautiful, with a compliance with necessity, as when he urges that "it is noble and necessary to gratify the good and healthy things of each body" (186c). He identifies the good with the healthy, and the bad with the sick. The word virtue does not occur at all in his speech. Neither does the word law, which played so large a role in Pausanias' speech. And the only time Eryximachus refers to soul in his speech is his early reproach of Pausanias for seeking love only in the souls of human beings (186a). Pausanias may have also reduced love to body, but he did so under the guise of a noble love. Eryximachus dispenses with any such beautiful cover.

When Eryximachus describes two Loves, he uses no traditional names of Greek deities, as had Pausanias. And he refers not to noble and base loves but to healthy and unhealthy conditions. It is the job of the doctor to bring things most at enmity in the body – opposite things such as hot and cold, dry and moist, or bitter and sweet – into concord. Through medicine the doctor induces changes so that bodies are in a state of harmony or health, even instilling love where it should be instilled and removing it where it should be removed (186b–e). What Eryximachus learns through his art, moreover, gives him the key to understanding all things. Since the two loves compete throughout the cosmos, "not only is medicine captained by the god [Love]," but other arts are as well (186e ff.). Eryximachus mentions gymnastics, farming, music, astronomy, and divination, concluding with the thought that Love has "a wide and great power," or rather "all power (*pasan dunamin*)" (188d).

It is not Love, however, in Eryximachus' analysis, that has such total power, but the arts that control the two loves, instilling and removing them, and being able to replace sickness with health, whether in the human body, in the seasons of the year, or in the relations between gods and human beings. Human control is clearest when Eryximachus describes the doctor, whereas when he comes to astronomy he describes it as a science rather than an art (188b). It does not seem possible that human art could control the revolutions of stars, the seasons, weather, frosts, hailstorms, or blights that Eryximachus mentions as concerns of astronomy (188a–b).[31] But when Eryximachus arrives at the final art that he discusses – divination – he combines the language of science with the language of art: inasmuch as divination "knows scientifically (*epistasthai*) erotic matters," it is "the craftsman (*dēmiourgos*) of friendship between gods and human beings." As such, divination would supplement, and perhaps supplant, the science of astronomy, for it would control seasons, plagues, and famines by crafting friendship with the gods. When Eryximachus says that the gods are "stronger" than we are, he refers less to the limits of our arts than to the power implied in our crafting friendship with them (188d). When he speaks of friendship between gods and humans, that friendship entails a kind of descent of the divine, insofar as the gods become subject to human art or science.

Eryximachus uses the language of medicine itself to explain divination's task – the "overseeing and healing of loves" (188c–d). The verb for healing is that from which the noun for doctor is formed: the doctor is literally the

---

[31] Nevertheless Empedocles, whose cosmic theory of love and strife in some ways resembles Eryximachus' theories, promises his students the knowledge that would give control of the weather. *Ancilla to the Pre-Socratic Philosophers: A Complete Translation of the Fragments in Diels, Fragmente der Vorsokratiker*, Kathleen Freeman (Cambridge: Harvard University Press, 1948), 64, fragment 111, and Ludwig, *Eros and Polis*, 72 n. 7.

one who heals, and healing is practicing medicine. The art of divination for Eryximachus is a form of medicine. Not Love but an imagined human art controls the two loves, and procures the greatest good for human beings by controlling them. Eryximachus himself begins his speech admitting his intention of "revering" (*presbeuomen*) his own art (186b).[32]

Whereas Pausanias' speech attempts to leave room for himself among the noble lovers, who encourage virtue in their beloveds, Eryximachus' place in his cosmological scheme is not as a lover at all. Indeed, lovers and beloveds hardly enter Eryximachus' speech, as he speaks of the arts and the harmony they produce out of discordant elements. In his speech, Eryximachus occupies the place of the artisan who can control love for the sake of human benefit. Just as Eryximachus' beloved Phaedrus praised the self-sufficient virtue of Achilles, Phaedrus' lover Eryximachus praises the self-sufficient knower, who has "all power." Eryximachus does not even try to connect his knowledge or art with love, or to present those who possess erotic arts as themselves erotic. He gives no hint that he is praising love from the point of view of a lover, as did Pausanias, rather than that of an artisan or craftsman able to benefit humanity as a result of his knowledge and skill. Eryximachus' being a doctor seems unconnected to his being a lover. Indeed, we wonder why someone with such total power would be a lover at all.

Only with the dramatic details that Plato supplies us – Eryximachus' relationship with Phaedrus – do we hear in his speech a lover's plea. Like Pausanias, Eryximachus appeals to both his beloved and his city. Pausanias implicitly addresses his beloved, urging him that it is noble for him to accept a lover who will educate him in virtue. He also addresses his city, urging that the cultivation of lovers and beloveds whose relationship aims at the noble is the very purpose of its laws about love. The seediness of his speech hides under the guise of a kind of political theorizing about the laws concerning love that reveals the superiority of Athens to other cities. So too does Eryximachus implicitly speak to his beloved: if we get together, I can promise you health, power, contentment, as a result of my art. And to his city he says that the very understanding of nature and art that allows him to benefit his beloved, and is therefore the basis of their relationship, also confers the greatest benefit on cities, inasmuch as it permits the control of all things through knowledge or science. The seediness of *his* speech hides under the guise of an understanding of the cosmos that benefits humanity. It is no accident that Eryximachus' beloved is concerned with his health. This beloved and his lover certainly go together, and they have a harmonious life together, one that hardly indicates the noble love about which Pausanias spoke. Indeed, the harmony between Phaedrus and Eryximachus – that of an amoral self-interestedness – exemplifies the cosmological harmony Eryximachus' art intends to accomplish.

Eryximachus turns away from Pausanias' concern with the laws or conventions of Athens to the cosmos itself. His speech is more ambitious, although he appeals to bodies rather than to souls, to comfortable preservation that the arts can provide rather than to nobility, and to health rather than to virtue. Phaedrus' speech, we have seen, culminates in an assertion of self-sufficiency in relation to the divine, Pausanias' culminates in clever rhetoric that hides seduction, and Eryximachus' in an art that provides the key to understanding and controling the cosmos, all masquerading as pious praises to the god to whom human beings owe the greatest goods.

Plato confirms Socrates' argument in the *Apology* that the corrupters in the city are many (*Apology* 25a–b). But here he also shows us their sophistication. Socrates' speech on Love, as we shall see, is a response to theirs. They constitute the intellectual milieu in which he lives his philosophic life and to which he responds. And the corrupters even appear similar to Plato's Socrates himself. Like Phaedrus, Socrates revises traditional poetry about the gods and heroes, in the direction of a virtuous self-sufficiency (*Republic* 387d). Like Pausanias, Socrates speaks of wisdom and virtue and philosophy, education and the care of souls, and even the task of the highest sort of lover to educate his beloved (*Phaedrus* 253b). Like Eryximachus, Socrates seeks a knowledge of the whole and even claims to possess an erotic art (*Phaedo* 96a ff. and *Phaedrus* 257a). Before Socrates distinguishes himself from these men, however, the poets have their turns, and present their own wisdom in their speeches in praise of Love. And just as Aristophanes aimed his comic art at Socrates' pretension in the *Clouds*, Plato's Aristophanes now aims his comic art at the pretensions he has just heard.

ARISTOPHANIC COMEDY

Because his hiccups do not stop until he applies the doctor's cure of sneezing, Aristophanes "wonders that the orderliness of the body calls for such noises and garglings" (189a). In effect, he wonders at what

Eryximachus has combined – a disorderly nature and a powerful art that orders it. If nature is as disordered as Eryximachus presents it, could art be powerful enough to order it? Or if art can produce the order that Eryximachus promises, can nature be as disordered as he presents it?[33] Aristophanes implies Eryximachus' inconsistency: he has neglected either the limits of art or the potential of nature. His own speech will dwell on the former.

By giving Aristophanes hiccups, Plato makes him resemble a character in one of his own plays. In Aristophanes' *Clouds*, Strepsiades is not able to give the proper greeting to Socrates' new gods, a chorus of Clouds, as they come onto the stage, because he has to relieve himself (*Clouds* 295–96). Aristophanes' mockery lies in the contrast between the solemnity of the occasion, as Socrates' new divinities descend from heaven, and the bodily necessities that determine Strepsiades' actions. Now, in the *Symposium*, Aristophanes himself is prevented by a bodily necessity from speaking, and even from speaking in worship of a god, one that the encomiasts suppose has not hitherto been recognized sufficiently (177a–c). The speeches on Love thus far reported have been overblown, pretentious, and even impious. Phaedrus' culminates in a praise of a self-sufficient virtue that human beings achieve through their own efforts, without the inspiration of the gods (180a–b). Pausanias' interprets Athenian law so that it discriminates between a noble and a base Love, both stemming from the gods, and supports the one and discourages the other (182d ff.). Law, in other words, does for humans what the gods do not.[34] And now, during Eryximachus' speech about the control that human art or science exerts over the cosmos, and even over the gods, comes the inarticulate noise of Aristophanes' hiccups.[35]

In contrast to the purportedly noble lovers and beloveds that Phaedrus and Pausanias describe, and Eryximachus' powerful craftsmen, the proudest of Aristophanes' characters fail in their enterprise, have no concern with education, and develop no arts. They do not even

---

[33] Focusing on this side of Eryximachus' speech, Saxonhouse understands Eryximachus' vision to be one of "a natural harmony and a benevolent nature." *Fear of Diversity*, 165. Lutz and Ludwig, in contrast, focus on Eryximachus' view of the great power of art. Lutz, *Socrates' Education to Virtue*, 62, and Ludwig, *Eros and Polis*, 71–72.

[34] Victorino Tejera suggests that "a precipitating cause of Aristophanes' attack of hiccoughs was the *dishonest* cynicism of Pausanias' self-serving sophistry." *Plato's Dialogues One by One: A Dialogic Interpretation* (Lanham, MD: University Press of America, 1999), 438.

[35] Similarly, in Aristophanes' *Frogs*, a chorus of frogs, whose sounds includes croaking, resounds in the background as the god Dionysus travels to Hades and thus defies the limits of death in order to rescue a poet (*Frogs*, 209–10, 220, 225, 235, 239, and 256).

have human shape. Aristophanes offers to tell not of their deeds but of their sufferings (189d; cf. *Phaedrus* 245c). In the earliest times, "the form of each human being was round all over, with back and sides in a circle," each with four arms, four legs, and two faces looking in opposite directions. The circle-beings, which include male, female, and mixed types, are able to walk upright, but their fastest movement is tumbling in a circle. Although these beings who tumble about like roly-polies seem hardly the stuff heroes are made of, they were, Aristophanes relates, lofty and proud, and attempt an ascent to heaven to assault the gods. Because the gods do not want to destroy them and thereby lose the honors they receive from human beings, Zeus punishes them by cutting them into two. But these newly divided beings have no time for the gods. Overcome by intense longing for their other halves and their desire to grow together again, they begin dying off in each other's arms due to hunger and inactivity, unwilling to do anything apart. In Aristophanes' account, love is the desire to restore a lost unity, which arises out of our deservedly maimed condition. Without the gods' intervention, love leads to death. Taking pity, Zeus moves their genitals to their cut sides so that through sex they might preserve the race, and finding some relief from their longing "turn to deeds and care for the rest of life." Love "attempts to heal human nature" by making one out of two, but there is no healing (190b–191d).

Punished by the gods for their overreaching, our ancestors no longer look to heaven, but only to the earth, as they wander about searching for their other halves. Their motion is that of upright human beings, but their forms bestow no dignity. Greek tradition, in contrast, tells of Oedipus' answer to the riddle of the Sphinx that understands the human being in his prime – he moves erect on two feet, and can therefore look ahead as he walks through life, and even up to the heavens.[36] But Aristophanes' two-footed human beings, who walk as we walk, are only halves. The gods position their faces not so that they can look where they are going, and surely not so that they can look up, but rather so that they look down at their navels and remember their punishment. The half-beings are aware of "riddles": they "divine" that they want something but they cannot say what it is (192c–d). They do not solve riddles. The ones who look up in Aristophanes' story, the

---

[36] Seth Benardete, "Sophocles' *Oedipus Tyrannus*," in *Ancients and Moderns*, ed. Joseph Cropsey (New York: Basic Books, 1964). See also Leon Kass, *Toward a More Natural Science* (New York: The Free Press, 1985), 286–88.

circle-beings, do so not by walking as upright beings, but by rolling around like balls. Their view of the heavens is momentary and unsteady, and since they have pairs of eyes on both sides of their heads, they cannot see the heavens without at the same time seeing the earth. They resemble the disciples of the Socrates whom Aristophanes creates in the *Clouds*, who bend over investigating the things under the earth, while their asses do astronomy (*Clouds* 193–94). The vision of the high cannot be severed from a vision of the low, and nothing in-between gets much attention.

Aristophanes' tale about pride and its fall mocks the pretensions of the previous speakers. In contrast to Phaedrus, Aristophanes leaves little room for heroic virtue, at least in the current state of human life. He attributes courage and manliness only to the acts of boys embracing their male lovers (192a). Unlike Pausanias, Aristophanes does not refer to education or nobility. As to law, it appears not as a means of encouraging noble love, as it had for Pausanias, but only as compulsion contrary to desire (191b). Unlike Eryximachus, Aristophanes says nothing of art, knowledge, or science possessed by humans; the only artisans he mentions are gods (190e and 192d). It is Love who is "a doctor" who "cures" the ills of humanity (189d).[37] Aristophanes uses "mind," or "intelligence" (*nous*) only in idiomatic expressions,[38] and his human world is virtually speechless, as Plato renders Aristophanes himself by giving him hiccups. There are no lovers and beloveds, so that one must persuade the other, as in Pausanias' speech (182b): each half is equally lover and beloved, equally attracted to the other half. Persuasion is unnecessary, and the desire of the lovers is manifest in embracing or in sex, not in conversing. It is not clear, in fact, if Aristophanes' embracing lovers have the distance from each other even to see each

[37] Strauss, *On Plato's Symposium*, 123 and 130. Ludwig points out the resemblance between Aristophanes' circular beings and Empedocles' description of an earlier epoch of asexual reproduction when people were "born with faces and breasts both front and back." Ludwig raises the question of whether Aristophanes' speech constitutes "a gentle satire aimed at the doctor through exploitation of one of his sources." *Eros and Polis*, 71–72. Moreover, with his emphasis on natural science, Eryximachus resembles the protagonist of the *Clouds* whom Aristophanes mocked; see Plochmann, "Hiccups and Hangovers in the *Symposium*"; Bloom, "Ladder of Love," 98; and Lutz, *Socrates' Education to Virtue*, 62.

[38] Aristophanes says we should choose a beloved "to our taste" (literally, "to our mind," 193c–d), and that those descended from males "pay no attention to" (literally, "do not have their minds on") marriage and children (192b). See Benardete, *"Plato's Symposium,"* 59, and Strauss, *On Plato's Symposium*, 132. Cf. Pausanias' speech, 181b–d. Also note the advice Eryximachus gives to Aristophanes at 189b–c.

other, much less converse. They do not want to know the one they love but to become one with each other.[39] In fact, Love is not of the other, but of the whole they might form (192e–193a). In Aristophanes' story only the gods speak (190c–e; 192d–e). It is not sex with the other that each wants; the soul of each plainly wants something else, but as to what, it is "incapable of saying" (192c–d). Aristophanes' humans are as inarticulate as Pausanias' Boeotians (182b).

In contrast to the first three speakers, Aristophanes restores the power of the gods. In his story, Zeus contrives a plan about what to do with the rebels, and he elicits Apollo's help. But while the gods play a crucial role in Aristophanes' tale, their role is to punish, to assure that humans remain in the weakened state in which they are no longer a threat. With the gods' oversight, humans no longer think any such "high thoughts" as those that moved their ancestors (190b). We learn from the experience of the circle-beings that there is no ascent for us, and that the gods descend only to punish. Aristophanes, in effect, restores the "snowy Olympus" and "murky Tartarus" that Phaedrus in his assertion of human sufficiency excised from Hesiod's poem (178b), but he places Olympus so out of reach that humans simply live in murky Tartarus. Aristophanes' human beings are shades of their former selves. While Phaedrus concentrates on the human in the absence of anything above or below, Aristophanes restores the high at the cost of separating it from anything below it. Disconnected from anything above, the human disappears, along with the soul, and only high and low are left, with no middle ground. The only time that Aristophanes uses the word "soul" in his speech is when he says that the soul is "incapable of speaking" (192c). If the circular beings had souls that were not reducible to their bodies, they could not be severed into two. Humans long for unity, but it is only a corporeal unity with their other halves. Aristophanes expresses only the half, only our desire to be with, even to be one with, the person we love, and not our desire to know or even to see that person. There is no conversation between Aristophanes' lovers. Touching predominates over sight. Aristophanes' speech leaves no room for philosophy; longing or desire has nothing to do with wisdom. That sneezing and gargling can cure hiccups suggests to Aristophanes not that nature is orderly enough to allow such cures but that nature is disorderly enough to need them.

Aristophanes' characters in his *Symposium* speech are, as Aristotle said of comic characters, inferior to and uglier than ourselves *(Poetics,*

---

[39] Strauss, *On Plato's Symposium*, 140 and 150.

I.v.1–2; I.ii.7). But if we see only the inferiority of those on the comic stage, we might not see ourselves in them. Laughing at them would foster only a sense of superiority. Our laughter would be, as Hobbes describes all laughter, "a sudden glory,"[40] and we would resemble our circular ancestors, who no doubt misled by their physical shape suppose they belong in heaven. If the comic poet were attempting to moderate pretension, he would fail. On the other hand, if Aristophanes' comedy reminds us of our pretensions, as the wrinkles left by Apollo are intended to do for the half-beings, and we see ourselves reflected only in what is inferior to ourselves, his mockery runs the risk of demoralizing. And there could be no laughter; it is a fact that no one at the symposium laughs at Aristophanes' speech (193e; cf. 222c). Forever doomed to physical separation from what they love and with eyes only for their incompleteness, Aristophanes' humans never look to heaven. It is not surprising that scholars have considered Aristophanes' presentation of human beings in this speech to be tragic.[41] And yet Plato's Aristophanes, in the words of Saxonhouse, does not "uplift us with the beauty of our necessary tragedy." He evokes fear and pity, "not by beautifying the fearful, but by depicting the ugly."[42]

Aristophanes restores the divine, in the face of the sophistic enlightenment of the previous speakers, but in a way that makes it inaccessible to human beings. His move reestablishes limits for human life. Agathon, who speaks next, assumes that the divine is accessible to human beings such as himself, as demonstrated by the ability of his poetry to move audiences. Loved by the god, the poet becomes one with him. Aristophanes' Zeus remains vigilant against human hubris, while Agathon's god, Love, loves the poet, Agathon himself. There are no limits.

TRAGIC VICTORY

Before Agathon has a chance to speak, Socrates, who has not been reported as saying anything since the encomia began, interrupts the

---

[40] Thomas Hobbes, *Leviathan*, ed. Michael Oakeshott (New York: Collier Macmillan, 1962), 52.

[41] For example, Ludwig, *Eros and Polis*, 56; Lutz, *On Socrates' Education to Virtue*, 71; Waller R. Newell, *Ruling Passion: The Erotics of Statecraft in Platonic Political Philosophy* (Lanham, MD: Rowman and Littlefield, 2000), 74; Rosen, *Plato's Symposium*, 157; and Strauss, *On Plato's Symposium*, 141.

[42] Saxonhouse, *Fear of Diversity*, 163–64; see also Nussbaum, *The Fragility of Goodness*, 172–73.

flow of the speeches to provoke a discussion with Agathon (194a). Socrates introduces the distinction between the senseless many who are judges in the theater, and the sensible people who are better judges, almost as if he were trying to wean Agathon from the popular applause of his drama and find a common ground between them. Phaedrus, "the father of the *logos*," however, intervenes to keep the agreed-upon encomia to Love on track. He foresees the end of the speeches about Love if Socrates has anyone with whom to converse, especially someone beautiful (194d). Agathon's praise of Love thus replaces the conversation that Socrates sought. The tragic poet will have his say, and Socrates must wait.

Agathon begins by criticizing all the previous speakers, for not one of them knows "the correct way" of making an encomium. Those speakers include not only the well-established poet who has just spoken but also his long-time lover Pausanias.[43] Instead of praising the god, Agathon claims, the others have been simply explaining how happy human beings are for the goods the god gives them. The arrogant Agathon, paradoxically, locates the superiority of his speech in its greater piety, for in contrast to the others Agathon will say what sort of god Love is, and only then the gifts he bestows (194e–195a).

Agathon has not, however, offered to define his terms at the outset. He will say "what sort" Love is, not what Love is.[44] When he proceeds to describe Love as beautiful and good, we are reminded of Polus, student of the famous rhetorician Gorgias, who when asked what art Gorgias teaches claims merely that it is "the most beautiful of arts," offering a reply to which Socrates objects (*Gorgias* 448c). By the end of his speech, Agathon produces a rhetorical flourish characteristic of Gorgias, to which Socrates calls attention (198c). Agathon, the rhetorician–poet, deals with externals, with the appearances, the beautiful attributes of Love, and Love's virtues, or the manifestations of his goodness. For Agathon there is nothing beyond the appearances. The world belongs to the poets.

Love is beautiful, Agathon argues, inasmuch as he is young, delicate, supple in form, and of beautiful hue. Love's youth is clear from his

---

[43] By contrast, Eryximachus, whose bold speech praises the power of art over the cosmos, begins with a kind of deference to Pausanias, who spoke before him (185e–186a). In contrast to Phaedrus and Eryximachus, the other lover and beloved present at the *Symposium*, Agathon and Pausanias never speak to each other during the evening (see, e.g., 176c and d, and 177a and c).

[44] Strauss, *On Plato's Symposium*, 156; Bloom, "Ladder of Love," 117; Rosen, *Plato's Symposium*, 181.

avoiding the old, and always keeping company with the young, and of course with the beautiful. Thus holds the old saying, Agathon notes, "like approaches like" (195b). Agathon not only corrects Phaedrus for saying that Love is the oldest god (195b), but he implicitly denies Pausanias' distinction between a noble (or beautiful) Love and a base or vulgar one. For Agathon, all Love is beautiful. Like the young Socrates reproached by the old philosopher Parmenides, Agathon neglects the ugly (*Parmenides* 211c–e; see 197b). He ignores Pausanias in another way as well: Agathon's older lover could hardly find a place for his own love in his beloved's paean to youth.

When Agathon uses the old saying, "like to like," he is not using it in the usual way – to describe those who love each other. The ones who are alike are Love, who is young, and the young, whom Love loves. Agathon's speech is not about human lovers and beloveds, but about the "god" and his favorite. We learn exactly who this is when Agathon demonstrates the "wisdom" of the god: Love must be wise, he argues, since to inspire poets, Love himself must be a poet. After all, what one does not have or know, Agathon observes, one could not give or teach to another (197a). For Agathon, wisdom becomes indistinguishable from poetry. And it is not just the young, but the young poet – Agathon himself – whom the god most loves. In terms of Climacus' analogy between the god and the king who loves a lowly maiden, the god is able to arrange for the consummation of his love by means of the ascent of his beloved. But neither Agathon's god Love nor Love's inspired poet recognize the problems in their relationship that Climacus points out (*PF* 29–30). In Agathon's speech, the god shows no signs of being troubled by his glorification – and hence transformation – of his beloved poet, nor is the poet inspired by love troubled by his good fortune. He is no more concerned about the source of his poetry (see *PF* 30) than is Agathon by what he might owe to others, whether it be Pausanias or the crowd whose applause he craves. And Agathon in his encomium eagerly celebrates the inspiration that for Phaedrus qualifies the lover's virtue.

Agathon's arguments for the other "virtues" of Love are reminiscent of the sophistical reasoning of the Unjust Speech in the *Clouds* (1036 ff.). Love is just, Agathon argues, because all consent to his rule, moderate because he rules all other desires, and courageous because he conquers even the divine warrior Ares, who fell in love with Aphrodite. In this account, virtue is hardly distinguishable from its opposite, since the reign of Love means the end of right, when justice is reduced to consent, the end of self-restraint, when all desires yield to Love, and of courageous deeds, when the most warlike leaves his armor outside the bedchamber. Like the Unjust Speech, Agathon in effect recommends vice as the path to happiness, and takes comfort in that the gods too follow this path (cf. *Clouds* 1045–52, and 1079–82).

In response to Eryximachus, Agathon reclaims the arts: the arts are not human ways of overcoming discord in bodies, as Eryximachus proposes, but grow from a divinely inspired love of beauty (197a–b). Agathon thus gives Eryximachus' "erotic arts" a different meaning, as he displaces the "knowledgeable" Asclepius, whom Eryximachus admires, with a love-inspired Apollo as the founder of medicine (cf. 197b with 186e). Agathon may "honor" his art, as Eryximachus does his (196d), but for Eryximachus, the arts control noble and base loves, and inculcate the one and remove the other. But Agathon makes no distinction between noble and base. In contrast to Aristophanes, Agathon refers to the soul, for it is, he says, the dwelling place of Love for both gods and humans (195e; 196b). But like Aristophanes, he is completely silent about mind or intelligence. All that Love must do to "teach" is to "touch."[45] Unlike Pausanias, who describes how the noble lover must persuade his beloved, and Aristophanes, who has gods speaking at least to each other, no one speaks in Agathon's speech. There is no need, no purpose for speech. Agathon's encomium culminates simply in the inspired poet, who is blessed, and whose love of beauty leads him to create to the applause of others. The poet is both lover and beloved. He has, and needs, no other half, even if he wants his audience to recognize his "self-sufficiency." While both Socrates and Aristophanes refer to Agathon and Pausanias' relationship (177e and 193c), Agathon never mentions Pausanias' name. Like Achilles in Phaedrus' speech, he seems to be alone in the Isles of the Blessed, but without having to follow his lover to death.

Agathon may be the first speaker to focus on Love as a god, but god and human merge. Thus his model for Love is the young lover, or poet, possessed by the god, who creates out of love for his own beauty.[46] He is both lover and beloved, as self-contained as Aristophanes'

---

[45] See Agathon's opposition between those for whom the god becomes a teacher and those whom the god does not touch, 197a. As Rosen notes, "Agathon continues to believe that wisdom may be imparted by touching." *Plato's Symposium*, 187.

[46] After Agathon stops speaking, the narrator reports, the company applauds "inasmuch as the youngster had spoken so appropriately to himself and to the god" (198a). What is appropriate to the one is appropriate to the other.

embracing lovers long to be.[47] Socrates sees into Agathon's character when his description of his "lofty-thinking" (*megalophrosunē*, 194b) echoes Aristophanes' reference to the hubristic "lofty-thinking" of the circle-beings (190b).

In their different ways, each of these poets understands human fulfillment as radically idiosyncratic. Aristophanes' humans seek their other halves, not any knowledge or wisdom that transcends their own and that they might hold in common with others. The circle-beings have their lofty thoughts, but "mind" has no place in the lives of the human beings produced by the cutting. For Aristophanes, philosophy is not possible, whereas for Agathon it is not necessary, since Love is the sufficient condition for wisdom. Wisdom comes immediately, through divine inspiration, and it is expressed immediately through the poet's creation. There is no striving, no conflict, no possibility of failure. Agathon thus leaves no place for suffering. As Bloom observes, in Agathon's speech "all the harsh things have been overcome by the soft and gentle ones."[48] His poetry produces tears no more than Aristophanes' produces laughter.

Can Agathon really be a tragic poet? According to Aristotle, tragedy portrays characters nobler (or more beautiful) than ourselves (*Poetics* I.ii.7 and I.iv). Because even the noble suffer terrible things, tragedy may lead to despair about the human condition. If tragedy beautifies the suffering of tragic figures, however, and moves us with that beauty, beauty appears sufficient. Not even suffering can destroy it. To understand suffering as beautiful is to see it from the perspective of the observer rather than that of the sufferer. After all, when we watch a tragedy, we suffer *with* its tragic figures. Suffering with another is not the same as suffering, for it requires distance as well as identification. Tragic characters learn by suffering (see Aeschylus, *Agamemnon*, 174–78), but we learn by their suffering. Tragedy might lead its audience to hope, inordinate hope, rather than to despair. Just as comedy might bind us to necessity more than is necessary by letting us see ourselves in our inferiors, tragedy might lead us to suppose that we can be free from suffering. Tragedy's contrivance, the god in the machine (*mechane*, see 191b), who appears at a play's end to resolve conflict and reestablish order, is not the corruption of tragedy that Nietzsche claimed but its logical development.[49] Later that evening, the drunken Alcibiades

[47] For characterizations of Agathon, see Rosen, *Plato's Symposium*, 169; Bloom, "Ladder of Love," 120; Benardete, "Plato's *Symposium*," 188–90.
[48] Bloom, "Ladder of Love," 112, 116, and 121.
[49] Nietzsche, *The Birth of Tragedy*, 111.

warns Agathon not to suffer the deception from Socrates that he himself suffered. It is only a fool, Alcibiades says, who learns from suffering (222b). This tragic poet whom he addresses, however, already supposes a world beyond suffering, which he describes in his speech. He has already heeded Alcibiades' advice. It is, in fact, the message of his own speech.

SOCRATES' TURN

When Agathon stops speaking, "all present applauded vigorously," echoing the applause Agathon must have received from the thirty thousand Greeks the evening before (198a; cf. 175e and 194b). Agathon's poetry moves both Athens' elite and its demos, however exclusive that elite may view its current gathering (see 212d). Like the Just Speech in the *Clouds*, Socrates seems to be confronted with the practically universal corruption of his city (*Clouds* 1088–1104). But while Socrates joined the audience to watch Agathon's recent victory in the theater (194b), he does not now concede victory to the poet. He thought that encomia select the most beautiful of the truths about the topic, he tells them, but he has learned from listening to their speeches that praising means saying the greatest and most beautiful things regardless of whether or not they are true. They are all no better than ignoramuses, Socrates implies, performing before ignoramuses, while acting as if they were doing something grand (198d–199a; see *Phaedrus* 260b–c). It is surprising that Socrates' insult does not provoke the outrage or disturbance that threatens in the *Apology* (20e and 30c). When Socrates requests that the symposiasts allow him to tell the truth in his own way, they agree. They are either remarkably polite or they want to hear what he has to say.

Socrates begins by asking Agathon a few questions. Socrates calls Agathon upon stage – not to be admired for his tragedy by thirty thousand Greeks (175e, 194b) – but like a tragic figure to have his error about Love exposed and corrected. "Is love of something or of nothing?" Socrates first asks Agathon. Before letting him take a stab at the question, Socrates explains that he does not mean to ask whether love is love of a mother or a father (199d). Incest, the classic crime in Greek tragedy, is implicit in Agathon's endorsement of love as "like to like." One is most like one's own. Agathon's understanding of the lover as self-sufficient, his love directed at himself and his own productions, makes Love incestuous. Socrates' warning about an answer he does not want to his question is therefore appropriate for Agathon. And implicitly it corrects Aristophanes' presentation of Socrates in the *Clouds* as someone who teaches that incest is natural and the sacred sanction against it merely conventional (*Clouds* 1371–77, 1427–32, 1443–46).[50]

Thus not only Socrates' allusion to incest, but his very question, is a good one for Agathon, who identifies lover and beloved (see 204c). For Agathon, love is, in a way, of nothing, as it is not directed to an object outside itself. When Socrates asks whether love is of something or of nothing, he asks whether Love resembles something that can be understood only in relation to something other than itself. For example, a father is a father of someone, and a mother is a mother of someone, of a son or a daughter. Socrates' examples call attention not only to relationship, and therewith mutual dependence, but to the relationship between parents and their offspring. What one generates is both one's own and also other. Agathon's view of generation, focusing only on the poet's creations, is blind to the latter.

Following the pattern of Socrates' examples, Agathon agrees that love is "of something," of that which it desires or loves, of what it does not have or possess and of which it is in need. Agathon himself said, Socrates points out, that matters were arranged by the gods through a love of beautiful things. Love, he implied, is love of beauty. And so Love lacks and is in need of beautiful things, as well as good ones, Socrates adds, inasmuch as the good are beautiful. Love, then, is neither beautiful nor good (200a–201b).[51]

Agathon admits he knew "nothing" of what he was saying (201b). But if Agathon knows nothing at all, and if there is no truth in his beautiful speech, he has no way out of his perplexity. He is truly at a loss, as Socrates so often claims of himself, and needs in effect a miracle, a "god

[50] I therefore disagree with Bloom that Socrates' allusion to incest reveals more about himself than about Agathon, a sign that "Socrates will think more shamelessly" than his conventional interlocutor. According to Bloom, Agathon "keeps Eros within the bounds of the conventional," whereas Socrates reminds us of what "is naturally possible [but] forbidden by the gods," "Ladder of Love," 125. But it is Socrates who claims not to mean incest when he asks about Love, who therefore reminds Agathon that some things are forbidden. Rosen, in contrast to Bloom, argues that Socrates' allusion to incest is directed against Agathon, but nevertheless comes close to Bloom's position about the shameless character of philosophy when he distinguishes incest as "the self-destructive aspect of the desire for divine perfection," rightly to be feared, and concludes that "those who wish to be gods or *causa sui*, must come to terms with, or laugh at that fear." *Plato's "Symposium,"* 214–15. Both Bloom and Rosen accept Aristophanes' view of Socrates on this issue.
[51] For discussions of the "logic" of this argument, see Nussbaum, *The Fragility of Goodness*, 176–81; and A. W. Price, *Love and Friendship in Plato and Aristotle* (Oxford: Clarendon Press, 1989), 18–20.

in a machine" to help him. But Socrates typically proceeds to search
after proclaiming his perplexity, and now he has recourse to a contrivance, a kind of god in a machine, who enters in a tale that constitutes
Socrates' speech about Love. As in Kierkegaard, there is a sort of
descent on the part of a teacher, Diotima, to the learner Socrates. But in
Socrates' tale, the "god in the machine" is not a god, but a foreign
priestess, Diotima, who "taught him erotic matters" (210d). Conjuring
someone more than human but less than divine, Socrates completes
his drama by serving as a messenger from an oracle. Like oracular
pronouncement in tragedies (see, e.g., Sophocles, *Oedipus Tyrannus*
787–93; 1176–77), Socrates offers truth to those who inquire, although
that truth does not lead to tragic doom.

SOCRATES' PROPHETESS AND THE DAEMONIC

Diotima resembles the goddess of Parmenides' poem, who educates
him, just as Socrates says Diotima taught him.[52] Socrates' prophetess,
however, is not a goddess but a human prophetess, and she educates the
young Socrates not about "what is," as does Parmenides' goddess, but
about what lies between divine and human. Her argument is this: That
Love is not itself beautiful and good does not mean that he is ugly and
bad. Rather, he is between god and mortal, and a great daemon, for the
daemonic, which includes all divination and prophecy, serves as a link
between the gods and mortals, carrying messages and prayers in both
directions, because "god does not mix with human." Thus the daemonic
"in the middle [of humans and gods] fills up the interval so that it binds
together the whole itself" (201–203a). Without daemons there would be
no link between the parts of the whole, and therefore strictly speaking
no whole.

As the link between humans and gods, the daemonic takes the place
of Eryximachus' "craftsman of friendship between gods and humans"
(188d) – and therewith responds to Eryximachus' view of all powerful
human arts and sciences that bring harmony to hostile and discordant
elements in nature. Whereas Aristophanes questions whether such a
disorderly nature as Eryximachus presents is amenable to the control
he describes, Diotima questions whether a nature so amenable could
be as disorderly as Eryximachus describes it. If it is not, it is not as
much in need of a "cure" as Eryximachus supposes (see 188d, where

[52] Saxonhouse, *Fear of Diversity*, 174 n. 16.

Eryximachus refers to the function of prophecy as "curing"), and "all power" does not belong to the arts. The comic poet responds to Eryximachus by mocking his hubris – placing the divine out of the reach of the craftsman whom Eryximachus thought could control it. Socrates' response, in contrast, concedes to Eryximachus the possibility of a beneficial relation between human and divine. At the same time, Diotima contrasts the "daemonic man" who is wise in the association and converse between gods and humans with the vulgar man wise in arts and handicrafts (*cheirourgias*) (203a), echoing Eryximachus' reference to the craftsman (*dēmiourgos*) of friendship between humans and gods.[53] Eryximachus' deeds are those only of a "handyman," who prescribes for Phaedrus without knowing what is truly good (see *Laches* 195c ff.).

Diotima's account of love as an intermediary between human and divine also addresses both Aristophanes and Agathon. In Aristophanes' speech, the gods enforce the distance between the divine and human, who do not touch, unless it be by means of Zeus's punitive knife. Agathon, in contrast, collapses human and divine, for the beautiful lover is possessed by the god, and out of his love of beauty, he creates. Diotima addresses both of them by establishing a distance between human and divine, without losing the connection between the two. Diotima's daemonic binds gods and mortals together. Middles are double-edged, as illustrated by the midpoint of a line, which both joins two line segments and separates them. As intermediary between mortal and immortal, the daemonic links what Aristophanes left asunder, at the same time that it separates what Agathon collapsed. Diotima has in effect combined the comic poet's emphasis on lack and need with the tragedian's identification of the beautiful and the good with one's own. When lovers strive for their own, they strive for something higher, outside themselves. Diotima's formulation allows us to see Aristophanes' and Agathon's as halves, each in need of the other. The "stranger lady," as Socrates calls her, provides a link between the speeches of the two poets, without which they are alien to each other, their views of the world in seeming opposition.[54]

Thus it is appropriate that Aristophanes' and Agathon's speeches lie side by side, even though it was due only to Aristophanes' hiccups,

---

[53] Socrates uses a similar expression in the *Apology* to describe those artisans whom he examined for their wisdom, *cheirotechnas*, "manual artisans"(*Apology* 22c).

[54] Ludwig also understands Diotima's task as "resolving the tension between love of beauty and love of one's own by somehow combining the two or otherwise overcoming the dichotomy." For his thoughtful argument that Diotima's attempt fails to do so, see *Eros and Polis*, 216–20.

or to chance, that he spoke before Agathon rather than before Eryximachus. No seating plan of the evening's host put them there. Of course, underlying the "chance" that befalls Aristophanes is Plato's art. The switch between Aristophanes and Eryximachus lets us see more clearly Plato's hand than if they had been sitting next to each other from the first. When Aristodemus arrived uninvited, Agathon seats him by Eryximachus, thus keeping the place besides himself free for Socrates (175a). Plato's master manipulation, however, joins Agathon with Aristophanes. It is as if he says to Agathon what Alcibiades says to Socrates when he spies him sitting next to Agathon: "Why did you take a seat here and not by Aristophanes or someone else who is laughable and wishes to be?" (213c). Plato corrects not only Agathon's notion of the proper seating but Alcibiades' as well. Socrates does not belong with either Agathon or Aristophanes alone, but only with both together.

To join the two poets, however, is not an easy matter. Diotima does so only by introducing the daemonic – something that links divine and human. To serve this purpose, which neither divine nor human can perform, the daemonic must differ from each of them. Yet if the daemonic has nothing in common with those things it links, it would have no point of contact. Presumably it differs from each of the things it connects by virtue of its being mixed of elements possessed by both of them. But a link is necessary between god and human, Diotima says, because god and human do not mix. Can they, then, be mixed in the daemonic?

Diotima highlights the difficulty of the intermediary by speaking of it as what lies between god and "mortal" (202e), using the word not for human being, but a word related to the verb "to die." How can one be in-between mortal and immortal? To say that one's mortal part dies whereas one's immortal part lives forever confirms that something can be only one or the other. If something is needed to bind together mortal and immortal, it must be composed of both, rather than only one or the other: if only mortal or immortal, the binder would need something in turn to bind it to the one unlike itself. On the other hand, if the binder were both mortal and immortal, it would need something to bind itself together. The same difficulty emerges when Socrates asks Diotima, "Who are Love's father and mother?"[55] Since god and mortal do not mix – indeed, that is why there must be some third to join them

---

[55] There exist various accounts of Love's parents. See Bury, *The Symposium of Plato*, 22, note on 178b.

(203a) – Love's parents must both be one or the other to mate. But if they are one or the other, how could they generate an in-between?[56]

Diotima acknowledges that answering Socrates' question about Love's parents is "a somewhat long affair" (203a–b). She responds with a tale about Love's birth. As we might expect if god and mortal do not mate, Love's mother, Poverty, and his father, Resource, are more alike than their names at first suggest. Poverty in the story is very resourceful, as she "plots" to lie by the drunken Resource to conceive Love (203b–c). And Resource himself is in need of her to bring forth his offspring: a resource is a resource not in itself but only for the sake of some purpose. The common translation of the Greek word for "resource" as "means," or "way," indicates that it must be understood in terms of a relation, just as, to use Socrates' earlier illustration, a mother or a father is a parent of someone. But if Poverty and Resource are mixed beings, who are *their* parents? Diotima's tale therefore reproduces the question: how can one account for something between mortal and divine?

The tale does move the issue forward, however, in one way. When Diotima first establishes the possibility of middles, she refers to correct opinion, which partakes of wisdom inasmuch as it is correct, but of ignorance inasmuch as it cannot give an account of why it is correct (202a). But how do we know that correct opinion exists? Perhaps all opinion is false opinion. Correct opinion can be identified only from the outside, only by someone who has knowledge. If correct opinion knew its correctness, it would be knowledge and not opinion. Or, if it understood that it was opinion and not knowledge, it would question its correctness, or become philosophy. When Socrates inquires about Love's parents, he questions the intelligibility of an intermediate, which could exist as a link between human and divine only if it were not needed as a link, only if human and divine could mix. Socrates' question thus demonstrates not only that he knows that he does not understand, but also that he understands the problem. To answer Socrates' question, Diotima gives a mythical account of Love's parents that connects Love to philosophy. As the offspring of Poverty and Resource, Diotima says, Love is like his mother "always poor," and like his father "a plotter after the beautiful and the good"; he is "in-between ignorance and wisdom," and thus "philosophizing throughout life" (203d–e). Philosophy

---

[56] This difficulty explains why one might assume that Poverty is mortal and Resource divine, as scholars not surprisingly tend to do. See Bury, *The Symposium of Plato*, xl; and Lutz, *Socrates' Education to Virtue*, 87.

replaces correct opinion as the "middle" between ignorance and wisdom: in seeking wisdom the philosopher is not yet wise, nor is he so ignorant that he doesn't know that he doesn't know (204a–b). Inasmuch as Diotima's story about Love's origins responds to Socrates' questioning, it is appropriate that she describe Love as if he were modeled on Socrates: scheming after the beautiful and the good, a great hunter, and desirous of wisdom (see *Lysis* 218c).

Until now in the *Symposium*, philosophy has received no discussion and little notice. Although the guests at Agathon's party await Socrates' arrival, and Agathon in particular keeps a place for him on the couch by his side, those present at Agathon's leave little place for Socrates and his way of life in their encomia to Love. It is only Pausanias who makes reference to philosophy: it is for the sake of virtue and philosophy, he claims, that a boy might gratify his noble lover and engage in sex for the sake of his education (184d). But he does not connect philosophy with Love: for him the lover/teacher is not moved by philosophy, while it is the beloved who is seeking wisdom. Agathon claims that Eryximachus' account of medicine requires him to come to the defense of his own art (196d–e). But Socrates, even before Alcibiades comes to accuse him, comes to the defense of his own life.

By introducing philosophy into the discussion, Diotima is able to shed light on Love. Just as ignorance alone cannot explain philosophizing, lack alone cannot explain love of the beautiful. If Love is neither beautiful nor ugly, and desires what it lacks, it would desire the ugly as much as the beautiful. There must be something beautiful about the love of beauty. Moreover, human complexity is manifest not only in our seeking knowledge but also in our generating or giving birth. As resourceful and needy beings, we give birth, the former attribute making generation possible, the latter making it necessary. Simple emptiness could not give birth, for it would have nothing to give. Nor would anything sufficient unto itself require generation for its fulfillment. It is when the (needy) lover meets someone with a beautiful soul, Diotima says, that he is "resourceful" in speaking to him about virtue and about what a good man should be and pursue (209b–c). Need finds resources within itself, and resources generate speeches about what is good. Therefore Diotima's further revelations about Love as creative, generative, poetic, and even about lovers as pregnant build on her earlier statements about Love as in-between. It is only through her account of generation that Diotima will be able to explain how something can be "between" mortal and immortal.

LOVE AS GENERATIVE

Diotima reaches the generative character of Love in response to another of Socrates' questions. "Of what use is Love to humans?" Socrates is unable to say what the lover of the beautiful derives from beautiful things. Only when Diotima substitutes good things for beautiful ones does Socrates understand that Love is useful, because when we love the good things and they become ours, we are happy (204c–205a). Thus love is not of another half, or even of the whole, as some say, unless it happens to be good. Diotima makes a passing reference to Aristophanes' speech, qualifying his view that love is love of one's own. We would be willing, Diotima continues, to amputate one of our limbs if we thought it harmful to ourselves (205e). We love the good because we love ourselves.

When the "use" of love becomes clear, however, everyone appears to be a lover, for everyone desires good things for himself. When Socrates wonders at this result, Diotima explains it through an analogy between lover and poet, whose literal meaning in Greek is "maker." We give one sort of maker, the poet, the name of "poet" (*poiētēs*), whereas the term should apply to artisans of all kinds, just as we apply the term "lover" to only one sort of lover (205b–c). Even if our way of speaking obscures the similarities between things, however, it is also based on a perception of their differences. We single out poets from other craftsmen and lovers from other human beings for good reason.[57] The beautiful cannot be reduced to the good.

To love the good – which is to desire that the good be ours and that thereby we be happy – is to love ourselves. But this does not exhaust the experience of Love, as indicated by Socrates' question about Love's use. If Love merely led us to our good, its use would be unquestionable. Earlier in the evening Phaedrus had given examples of lovers who gave their lives for those whom they loved, such as Alcestis for Admetus (179b–c). Whereas to love the good is to love ourselves, to love the beautiful brings us outside of ourselves.[58] It is not that Aristophanes does not leave a place for the love of the good, when he defines Love as love of one's own (205e), but that he does not leave a place for love of the beautiful. Without the latter, love of the good merges into love of one's own. Diotima therefore does not

---

[57] As Bloom observes, when Diotima points out that only certain individuals are called poets, she "alerts us to the mysterious fact that poetry is privileged because it caters to the longing for the beautiful." "Ladder of Love," 136. See also Price, *Love and Friendship*, 43.

[58] Lutz, *Socrates' Education Toward Virtue*, 89.

explain Love simply in terms of the good, as opposed to the beautiful. Although she demonstrates the use of Love by reference to the good, she reintroduces the beautiful, arguing that the lover desires to give birth in the presence of the beautiful. Lovers are pregnant, she claims,[59] and are in a flutter when they approach the beautiful, for only the beautiful acts as midwife, providing relief from the pains of labor. By generation, by leaving behind something new in the place of the old, mortal beings partake of immortality. Even the beautiful itself may seem useful in Diotima's account,[60] but the generation that it makes possible leads us beyond ourselves. Parents are willing to do anything to preserve and nurture their young, "to fight to the finish . . . for the sake of those they have generated, and to die on their behalf; and they are willingly racked by starvation and stop at nothing to nourish their offspring" (207a–b).

It is fitting that Socrates invent a woman in order to answer the previous speakers, whose downplaying of generation, offspring, and children is consistent with their homosexuality. Phaedrus praises love for being parentless (178b), and Pausanias' Heavenly Aphrodite is motherless (180d). Pausanias implies the importance of generation, or at least relationship, in passing – if there are two Aphrodites there are two Loves, for "there is no Aphrodite without Love" (180d) – but takes no note of its implications. Eryximachus, who mentions cold and hot, bitter and sweet, and dry and wet among the elements that art reconciles, is silent about male and female.[61] Of the previous speakers, only Aristophanes describes the generation of offspring by men and women.[62] But he presents generation not as a need of the parents but merely as a by-product of their sexual embrace.[63] Although generation preserves the race (191c), it offers no satisfaction or fulfillment to the needy and imperfect beings

---

[59] There has been criticism of Plato for appropriating pregnancy for the male. (For reference to this literature, see Saxonhouse, *Fear of Diversity*, 176.) Diotima's striking statement, however, does not so much merge male and female roles in reproduction, begetting (*gennan*) and giving birth (*tiktein*), as acknowledge the complexity necessary for generation. In other words, Love has a father *and* a mother.

[60] See Harry Neumann's criticism of Diotima as a sophist and of her utilitarian account of the beautiful. "Diotima's Concept of Love," *American Journal of Philology* 86 (1965): 39–43; 47–48.

[61] For a discussion, see Saxonhouse, *Fear of Diversity*, 174 and 176–77; Rosen, *Plato's Symposium*, 70 and 100–02.

[62] Other than in the exchanges between Diotima and Socrates, the only occurrences in the *Symposium* of words related to generating (*gennan*) or giving birth (*tiktein*) are in Aristophanes' speech (191b-c).

[63] Lutz, *Socrates' Education to Virtue*, 69; Newell, *Ruling Passion*, 74; and Bloom, "Ladder of Love," 142.

seeking relief for their longing through sex. And while Agathon makes room for the poet's creations, they come solely from the inspired poet. No other human being inspires or contributes to his creations, for if Love bestows on him wisdom he needs nothing else. Agathon may present Love as the youngest god, but he does not even raise the question of his parents, unlike Socrates and some of the other symposiasts (cf. 195b with 178b, 180d, and, of course, 203a). His position that Love is the youngest of the gods, which requires comparison to other gods, immediately collapses into his statement that Love is "always young" (195b). That is why Love frequents only the young, those like himself. Agathon's presumption of self-sufficiency is related to his homosexuality, as is love of one's like to love of oneself. Socrates therefore invents someone other to address these men – a prophetess, whose inspiration distinguishes her from other human beings; a foreigner, who is a stranger in Athens; and, most important in this setting of male homosexuals, a woman who points dramatically to what is missing from the previous speeches by presenting all human beings, men as well as women, as pregnant. Replying to them all, the woman Socrates invents presents a view of generation at all levels of human life.

Diotima moves from the generation of children to the ways in which the desire for immortality is satisfied through fame. This was the goal of Alcestis in giving her life for Admetus and the goal of Achilles in dying for the sake of Patroclus, she points out, thus revisiting Phaedrus' two examples of those who sacrificed their lives. Alcestis was a lover of fame, not simply subordinate to her beloved husband, as Phaedrus presented her. And Achilles was similarly concerned with his own immortal remembrance and not, as Phaedrus thought, an exemplar of self-sufficient virtue. The "immortal memory" that Alcestis and Achilles sought for themselves is one "that we *now* hold" (208d) (emphasis mine). They are dependent on their community, and even on the poets. Like Aristophanes before him, Socrates addresses the hubris of the first speakers, though not by presenting the gods' mutilation of the circle-beings as punishment for their aspirations, but by insisting that their aspirations are achieved in the context of human community.

Diotima adds a third example of love-inspired virtue, whose memory has been preserved – that of a legendary Athenian king named Codrus who gave his life to save his city "on behalf of the kingdom of his children" (208d).[64] Whereas in Phaedrus' speech, lovers perform noble deeds

---

[64] That Athens' enemies were Dorians from whom Codrus saved his city by sacrificing himself has an ominous ring to those hearing the narration and expecting Alcibiades

because of the presence of their beloved and serve their cities only incidently, in Diotima's presentation lovers perform noble deeds in the presence of their city, because it is their city in which their memory is preserved. In her last example, moreover, the city has an even more prominent place because Codrus' city will be not only the home of his memory but of his descendants. Athens is the kingdom of Codrus' "children." Diotima emphasizes to Socrates that her new example is "your" Codrus, conceding that one might be especially interested in or pleased by virtue coming from one's own city (see *Apology* 30a and *Theaetetus* 143d). As the offspring of his mother, Diotima said earlier, Love is homeless (203d), but understanding Love as the desire for immortality through generation, paradoxically, gives Love a home.

Diotima next refers to the virtue of prudence as an offspring of the love for immortality, as well as a range of activities that sustain and flourish in political communities. Among the offspring most worthy of memory, she includes the education in virtue that Pausanias promised the young that noble lovers would give them. Whereas Pausanias' defense of a noble love turns on the lover's education of his beloved, he does not connect his being a teacher with his being a lover. Diotima does so. Those pregnant in soul, having conceived "prudence and the rest of virtue," seek a beloved beautiful in body and soul, and attempt to educate him by speaking to him about virtue and what a good man and his pursuits should be (209b–c). In this way, lovers give birth to that with which they were for a long time pregnant. The element of nurturing remains for Diotima even at the highest level, when she describes the ascent of the lover from the visible beauty of his beloved to the knowledge of beauty itself, permanent and unchanging, unmixed with anything ugly – "the perfect end" of the lover's labors, as a result of which he will give birth to and nurture not phantoms of virtue but true virtue. Just as nurturing completes generation, so does teaching complete love. Only when the lover gives birth to true virtue and nurtures it, Diotima concludes, does he become "dear to the gods and immortal, if it is possible for any human being" (212a). The lover's ascent may reach an "end" in knowledge of the beautiful, but that end is there- fore also a beginning. Whereas Aristophanes' embracing half-beings cared so little about food that they perished from hunger until Zeus took pity, when Diotima's lovers embrace beauty itself they "are ready to do

---

to appear before the evening is over. Those hearing the narration would know that Alcibiades was to sacrifice his city to the Dorians (Spartans) to save his own life (see Thucydides, 6.89.9 ff.).

without food or drink *if it were possible*" (cf. 191b and 211d; emphasis mine). They do not die. They generate. In response to Aristophanes, Diotima says that generation is not a mere by-product of lovers' desire for satisfaction, but the end of that desire, and even has a further end, nurture and education (see also *Phaedrus* 276e–277a).[65]

When Socrates presents Diotima's teaching that Love generates, and that generation – and nurturing – is a mortal's way to immortality, he reminds Agathon of death in a way that links mortals to their offspring, to future generations, and to their communities more generally. His acknowledging limitation, in contrast to Agathon's assumption of self-sufficiency, places human beings in political communities. Moreover, Diotima does not say merely that the lover nurtures his offspring, but that he does so "together" with his beloved (209c).[66] The beautiful beloved is necessary for the lover to give birth, and also to his nurturing of what they have generated together.

In her teaching about generation, Diotima does not merely remind Agathon of human dependence on others; she also reminds Aristophanes of the satisfaction possible within political communities. In Aristophanes' speech, the boldest and manliest types go into politics, but only after sex allows them to turn to the deeds of life necessary for the survival of the race (191c–d; 192a).[67] Manly virtue and politics are the servants of necessity, and the only available relief from longing is essentially private, as humans futilely seek recovery of their original condition. When Diotima replies to Aristophanes that we love our own only insofar as it is good (205e), she leaves room for a politics that strives to ensure that our own is good, a politics that goes beyond mere necessity or preservation as it comes to care about the character of what is preserved, of what lives on in memory. Insofar as the beautiful cannot be reduced to the good,

---

[65] Thus I disagree with those commentators who suppose that Diotima omits generation when she describes those who reach the end of their labors in their contemplation of the beautiful itself. For example, Bloom, "Ladder of Love," 147; Saxonhouse, *Fear of Diversity*, 173; Lutz, *Socrates' Education Toward Virtue*, 99–100; and Newell, *Ruling Passion*, 73. Neumann, in contrast, acknowledges the importance of generation for Diotima even at the highest stage of love, but argues that from a Socratic point of view this is a defect in her account inasmuch as beauty "is loved not for its own sake, but as the means by which mortals can give birth," "Diotima's Concept of Love," 39 and 41–44.

[66] Diotima highlights their mutual labor by using a fairly uncommon verb, *sunektrephein* (209c). The only other appearance in the Platonic corpus is in the *Menexenus*, where Socrates uses it of the city which helps to nurture the children of its soldiers who die in war (*Menexenus* 249a).

[67] Strauss, *On Plato's Symposium*, 149–50, and Ludwig *Eros and Polis*, 35 and 37. See also Newell, *Ruling Passion*, 73–74.

self-interested political action might be mediated by the beautiful. It is Socrates' intermediate position between lack and possession, and not the position of either of the poets, that leaves open this possibility for political life. The lovers whom Diotima describes generate and nurture, not only children, but also inventions of arts or crafts, works of poetry, laws of political communities, speeches about virtue, and even virtue itself in the souls of others (208e–212a). By including craftsmen, poets, and legislators, Diotima indicates the positive side of those whom Socrates claims in the *Apology* to have examined for their wisdom (*Apology* 29e–30a, and 31b). The understanding of love that underlies Socrates' philosophic life thus underlies political life as well. That is, the state between poverty and resource that accounts for the pursuit of wisdom and its generation in others through questioning them also accounts for the ongoing human activities that keep political communities alive and flourishing.

This lesson from Diotima is therefore not the backward-looking self-sufficiency of the doctrine of recollection that Climacus attributes to Socrates in Kierkegaard's *Philosophical Fragments*. Although Climacus refers to the passage from the *Symposium* about the lovers' giving birth to "many beautiful and glorious discourses and thoughts," he understands birth as only "an appearing of what was present." In "this birth," Climacus says, "the moment is instantly swallowed by recollection" (*PF* 31). Climacus ignores Diotima's emphasis on nurturing, which makes clear that the lover – or teacher – cannot disappear but has further work to do in the course of time. In the case of human offspring, this is obvious, and Diotima indicates the care that parents demonstrate when she talks of their readiness to go hungry, and even to sacrifice their own lives for their children (207b). But for Diotima, all forms of generation have this in common, precisely because what is generated must endure in time, if generation provides any satisfaction to our desire for immortality. And so Codrus gave his life for Athens in which the memory of his deed might be preserved (208d). His "disappearance" indicates not his independence, or self-sufficiency, but his dependence on others to care for what he has begun. It affirms, in other words, how essential enduring communities are to human fulfillment.

Socrates concludes his speech by claiming that he has been persuaded by Diotima, and that he will try to persuade others (212b). He would like to join the teachers, those who out of a love of beauty as well as out of a desire for immortality generate virtue in others (cf. 212a).[68] In the

---

[68] Although Socrates claims in the *Theaetetus* that as midwife he does not generate but only questions others, he also admits that he is in part the "cause" when those whom

Phaedrus, Socrates elaborates Diotima's teaching when he discusses the immortality possible for human beings in generating seeds in others through the "dialectical art" or the "art of conversation" (*Phaedrus* 276e–277a). When Socrates concludes his speech in the *Symposium*, Aristophanes objects to Diotima's implicit criticism of his speech (212c; see 205e). Socrates' is the only speech at the *Symposium* that summons discussion. Moreover, we soon get another view of Socrates as teacher, for Plato proceeds to bring into the dialogue one of Socrates' most famous students. Fortunately for our judgment of Socrates, Alcibiades is not Socrates' most famous student.

ALCIBIADES' DRAMATIC ENTRANCE

Socrates' brewing discussion with Aristophanes ends when Alcibiades joins the party, quite late, quite drunk, supported by a flute girl, and accompanied by other carousers.[69] His resemblance to the god Dionysus has long been noted.[70] For example, he is crowned with ivy as is Dionysus in Euripides' *Bacchae* (*Bacchae* 81–82).[71] Dionysus is the god of wine as well as of the theater, and just as Dionysus in the *Bacchae* intoxicates the city of Thebes to join in his worship (*Bacchae* 24–26; 186–88; 204–05; 221, 278–83), Alcibiades enjoins everyone at the symposium to drink (213e).[72]

---

he questions "give birth to many beautiful things" (*Theaetetus* 150 c–d). As to Socrates' practice of midwifery in that very dialogue, Theaetetus at the end declares that in his conversation with Socrates, "I for one have said even more on account of you than all I used to have in myself" (*Theaetetus* 210b). See Neumann for a different interpretation of this issue, and of its relevance to the *Symposium*, "Diotima's Concept of Love," 57.

[69] Rosen understands Alcibiades' interruption to represent "the impossibility of remaining in the presence of the divine through the medium of speech." *Plato's Symposium*, 279. But Alcibiades interrupts not Socrates' contemplation of the beautiful, and not even the account of the lover's contemplation of the beautiful, but Socrates' conversation with Aristophanes. Nor is it clear that Alcibiades does Socrates a favor by "rescu[ing] him] from the criticism which discussion of his speech would have engendered." *Plato's Symposium*, 279. True to form, Socrates generates a discussion.

[70] Helen Bacon, "Socrates Crowned," *Virginia Quarterly Review* 35 (1959): 424; John Anton, "Some Dionysian References in the Platonic Dialogues," *Classical Journal* 58 (1962–63): 50. At 218b, Alcibiades speaks of "a philosophic madness and bacchic frenzy" that possesses him. He understands philosophy, or at least his own experience of it, in terms of the god Dionysus.

[71] Rosen, *Plato's Symposium*, 287 n. 35.

[72] Geier points out that it is not until Alcibiades' arrival that the gathering becomes "a drinking party." Moreover, Alcibiades "introduces into the dialogue both the word for drinking partner, *sumpotēs* (212e4, 213b7, 216d7) and the word for drinking together, *sumpinein* (213a2). *Plato's Erotic Thought*, 53. By this means, Plato allows Alcibiades to give his dialogue a title.

He is a man who intoxicates the gathering when he joins it, just as Thucydides recounts his arousing Athens' *erōs* for the conquest of Sicily (Thucydides, 6.24.3). Whatever theatrical spectacle Alcibiades creates, the Athenians are no mere spectators of his drama but actors, and in this case sufferers. The ravishing and Siren-like traits Alcibiades will attribute to Socrates' speeches (215d–e) more accurately describe his own, at least on the momentous occasion when he moved Athens to follow him to Sicily. Like Homer's Sirens, Alcibiades promises the Athenians wonderful things, but lures them to their deaths (Homer, *Iliad* 12. 184–191).

Inasmuch as Alcibiades appears dressed like Dionysus, he seems to have come to judge the contest in wisdom that Agathon had proposed between himself and Socrates, "with Dionysus as judge" (175e). In fact, Alcibiades comes to crown Agathon for his victory in the tragic contests, but when he sees Socrates he takes some of the fillets he has just placed on Agathon's head to crown Socrates as well. He must do so, Alcibiades pronounces, because Socrates himself conquers everyone in speech, not only the other day like Agathon, but always (213e).[73] Alcibiades immediately thinks of speech in terms of conquest, and does not hesitate to play the judge. He sees to it that Socrates and Agathon share in the honors, as he sits between them on the couch (213b).

Alcibiades is not, however, altogether pleased to encounter Socrates at Agathon's. He greets Socrates by accusing him of "lying in ambush" for him, just as Socrates is "accustomed" to doing, and of appearing suddenly when Alcibiades least expects him (213b–c). Alcibiades' language here recalls his observation in the *Alcibiades I*, when Socrates first approached him, that Socrates always turns up wherever he happens to be (*Alcibiades I* 100d). But while Alcibiades sees Socrates turning up on the night of the symposium in terms of the past, their relationship is not as it used to be, for Socrates is hardly seeking out Alcibiades as he had earlier. It is in fact Alcibiades, not Socrates, who now turns up "suddenly" when least expected (cf. 212c with 213c). Alcibiades is mistaken in seeing Socrates in "customary" terms. Socrates has even come to the present gathering "having made himself beautiful" and "wearing fancy slippers contrary to his custom" (174a).

In the course of the banter between the two of them, Alcibiades claims that there can be no reconciliation between him and Socrates

---

[73] Bacon, "Socrates Crowned," 424 and 427; Anton, "Some Dionysian References in the Platonic Dialogues," 50; Rosen, *Plato's Symposium*, 287; and Strauss, *On Plato's Symposium*, 26 and 257.

and that he will get his revenge on Socrates later (213d). His expression of a desire for revenge connects him with Euripides' Dionysus in yet another way. In the *Bacchae*, Dionysus comes to Thebes to exact revenge on those who refuse to recognize him as a god, especially Thebes' ruler Pentheus, whose slight to Dionysus results in his being dismembered limb from limb (*Bacchae* 26–36; 43–48). Like Dionysus, Alcibiades does not bear slight easily, whether from Socrates – as his encomium reveals – or from his city when it charges him with impiety (Thucydides, 6.92.4). Of course, if Alcibiades' revelations about Socrates constitute his revenge, his is more playful than Dionysus' revenge on Thebes, for Alcibiades will only metaphorically tear Socrates apart by comparing him to a statue of Silenus and splitting it open (219e). And Socrates expresses the concern merely that Alcibiades may make him ridiculous (214e; cf. *Bacchae* 250).

The ruin Alcibiades brought to his city, however, is another matter. Plato alludes to his disastrous effect on his city not only by dressing Alcibiades like Euripides' Dionysus, who devastated a city that did not properly honor him, but also by showing him in various ways acting like a tyrant at the gathering at Agathon's house. After crashing the party, he changes the terms of the agreed-upon entertainment and issues orders to the company (213e and 214c–d).[74] As Schein points out, when Alcibiades claims the role of "leader of the symposium," *archōn poseōs* (literally, "leader of the drinking"), he uses a phrase that sounds like "leader of the city," *archōn poleōs*. Plato thus "reminds us of the actual political behavior of Alcibiades, who, it was thought, was aiming at making himself tyrant"[75] (see also Thucydides, 6.53 and 60–61). Although Alcibiades at first admits it is "necessary to obey" when he joins the other guests, he insists on not doing what they enjoin, but on praising Socrates (214b–d). A "praise" of Socrates it will be, although by its end Alcibiades admits that his speech is "mixed with blame" (222a).

ALCIBIADES' IMAGES OF SOCRATES

Alcibiades will praise Socrates, he says, through "likenesses" or "images," which may seem to be "for raising a laugh," but aim at "truth, not laughter." Alcibiades may be at the height of political power in

---

[74] Gary Alan Scott, *Plato's Socrates as Educator*, 123.
[75] Seth L. Schein, "Alcibiades and the Politics of Misguided Love," *Theta Pi* 3 (1974), 159.

Athens, but tonight he is playing the role of a poet in presenting Socrates through images. Socrates competes with Aristophanes and Agathon in describing Love, but Alcibiades, whose speech draws "images" of Socrates (215a), competes with Plato himself.[76] Alcibiades first compares Socrates to the statues of Silenus, an old man in Greek myth with the ears of a horse. Both Socrates and Silenus have ugly exteriors. And when the statues of Silenus are "split open into two," there are images of gods within. So too does Socrates, Alcibiades says, hide within himself images "divine and golden, altogether beautiful and wondrous" (216d–217a; 222a).

Socrates' "Silenus" guise, according to Alcibiades, is twofold. In the first place, Socrates pretends to love beautiful young men, disguising himself as a lover. But he is in fact "full of moderation" and does nothing but contemn all the things most people pursue (216d–e). In the second place, Socrates conceals his wisdom. His speeches "resemble the Silenuses when they are opened." While Socrates always talks about smiths, cobblers, and tanners, and claims that he is "ignorant and knows nothing" (221d–e; 216d), his speeches when opened are intelligent and contain "everything proper to examine for one who would be noble and good" (222a). Alcibiades admits that he himself was deceived in thinking Socrates his lover, and supposing that by giving Socrates sexual favors he would be able "to hear" all that Socrates "knows" (217a). That is, Alcibiades hoped to gain access to Socrates' hidden wisdom. Socrates thus pretends to be a lover, according to Alcibiades, when he is not. And he pretends to be ignorant, when he is not.

Alcibiades knows that there is something strange about Socrates' love (see 215a and also *Alcibiades I* 104d), for Socrates does not desire Alcibiades in the way that his other lovers do. And he senses that Socrates knows something in spite of his claim to ignorance. But like Agathon he supposes that what is not empty is full, and one who is not ignorant is wise.[77] Alcibiades therefore concludes that both Socrates'

---

[76] Nussbaum also notes this connection between Alcibiades and Plato, but suggests not a competition but that Alcibiades serves as "a poet, and an inspiring god of poets (Plato?)." *The Fragility of Goodness,* 193.

[77] In the *Alcibiades II,* Alcibiades denies that there is "some third condition in the middle of being wise and unwise, that makes a person neither one nor the other" (*Alcibiades II* 139a-b). Whoever the dialogue's author may be (many scholars think that the *Alcibiades II* was not written by Plato), he understood this important problem in Alcibiades' thinking. See also the "arguments" of the sophistical brothers in the *Euthydemus* (*Euthydemus* 276a–c).

eroticism and his claim to ignorance are disguises, external coverings that hide beautiful things within – moderation and wisdom. He arrives at the symposium too late to hear Socrates' recounting his lessons about Love from Diotima, and her correction of Socrates' youthful belief that if Love is neither ugly nor bad, it must be beautiful and good, and that if someone is not ignorant, he must be wise (201e–202a).

Alcibiades likens Socrates not only to Silenus but to the satyr Marsyas: as the satyr charms and possesses human beings by means of his flute, so too does Socrates ravish those who hear him by means of his speeches. When Alcibiades hears Socrates' speeches, he confesses, his "heart leaps and tears pour out." Indeed, even now, he must stop his ears against Socrates' words, for they practically paralyze him with shame for his way of life (215c–216b; see also *Alcibiades I* 132b–c).[78] The relation between Alcibiades' two images of Socrates, as Silenus and as Marsyas, is somewhat obscure. If the outer covering of Socrates' speeches is ugly and off-putting – his speeches about lowly shoemakers and tanners, and his claim to ignorance – how does Socrates so ravish his listeners? While Socrates' snub nose and protruding eyes may conceal a beautiful soul, Alcibiades does not emphasize these physical features of Socrates as part of his deceptive covering (215b), but rather Socrates' deeds and speeches. For Alcibiades, Socrates' deeds (his acting like a lover) and his speeches (his discussion of cobblers and tanners and his claim to ignorance) are the ugly cover. But deeds and speeches may be the manifestations of one's soul as well as its cover. When Alcibiades splits Socrates into two to find beautiful images inside, he throws aside the covering. Only the inside matters. And there is no likeness between the two, only difference.

Looking for the esoteric Socrates beneath the surface, Alcibiades understands Socrates' claim of ignorance as part of a false cover, not as Socrates' wisdom. He thus sees nothing true in Socrates' irony, which he understands as a deceptive claim to ignorance (216c and 218c; see also *Republic* 337a), rather than as a way of speaking that is appropriate to one aware of his condition between ignorance and wisdom.[79] Again,

---

[78] Although Alcibiades does not mention it, Marsyas' flute-playing did not have a happy outcome: after competing and losing in a music contest with Apollo, the god slew the satyr for his hubris. Whether he intends it or not, his image of Socrates is ominous.

[79] Scott points out that Socrates' claim to ignorance indicates not his mockery of human beings, as Alcibiades understands it (216e), but that Socrates' "present self-knowledge and present self are merely provisional." *Socrates as Educator*, 156. It also

for Alcibiades, there is no middle, this time between lying and saying the truth (see, e.g., 216a, 217b, 219b, and 222e).[80] There is only the ugly outer covering, the claim to ignorance, and the beautiful images of virtue within. The cover illustrates deficiency; inside, Socrates is "full" (216c).[81]

When Alcibiades proposes to offer sexual favors to Socrates in return for his wisdom (217a), Socrates denies that he has any such wisdom as Alcibiades supposes. Leo Strauss brings up the possibility that "Socrates has no hidden business, no hidden knowledge. Those beautiful statues within Socrates, of which Alcibiades spoke, are equally accessible to all through Socrates' speeches."[82] This is what Socrates himself claims in the *Apology* when he says that he never begrudged anyone, whether young or old, rich or poor, who desired to hear him speaking (*Apology* 33a–b). Of course, one must understand his speeches in order that Socrates' beauty be accessible. Since Alcibiades rejects any truth in Socrates' claim to ignorance, he supposes that Socrates refuses to share with him what he knows. When Socrates responds to him that they "will in the future, after deliberating, do whatever seems best to us two about these and other things" (219a–b), Alcibiades hears only a rejection of his proposal, not an offer of a different sort of relationship. Alcibiades' likening Socrates to Silenus' statues, with his language of disguise, obscures more than they reveal.

Not surprisingly, Alcibiades understands love in terms of ruling and being ruled, referring to Socrates' "wondrous power" and his own "abject slavery" to Socrates (215e, 216c, and 219e). When he begins to pursue Socrates, he imagines that the roles of beloved and lover have merely been reversed (217a–219c, 222b, and 213c; *Alcibiades I* 135d);[83] he has no conception of the reciprocal relation Socrates proposes when he

---

indicates Socrates' desire that his interlocutor affirm the truth for himself (see *Alcibiades I* 106 ff.).

[80] As Lutz comments, when Alcibiades attributes irony to Socrates, he "seems to mean that [Socrates' speech] was joking and playful and false." *Socrates' Education to Virtue*, 135. See, in contrast, Rosen's praise of Alcibiades' "brilliant description of Socrates' irony." *Plato's Symposium*, 309.

[81] Alcibiades calls Socrates "daemonic" (219c), but he did not hear Socrates' report of Diotima's lesson that the daemonic is an intermediate condition. He does not know the truth in what he is saying.

[82] Strauss, *On Plato's Symposium*, 273.

[83] For discussion, see Rosen, *Plato's Symposium*, 289; David M. Halperin, "Plato and Erotic Reciprocity," *Classical Antiquity* 5 (1989): 68–70; Scott, *Plato's Socrates as Educator*, 48; and Daniel E. Anderson, *The Masks of Dionysus* (Albany: State University of New York Press, 1993), 123.

speaks of their deliberating about what is good for them (219a). Pointing
to Alcibiades' language of domination and submission throughout his
speech, Scott observes of Alcibiades, "if he is not the master he must be the
slave." Feeling enslaved to Socrates, Alcibiades tries to dominate him.[84] If
there is no middle between emptiness and fullness, love can be only
subjection and domination. There is no space for reciprocity. Only
in-betweens can both love and be loved (see *Lysis* 40d–e).

Just as Socrates' attachment to him eludes Alcibiades' understanding
of love, so too do Socrates' conversations with others elude Alcibiades'
understanding of speech. Alcibiades compares Socrates as speaker to
"Pericles and other good rhetoricians whom he believed spoke well,"
but who did not have the same effect on him as Socrates did. He thus
knows there is a difference between Socrates and the others, but he does
not grasp the distinction that Socrates makes in the *Gorgias* between
rhetoric and dialogue or conversation (*Gorgias* 448e). He describes the
ravishing character of Socrates' speeches in a way similar to Socrates'
description in the *Protagoras* of lengthy rhetorical displays as opposed to
the briefer give and take of conversation.[85] He supposes that he can

---

[84] As Scott points out, Socrates' response to Alcibiades' proposition of exchange of
sexual favors for wisdom accuses Alcibiades of the desire to dominate: since you are
proposing to exchange bronze for gold, Socrates tells Alcibiades, "you're planning to
gain an advantage (*pleonektein*) over me" (218e), *Plato's Socrates as Educator*, 124. See
also Schein, "Alcibiades and the Politics of Misguided Love," 158–67, and Anderson,
The Masks of Dionysus, 114 and 122. After Alcibiades stops speaking, Socrates claims
that this is still true of Alcibiades (222d-e).

[85] The young Alcibiades is present in the *Protagoras* when Socrates makes this distinc-
tion, and even supports Socrates' preference for conversation over lengthy speeches
(*Protagoras* 336b-d; see also *Protagoras* 347b and 348b). Rosen understands Alcibiades'
remarks in the *Protagoras* to indicate that the young Alcibiades is more open to
Socrates than is the man in the *Symposium*. *Plato's Symposium*, 285. Bloom substantiates
Alcibiades' "image of Socrates as the sorcerer" by reference to "the golden speeches of
Socrates [that] can be found all over Plato's dialogues," such as his "great speech about
divine madness in the *Phaedrus*" and his speech inventing Diotima in the *Symposium*,
"The Ladder of Love," 159. We should also note, however, that those two speeches
address previous speeches in the works in which Socrates delivers them, and are
therefore part of a dialogue. Those speeches each give way to further conversation
(212c and *Phaedrus* 256c ff.). Moreover, Socrates' *Symposium* speech, like the *Symposium* itself, includes narration of dialogue. Only if one were to narrate (or dramatize) a
dialogue itself, with Socrates responding to particular interlocutors, could one preserve for a larger audience the dialogic character of Socrates' speeches and therewith
the crucial role of the particular addressee. By writing such dialogues, Plato differ-
entiates himself from Alcibiades by his awareness that we must take a second step in
understanding any "repetition" of a Socratic speech, inasmuch as it is addressed to a
particular individual or group of individuals.

simply hear what Socrates knows. He more often refers to Socrates' "speeches" than to his conversations or "dialogues" (see 213e, 215c–e, 218a, 221d–e, and 222a; cf. 217b). He does not reveal as much knowledge of Socrates as does Phaedrus, who warns the others of Socrates' preference for conversation lest Socrates' discussion with Agathon supersede the speech-making that was the agreed-upon entertainment for the evening (194d).

Alcibiades even insists that like Marsyas' tunes, Socrates' speeches can be reproduced by anyone with the same effect, "even if he be a poor speaker," and regardless of "whether the hearer be a woman, man, or lad." All are "struck out [of their minds] and possessed" (215b–e). He assumes that Socrates' conversations can be simply conveyed from one speaker to another, and seems unaware that they are responses to what an interlocutor says (see 173c and *Lysis* 211a).[86] It is therefore not surprising that Alcibiades supposes that engaging Socrates means a life of idleness or passivity, "sitting beside him until [he] grows old" (216a–b). If Alcibiades were correct about Socrates' speeches, he would be correct to run away as if from the Sirens, who promise knowledge to those who hear their song while in fact enticing them to their deaths (Homer, *Iliad* 12. 184–91; see also *Euthydemus* 263d–e).

---

[86] Alcibiades claims that Socrates' speeches possess him and others just as the worshipers of Cybele, the Corybantes, are inspired by wild music and frenzied dancing (215e). In the *Ion*, Socrates refers to the Corybantes to illustrate the effect of the poet's divine inspiration, which acts like a magnet, drawing first the poets, then the rhapsodes and actors, and then their audiences (*Ion*, 533d–536b; see also Lawrence, "Socrates and Alcibiades," 318). Of the inspired poets Socrates says that they are "out of their senses," and that "the god takes away their mind" (534b and c). Similarly, the rhapsodes and actors may act as "middles" between the poet and audience (536a), but they make no independent contribution to the process. The medium is not the message; in fact, it must be nothing at all. Socrates' interlocutor Ion, a rhapsode with an affinity for Homer, is not convinced, and "would wonder if [Socrates] could speak well enough to persuade him that he is 'possessed' when he praises Homer" (536d). Perhaps he perceives that if inspiration were as Socrates describes it, he could be equally inspired by all poets, not just Homer in particular (but consider *Ion* 534b). In any case, Socrates' speeches fail to persuade or "possess" their hearer, at least when they maintain his possession by an outside source (cf. *Crito* 54d and 46b). Consider also Alcibiades' denial and Socrates' insistence in *Alcibiades I* that the one who answers questions is responsible for the conclusions reached (*Alcibiades I* 106c, 109b–c, 112d and 113a). On that occasion Alcibiades does not see that Socrates' interlocutor has a crucial part to play in the conversation. Perhaps feeling the need for self-preservation in the face of a Socratic onslaught of questions, Alcibiades uses the Greek *ego* no fewer than seven times between 112e and 113b in that dialogue.

Rosen also points out that Alcibiades does not fully understand Socratic dialogue: "Alcibiades had said that Socrates always wins in speech (213e3); for him, the Eros of dialectic is essentially eristic. . . . [Alcibiades] does not give us an adequate example of dialectic."[87] But Rosen understands the "self-neglect" of which Socrates accuses Alcibiades (215c) to be "a form of selfishness which makes him run away rather than surrender to the selflessness of logos [speech, reason, argument]." For Alcibiades to follow the logic of the argument and to accept and obey its conclusions, according to Rosen, would be "a selfless defeat."[88] Rosen thus suggests that whereas Alcibiades misunderstands speech as selfish (for the sake of victory over another), speech is in fact selfless, something to which the eristic young man will not surrender. From this perspective, there appears no middle ground between the demands of the argument and our self-love. However, it may not be as easy to speak of the self-lessness of dialogue as of the selflessness of "logos."

If dialogue is simply an instance of speech, then what pertains to speech pertains to dialogue. And one gives oneself to the argument, whether it emerges in conversation or in a monologue of another. On the other hand, speech always implies dialogue, in the sense that speech is never abstract but always to another (even those speaking to themselves must imagine themselves as divided into speaker and lis-tener in order to do so).[89] Even when speaking to someone who listens silently, the speaker takes his listener into account, as he imagines his listener taking it in. Because speech is always directed to someone, speech itself is an instance of dialogue, however one-sided and partial any particular instance may be. Dialogue thus makes manifest the contribution of the other person or persons, something that rhetoric can easily obscure. When Socrates proposes that he and Alcibiades deliberate together about what is best for the two of them, he is not asking Alcibiades to surrender himself to the argument or the speech, but offering him a part. The problem the pair face is not that Alcibiades must give up his part, but that Alcibiades is not satisfied by any mere part (see, e.g., 213e, and 214c–d; *Alcibiades I* 104e–105c). After proposing the exchange of Socrates' wisdom for his sexual favors, Alcibiades asked Socrates to consider what was best for the two

---

[87] Rosen, *Plato's Symposium*, 309.
[88] Rosen, *Plato's Symposium*, 300.
[89] See Michael Davis, *The Autobiography of Philosophy* (Lanham, MD: Rowman and Littlefield, 1999), 70.

of them, but his proposition indicated that he himself had already decided for them (cf. 219a and 218c).[90] When Socrates responded that after deliberating they would do whatever looked best to the two of them (219b), he was not only offering a part to Alcibiades but claiming one for himself.

ALCIBIADES' PRAISE OF SOCRATES' VIRTUES

Most impressed by what he understands as Socrates' superiority to his own charms, Alcibiades presents Socrates' virtues in terms of "endurance" of painful situations rather than of any positive enjoyment of good things (219d; 220a).[91] Socrates' greatest virtue, according to Alcibiades, is his moderation, which causes him to "have no care for beauty, and to despise wealth, and any honor held blessed by the multitude" (216d–e). Alcibiades describes Socrates' endurance of hardship during military campaigns, including inclement weather and lack of food, and his ability to drink without becoming intoxicated. He compares Socrates to Ajax, whom Homer presents as good in defense, good at warding off the enemy rather than in pursuit, in contrast to Achilles, who was good at both (219e; see *Republic* 375a). As to Socrates' particular acts of courage, Alcibiades praises Socrates' saving his life at Potidaea. Alcibiades understands the episode to indicate Socrates' resistance and self-abnegation, for Socrates refused the prize for valor that Alcibiades urged the generals to give him, and insisted that it be given to Alcibiades instead. Finally, Alcibiades sees Socrates' courage in his self-control in the retreat at Delium, in his being "in his senses" or "collected" (221a). It is here that Alcibiades quotes the *Clouds*, for Socrates walked "strutting like a pelican, his eyes darting from side to side" (221b; *Clouds* 362). Indeed, Alcibiades appears to be describing Aristophanes' Socrates more than the Socrates of Plato's dialogues. Like Aristophanes, Alcibiades presents Socrates as ascetic, unerotic, and characterized by hardihood and endurance, and demanding such traits from his disciples (see *Clouds*

---

[90] See Rosen's discussion of Alcibiades' euphemism in this passage (*Plato's Symposium*, 307) as well as Anderson's observation that Socrates "in his reply ignores the submissiveness of the *eromenos* [beloved] implied in this passage." *The Masks of Dionysus*, 122–23.

[91] Strauss observes that Alcibiades in his description of Socrates conflates moderation, which "has to do with the right attitude toward pleasure," and endurance, which involves "the right attitude toward pains." For Alcibiades, "this virtue [endurance] swallows up everything." *On Plato's Symposium*, 274.

415–17, 439–42, and 737). His virtues, as Alcibiades presents them, are indistinguishable from his hubris (215b, 217e, 219c, 220b, and 222a).

When Socrates discusses courage with Laches and Nicias in the dialogue bearing the name of the former, Laches defines courage as endurance. Socrates responds that if endurance alone is courage, courage might be identical with folly (*Laches* 192d).[92] In the *Laches*, it is Nicias who argues that courage is knowledge, claiming that he derives his understanding of courage from previous conversations with Socrates (*Laches* 194c–d). Plato's Alcibiades has had such conversations with Socrates (216a; see also *Alcibiades I*), but the word for knowledge never occurs in Alcibiades' speech about Socrates. It is one of Plato's ironies, at Alcibiades' expense, that he attributes to Alcibiades' political opponent Nicias (see, e.g., Thucydides, 6.15.2), the elderly and cautious Athenian general and statesman, a fuller understanding of Socrates than to Alcibiades (see also *Laches* 187e–188a).

Alcibiades is not entirely silent, however, about Socrates' life of inquiry or philosophy. In fact, he introduces Socrates' philosophic heroics in Homeric language, revealing what the "strong man did and dared" (220c; *Odyssey* iv. 242).[93] Having "gotten a thought, Socrates stood on the same spot from dawn on, considering it, and making no progress would not let up," not moving until the following dawn. Alcibiades both admires and resents the self-sufficiency he attributes to Socrates. Consequently he ridicules it. Ionian soldiers in the Athenian army, after they finished their dinner, brought out their bedding – for it was summer – and slept

---

[92] Rosen, *Plato's Symposium*, 315.

[93] The phrase from Homer that Alcibiades uses to describe Socrates is spoken by Helen to describe Odysseus, when he disguised himself as a lowly beggar in order to sneak into Troy undetected. As Helen recounts, she was the only one able to recognize Odysseus, who eventually admits to her who he is and tells her "all the purpose of the Achaeans." No doubt that analogy appeals to Alcibiades inasmuch as the disguised Odysseus reveals himself and his secrets to the one who penetrates his disguise. However, Plato's irony may be again at Alcibiades' expense: in his pride (in seeing through appearances) Alcibiades compares himself to a woman who first betrays her people and escapes to Troy, and then betrays the Trojans in turn by not revealing Odysseus' disguise (*Odyssey* IV. 242–62). As Alcibiades will later become, first to the Athenians, and then to the Spartans, Helen is a double traitor. Helen seems even ready to betray the Greek cause again when their army hides within the "Trojan" horse: in the words of her husband Menelaus, Helen is "moved by some divine spirit" to circle the Trojan horse imitating the voices of the wives of the men within. The men, including Menelaus himself, have to be restrained by Odysseus from rushing out to their deaths at the sound of Helen's calls (*Odyssey* IV. 271–89). In recounting this episode, Menelaus thus indicates Odysseus' ability to see through and resist Helen's Siren-like charms that captivate his fellow Greeks.

outside to find out if Socrates would stand all night. Alcibiades presents Socrates' philosophic life as a silent show for dozing soldiers. His image of Socrates rivals Aristophanes' image of him suspended in a basket investigating the heavens (*Clouds* 218–32). Like Aristophanes' Socrates, Alcibiades' Socrates thinks by himself, rather than through his conversations with others. Alcibiades makes philosophy into a test of endurance (see 219e). Moreover, in his description of Socrates' all-day and all-night contemplation, Alcibiades simply assumes that Socrates stood immobile thinking because he was "making no progress." He cannot imagine the possibility that Socrates was transfixed because one success followed another, or that he was absorbed in such pleasures.[94] He promises to reveal Socrates' inner beauties, but he sees little more than do the Ionian soldiers. Whereas Plato's Socrates claims to have been persuaded by Diotima, who emphasizes the generative character of love, and of philosophy (212b), Alcibiades understands philosophy as idle and unproductive. At the outset of his speech, he claims that his images of Socrates are meant to reveal the truth, not to provoke laughter (215a). But when he finishes speaking, as Aristodemus reports, there is laughter (222c). He can compete only with Aristophanes, not with Plato.

Alcibiades' presentation of Socrates' virtues thus stems from his belief that Socrates' ugly exterior hides beautiful things within, that Socrates' self-presentation as a lover hides his moderation, and that his claim to ignorance hides his wisdom. Socrates' virtues are, in sum, those of a self-sufficient man, who consequently disdains those things the majority of human beings pursue, such as wealth, honor, and beauty. Socrates is self-contained, unaffected either by summer or winter, for example, or by whether his drink is water or unadulterated wine (220a). His courage in saving Alcibiades' life and insisting that the latter receive the prize of valor is a sign of his self-denying superiority to others, not of his

---

[94] The only time that Plato's Socrates, in contrast to Alcibiades', engages in such a trance-like state of contemplation is on the way to Agathon's symposium, and his stop delays his entrance only for a short time. Although Socrates arrives late to dinner, he is not so late that he misses it entirely (175a–b; 175e–176a). No self-absorbed contemplation keeps him from a party with the intellectual and cultural elite of the day. Rosen notes the difference between Socrates' lengthy contemplation that Alcibiades describes and the briefer one just before the party, but draws the opposite conclusion. "The banquet and its participants," he writes, "make up a more pressing external circumstance for Socrates than the military campaign and his fellow soldiers." *Plato's Symposium*, 313. Like Alcibiades, Rosen presents Socrates as moved by compulsion rather than attraction. Socrates' admirer Aristodemus, who is present at the party, tells Agathon that while such states of contemplation are "customary" for Socrates, Socrates "will come presently" (175b).

love.[95] Finally, his thinking renders him immobile. If justice is a virtue that involves one's relations with others, it is not surprising that Alcibiades does not think to attribute it to Socrates. In his *Nicomachean Ethics*, Aristotle says that we do not attribute justice to the gods (*NE* 1178b10–15). What sort of contracts would gods make, for example, or to whom do they owe anything? Alcibiades views Socrates as if he were godlike.

Alcibiades concludes his speech by warning Agathon not to be deceived by Socrates' pretense to be his lover, and thus not to suffer what he and many others have suffered (222b). The alternative to a painful relation with Socrates for him is not a pleasant one, but avoidance. He has seen in Socrates primarily the virtue of endurance, and it is not one that he finds entirely attractive.

AFTERMATH

Socrates claims to detect Alcibiades' underlying intention in his warning to Agathon not to be deceived by Socrates' attentions. Alcibiades' speech, Socrates insists, is only a screen to set Agathon and Socrates at odds, so that Alcibiades might remain Socrates' only beloved, and Agathon's only lover (222c–d). That is, Alcibiades wants no competitor to come between either him and Socrates, or him and Agathon. When Alcibiades first sat next to Agathon, Agathon invited him to recline "in the third position." Placing himself between two already on the couch, Alcibiades is clearly the third. But at Agathon's words, Alcibiades inquires, "who is the third?" (213b). He is not one who joins others, but the one whom others join. As do many of Plato's characters, he says more than he knows.

When Socrates appeals to Agathon not to let Alcibiades part them, Agathon declares that he will move from one side of the couch to the other in order to be next to Socrates (222e). Socrates has seized control

---

[95] Socrates did, after all, save Alcibiades, and not just, in Vlastos' terms, the good qualities that he shares with others. As in other instances, Bloom follows Alcibiades' lead in his understanding of Socrates: in rescuing Alcibiades, Socrates "acted *comme il faut*. He was nearby." Socrates thus helps Alcibiades, according to Bloom, "because the deed was forced on him; and he knows that many accidents occur in life, which if one tried to escape, one would live in constant, demeaning fear." "The Ladder of Love," 168. Bloom thus traces Socrates' deed to the same kind of self-sufficiency and independence that Alcibiades depicts in Socrates. For further discussion, see my "Philosophy and Empire," 517–21.

from Alcibiades. If Agathon moves, Socrates will lie in the middle between Alcibiades and Agathon, and perhaps metaphorically between Alcibiades' imperialistic politics and tragedy. We do not know, however, whether Socrates succeeded in moving Agathon to his side, because a crowd of revelers bursts in on the scene, for "someone went out" and left the door open (223b). Who left? The person walking out could not be Aristodemus, who soon falls asleep right there, nor Phaedrus or Eryximachus, who leave soon after the revelers bring chaos. The two poets and Socrates remain the last ones speaking. Of the named guests, only Alcibiades and Pausanias are unaccounted for. Pausanias would have every reason to leave: not only has he borne the insults of Agathon's speech, but he now hears Alcibiades' assertion of Socrates' intentions toward Agathon, and sees his beloved move to sit beside Socrates.

Perhaps it is Alcibiades, however, who left the door open as he departed.[96] From this point forward in the dialogue, he is not mentioned again. We do not hear when, or with whom, or even if he leaves. He is forgotten. When Agathon moves over to Socrates' side, Alcibiades' moment is over. It is brief, as will be his command in Sicily. If he leaves, his departure is quiet, unperceived or at least not reported by the narrator. Alcibiades' sway is less than he would like it to be, for Agathon chooses not to follow his advice to flee Socrates, and Socrates seems to be showing more interest in Agathon than in his former beloved.

More important, the drunken revel and chaos that Aristodemus now reports recall the night that a group of Athenians (in which Alcibiades, as well as Phaedrus and Eryximachus were thought to have participated) desecrated the statues of Hermes. Since Phaedrus and Eryximachus are among the first to leave Agathon's party after the revelers enter, and Alcibiades disappears, we suspect that the three of them are off to mutilate the Hermae. When Alcibiades refers to the Silenus figures with which he compared Socrates, he identifies them as those found in the shops of "herm sculptors" (215b).[97] Plato also has

---

[96] This is also the suggestion of Geier: inasmuch as "very many" revelers enter, Alcibiades' performance leads to "the complete domination by the 'many.'" *Plato's Erotic Thought*, 57.

[97] The word Alcibiades uses for statuary shops, *hermoglupheia*, is not a common one, but occurs only here in extant Greek literature. It means, literally, the place of those who carve statues of Hermes, and therefore of those who carve statues more generally.

Alcibiades call Socrates "a god-send," in Greek a *hermaion* (217a), and then has him break Socrates apart by comparing him to a statue of Silenus. Regardless of when the desecration actually occurred, however, or even whether Alcibiades actually participated in it, such allusions suggest Plato's judgment of Alcibiades' culpability for crimes against his city and for its ultimate ruin.[98]

Alcibiades might have had one more chance to see Socrates from Plato's perspective, when Socrates spends the rest of the night in conversation (223c) after most of the guests leave or fall asleep. But there is no sign of Alcibiades. Like the all-night vigil Alcibiades describes, Socrates stays up all night, but in this case Socrates is not thinking alone. Rather he is discussing comedy and tragedy with the two poets present at the symposium. After writing a series of speeches delivered to an indefinite number of guests (180c), Plato concludes his work by reminding us of how Socrates directs his arguments to his particular addressees, in this case, those who because they are poets are most likely to contribute to and to benefit from such a conversation.

The evening being late, our narrator Aristodemus nods off and catches only the drift of Socrates' discussion with the poets: Socrates is compelling Aristophanes and Agathon to agree that "it belongs to the same man to know how to compose comedy and tragedy," and that "whoever is by art a tragic poet is also a comic poet" (223d). In light of the prominence of Aristophanes and Agathon at the symposium, the dialogue's conclusion is no mere "side issue" (see 222c). Although our sleepy narrator misses the details of the argument, Socrates' speech about Love helps us to understand its meaning. When Aristophanes presents human beings as poor, in need of resources to satisfy their longings, he does not see the possibility of a marriage between Poverty and Resource. His speech is notably silent about the beautiful. But Poverty begets nothing without Resource. In Agathon's account, by contrast, the lover, inspired by Love, generates, but he generates alone,

---

[98] Rumors of Alcibiades' involvement in the breaking of the Hermae, as well as of his revelation and desecration of the Eleusinian mysteries, aroused the public's fear of his tyrannical ambitions and ultimately led to the official charges against him (Thucydides, 6. 27–28). Plato alludes to the latter charges against Alcibiades as well when he has Alcibiades present his revelations of Socrates' inner nature as if he were revealing secrets to the uninitiated (e.g., 218b). For speculations about the connection between the charges and the *Symposium*, see Bloom, "The Ladder of Love," 72; Strauss, *On Plato's Symposium*, 1, 15, 24, 40, and 287; and Rosen, *Plato's Symposium*, 285.

and there is no nurturing or education. He is not aware that Resource does not beget without Poverty. Without Diotima's contribution, the low (comedy) loses its connection to the high, and the high (tragedy) loses its connection to the low. Without an understanding holding comedy and tragedy together, neither stays in its place. There is no laughter without Resource, nor tears without Poverty. Poetry degenerates either into the demoralizing world of Aristophanes' speech or the saccharine one of Agathon's. The former's "comedy" resembles a degenerate form of tragedy, in which suffering lacks nobility, while the latter's "tragedy" resembles a degenerate form of comedy, self-content only by blinding itself to the ugly.[99] To Aristophanes, Diotima insists that Poverty can marry Resource (restoring the laughter), and to Agathon that Resource must marry Poverty (restoring the tears). She thereby demonstrates the connection between comedy and tragedy, while preserving their difference. The same poet might therefore compose both, inasmuch as both are based on the connection between the beautiful and the ugly, a connection implied in Diotima's account of the intermediate status of Love. To preserve tragedy, the poet must understand that Love is not simply beautiful. To preserve comedy, he must understand that Love is "of something," not just of oneself. Socrates, in fact, said the former to Agathon in the discussion that preceded his account of Diotima's lessons. And Socrates was about to discuss the latter with Aristophanes when Alcibiades interrupted (212c).

Socrates thus returns at the end of the evening to the discussion he was about to have with Aristophanes when Alcibiades entered, but now he includes Agathon as well. Perhaps the appearance of Alcibiades' hubris has made both poets more amenable to Socrates' position. Agathon has just been reminded of the tragic connection between learning and suffering by Alcibiades' revelation of his own learning through suffering in his relationship with Socrates. Agathon is moving closer to Socrates on the couch when the revelers enter. Aristophanes has seen from Alcibiades' speech that resentment and outrage rather than moderation occur when human beings find the divine inaccessible, as Alcibiades finds the "divine and golden" images, the beautiful and wondrous possessions that he thinks Socrates conceals within himself (217a). Mockery of the high does not restrain hubris but turns it toward the celebration and indulgence of private satisfactions, in which so many of Aristophanes' comedies culminate.

---

[99] This latter was in fact Nietzsche's observation about Euripides' – and Agathon's – tragedy. *The Birth of Tragedy*, 92.

Aristophanes surely intended to defend political life by his critique of Socrates in the *Clouds* (see, for example, *Clouds* 549–625). However, to mock pretensions to the high, whether those of Socrates in that play, or those of our circular ancestors in Aristophanes' speech in the *Symposium*, leaves life absorbed by the low, just as Agathon's denial of need and suffering leaves Athens vulnerable to Alcibiades' vision of world empire. Perhaps it was Plato's conceit that his dialogues might have shown Alcibiades an image of Socrates' philosophizing that Alcibiades could have made his own, and thus saved Athens from Alcibiades in a way that Socrates did not.[100]

Plato's dialogues, of course, were not available to Alcibiades. The historical Alcibiades arrives too early to read Plato, just as Plato contrives it that Alcibiades arrives too late at the symposium to hear Socrates' praise of Love and its connection to philosophy and to generation. By writing dialogues, Plato made it possible for readers to arrive on time. Perhaps this is why Plato can conclude the *Symposium* with Socrates' argument that a poet who can compose tragedy can compose comedy as well.

THE INCOMPLETENESS OF THE *SYMPOSIUM*

Although the poets are open to Socrates' arguments – for Aristodemus reports that Socrates "is compelling them to agree" – they also are "barely following due to their drowsiness." First Aristophanes and then Agathon fall asleep. "Having put them to bed," Socrates leaves, with Aristodemus following "as he was accustomed" to doing. Socrates spends the day, Aristodemus further reports, "just as he did at any other time," and "toward evening went home to rest" (223d). The exciting gathering gives way to ordinary or customary life, even if Alcibiades would within the year lead Athens to Sicily, and Socrates would eventually be executed. The incomplete conversation, and our uncertainty about how much his interlocutors understand before they fall asleep, contribute notes of sadness. Aristodemus only "follows" Socrates; "the two go together" no more than they arrive together at the party. The *Symposium* offers us an unfulfilled promise, as does the relationship between Socrates and Alcibiades. Something is missing in the *Symposium*.

At Phaedrus' suggestion, the *Symposium* revolves around encomia to Love. If something is missing in the *Symposium*, it is because love is not

---

[100] For a different speculation, see Benardete, "Plato's *Symposium*," 198–99.

enough. It is not enough for lovers, in the first place, who want to be loved in return. At least this is true of Pausanias, who uses the word "friendship" in his speech more than anyone else does at the *Symposium*, and even refers to the friendship of a beloved for his lover (182c and 183c). In the case of the nobler of the two love relationships he describes, Pausanias imagines friendship developing between lover and beloved (182c, 184b,185a), although its basis is only unlike and dubious goods. His beloved Agathon, whose speech, as we have seen, abstracts from human love relationships, locates friendship only on a grander level, attributing it to the reign of Love over the gods (195c).

Socrates' expertise in matters of love, insofar as it comes from Diotima's lessons, has little to do with reciprocal relationships. It is not that the lover loses himself in the contemplation of the beautiful, for, as I have argued, the end of his labors includes generating and nurturing offspring. Lover and beloved, moreover, nurture the offspring of their union together (209c). It is in this context, in fact, that the word for "friendship" (*philia*) makes its sole appearance in Socrates' speech. When the offspring are the works of poets or legislators, Diotima tells Socrates, the association between the lover and his beloved is closer than when they share children in the ordinary sense, and their "friendship" more secure "inasmuch as they share children that are more beautiful and deathless" (209c). Friendship emerges and is solidified through offspring; lover and beloved are a pair only because there is a third they share and nurture. Diotima does not say, however, that the beloved loves in return. When Diotima refers to Achilles' "dying after" Patroclus, she claims that Achilles acted out of love for immortal fame (208d). No more than did Phaedrus, does she appeal to their friendship.

Socrates may have loved Alcibiades, but they do not become friends, even if Alcibiades begins to act the lover in turn. His doing so appalls Alcibiades, and as we have seen he runs away from Socrates. Love's fulfillment requires friendship. In the *Phaedrus*, in contrast to the *Symposium*, Socrates gives an account of how the beloved becomes a lover, loves in return, and how both see themselves in the other (*Phaedrus* 252d–253a and 255d). And Socrates refers to them as friends (256c). In that dialogue, Socrates therefore links love with self-knowledge and friendship. It is in the *Phaedrus* that Socrates acknowledges that he does not yet know himself, and that his attempt to do so in obedience to the command on the temple at Delphi leaves him no leisure for anything else (*Phaedrus* 229e). Socrates implicitly connects his pursuit of self-knowledge to others when he explains why he does not often leave the city: he is "a lover of learning," and "country places and trees won't teach [him] anything, unlike human beings in the city" (*Phaedrus* 230d). He also connects his pursuit of self-knowledge to pious speech. Socrates not only traces his inquiry to the words "Know thyself" on the temple at Delphi, but also refuses to take time away from his search to know himself in order to demythologize the stories of the gods (*Phaedrus* 229c–230a). Most obviously, his long speech about love in the *Phaedrus*, his palinode, is an example of pious speech, since it recants a speech that blasphemes love (*Phaedrus* 242d–243b).

In bringing together the themes of reciprocity, self-knowledge, piety, and the philosopher's indebtedness to others in the city for their teaching him, the *Phaedrus* deepens the understanding of Love and philosophy that we find in the *Symposium*.[101] Moreover, in its presentation of reciprocity between lover and beloved, the dialogue points us toward friendship, which is missing both from the relationships between the various couples in the *Symposium*, including that of Alcibiades and Socrates, and from that dialogue's encomia to Love. Phaedrus may seem the least likely of the *Symposium*'s guests for a friendship with Socrates, given his emphasis on the useful in his encomium to Love. And yet Socrates addresses him as "dear [*phile*] Phaedrus" when he first sees him in the *Phaedrus*, using the adjective for friend, *philos* (*Phaedrus* 227a).[102] It turns out that he and Socrates share a love of speeches, and by the end of the dialogue Phaedrus expresses a wish to be included in a prayer of Socrates', "for friends have all things in common" (*Phaedrus* 279c).

Since the *Phaedrus* is dramatic rather than narrated, we depend on no dozing narrator such as Aristodemus (223d) for that final conversation in the *Phaedrus*. That conversation discusses not only the speeches about love that have been delivered in the *Phaedrus*, but also the speeches of the politicians, the laws they write, the rhetoric taught by the teachers of rhetoric, and a genuine art of rhetoric that knows the souls of its addressees. Whereas Socrates' conversation with the two poets at the close of the *Symposium* ends when they fall asleep (223d), in the *Phaedrus* Socrates and his companion resist the sleep-inducing

---

[101] Charles L. Griswold, Jr. makes a similar argument about the relation between the *Phaedrus* and *Symposium*, in *Self-Knowledge in Plato's Phaedrus* (University Park: Pennsylvania State University Press, 1996), 19–20. Griswold points out that "self-knowledge is not mentioned at all in the *Symposium*," 19.

[102] Griswold notes Socrates' frequent use of the expression "dear Phaedrus" in that dialogue. *Self-Knowledge*, 26.

hum of the cicadas overhead and the noontime heat in order to converse (*Phaedrus* 259a and d). The young man who knows of Socrates' inclination to conversation rather than speeches, and causes Agathon to postpone his conversation with Socrates (194d–e), now has one himself with Socrates in a dialogue bearing his name. When we turn to the *Phaedrus*, we are still seeing the aftermath of the *Symposium*.

3

Self-Knowledge, Love, and Rhetoric
(Plato's *Phaedrus*)

The issue of self-knowledge arises in the *Phaedrus* in various ways. This is the dialogue in which Socrates says that he follows the injunction to "know thyself" that is written on the temple at Delphi, and that this task leaves him no leisure for other things (229e).[1] Later, he describes how lover and beloved come to see themselves in each other as a result of their love. And in the last half of the *Phaedrus*, he and Phaedrus discuss the three speeches about love that they have just delivered in the first half of the dialogue. The self-reflective character of the *Phaedrus* is highlighted when contrasted to the *Symposium*: instead of engaging in a discussion of their own speeches, the symposiasts are treated to stories about Socrates from a drunken Alcibiades, who has been disappointed in love. Although Socrates talks to the poets at the end of the evening about comedy and tragedy, they are falling asleep.

Because Socrates' and Phaedrus' discussion of rhetoric includes a discussion of writing, moreover, the *Phaedrus* serves as Plato's reflection on his own activity of writing dialogues. Socrates in fact offers a standard of good writing: it should be constructed as if it were a living animal, "neither headless nor footless, but with middle [parts] and extremities, written appropriately to each other and to the whole" (264c). In light of this standard, which Socrates refers to as "speech-writing" or "logographic" necessity (264b), scholars are struck by the "apparently disjointed character" of the *Phaedrus* itself, insofar as it is divided between a series of speeches about love and a conversation about

---

[1] References in parentheses in this chapter, unless otherwise noted, are to Plato's *Phaedrus*. translations from the Greek are my own, although I have relied on James H. Nichols, Jr., *Plato Phaedrus*, translated, with introduction, notes, and an interpretative essay (Ithaca: Cornell University Press, 1998).

rhetoric.[2] Plato's dialogue seems to fall short of the standard for good writing that is articulated in the dialogue itself. Even more puzzling, Socrates gives an implicit criticism of Plato's very act of writing when he argues that the written word is inferior to the spoken word because it is unable to defend itself, does not respond to particular addressees, and merely repeats the same thing over and over again (275d–e).

These problems, however, pale before an even greater difficulty the dialogue poses – its seeming praise of madness. After making a speech criticizing love for its lack of "intelligence and moderation" (241a), Socrates declares that he blasphemed against Love, and must recant. His recantation claims that the greatest goods come to human beings from madness sent by the gods, including love as well as prophecy and poetry. Gregory Vlastos finds this view of love as a form of madness on the part of the "ultrarationalist" Plato to be "extraordinary."[3] With considerable understatement, R. Hackforth similarly observes that Socrates' "exaltation of 'divine madness' over rational prudence" is "hardly in character with the Socrates we know" from Plato's earlier dialogues.[4]

Some scholars have attempted to downplay this seemingly positive presentation of madness. James Arieti, for example, claims that Socrates' speech about madness in the *Phaedrus*, along with his earlier speech critical of love, simply serve to illustrate rhetorical techniques, and should not be taken seriously as endorsing any view of love.[5] William S. Cobb contrasts Socrates' praise of mad poets and prophets here with his criticisms of them elsewhere for lacking understanding of what they are doing (e.g., *Apology* 22c and *Laches* 198e–199a), and finds elements of irony in Socrates' apparent endorsement of madness. As to love itself, Cobb argues that it resembles the other kinds of madness only

[2] William S. Cobb provides a brief survey of ways in which scholars have tried to find unity in the dialogue. *The Symposium and the Phaedrus: Plato's Erotic Dialogues*, trans. with introduction and commentary (Albany: State University of New York Press, 1993), 139–41.

[3] Vlastos, "The Individual as Object of Love in Plato," 27 n. 80. See also Gerasimos Santas, "Passionate Platonic Love in the *Phaedrus*," *Ancient Philosophy* 2, no. 2 (Fall 1982):105–14.

[4] R. Hackforth, *Plato's Phaedrus*, translated, with an introduction and commentary (Cambridge, UK: University of Cambridge Press, 1952), 14.

[5] James Arieti, *Interpreting Plato: The Dialogues as Drama* (Lanham, MD: Rowman and Littlefield, 1991), 190 and 193. See also Cobb, *The Symposium and the Phaedrus*, 149–50; and C.J. Rowe, "The Argument and Structure of Plato's *Phaedrus*," *Proceedings of the Cambridge Philological Society*, 32 (1986): 110 and 119–20.

in being god-given and so is "not madness in the sense of a condition that violates or transcends the limits of rationality."[6] Charles L. Griswold's analysis of the palinode produces a similar conclusion: at least at the highest levels, either reason is erotic or love is rational, and this is the key to "the thesis that philosophy is divine erotic madness."[7]

Whereas Cobb argues that the discrepancy between appeals to reason in other dialogues and the palinode's praise of madness calls into question the latter, Nussbaum finds in this discrepancy evidence of a change in Plato's thought. She argues that the *Phaedrus* serves as Plato's recantation of his more rationalistic positions found in dialogues such the *Republic* and the *Phaedo*, which he embodied in Socrates' earlier speech in the *Phaedrus* in order to retract. Socrates' recantation is Plato's recantation. Nussbaum attributes Plato's "reevaluations" of his earlier "Socratic" position to his "own passionate devotion to Dion."[8] Whereas she argues that Plato confronts us in the *Symposium* with a tragic choice between Socrates and Alcibiades, between which it is impossible to choose, by the time he wrote the *Phaedrus* love triumphs over tragedy. Similarly, Hackforth argues that "Plato is a compound of rationalist and poet," and that "in the *Phaedrus* the poet definitely gets the upper hand."[9] The compound appears to dissolve for Hackforth, just as the tragic tension dissipates for Nussbaum.

Plato raises the question of reason and its limits not only with the dialogue's positive assessment of god-given madness, but also by the prominence of myths in the *Phaedrus*. The issue first comes up in the dialogue as a result of its setting in the countryside, which Phaedrus supposes is close to where Boreas is said to have abducted Oreithyia (229c). Socrates offers a myth about the soul's pre-existence in the palinode (at 253d; see also 265c), and even in the course of his discussion afterward with Phaedrus, finds occasion to tell two other

---

[6] Cobb speculates as well that Plato may be simply appealing to common opinion in Socrates' description of love as madness. *The Symposium and the Phaedrus*, 149–50.

[7] Griswold, *Self-Knowledge*, 67.

[8] Nussbaum understands Socrates in the *Phaedrus* to be a Platonized Socrates. She speculates that in the characters Phaedrus and Socrates, Plato represents Dion and himself. *The Fragility of Goodness*, 212 ff. and 228–29; cf. 198. Graeme Nicholson argues that "by setting out an extreme anti-erotic position to be refuted," Plato "is cleansing himself of whatever intellectualism he may have had in his younger days." *Plato's Phaedrus: The Philosophy of Love* (West Lafayette, IN: Purdue University Press, 1999), 122.

[9] Hackforth finds Plato's "non-rational, mystical side" even in what he regards as earlier portrayals of Socrates, and refers us to the mystical experience of philosophy that Plato describes in his Seventh Letter (341c), *Plato's Phaedrus*, 61, see also 14–15, and 72 n. 1.

tales – one about the cicadas who are singing as he and Phaedrus converse, another about two Egyptian divinities who disagree about the benefits of writing (259b and 274c). Hackforth expresses a view prominent in the scholarship on Plato when he states that Plato's myths capture "the vision of a poet whose images ... spring from a non-rational intuition" when reason reaches an impasse.[10]

The prominence of non-rational or even irrational elements in the *Phaedrus* is not surprising in the dialogue in which Socrates acknowledges his inability to understand himself. Yet Socrates claims that his perplexity about himself leads him not to a mystical experience but to an all-consuming pursuit of self-knowledge, so consuming that it leaves him no leisure for rationalizing the myths about the gods (229d). By the same token, however, by holding him to inquiry his task keeps ecstatic experience such as the inspired poet's at bay. Thus he claims to leave his first speech about love unfinished, for he is "already speaking in hexameters" and does not want to be possessed by the nymphs to whom Phaedrus has exposed him (241e). And whatever inspiration he claims in the course of the dialogue, his very claims imply reflection on his experience that remind him of himself (234d; 235c–d; 238c). Socrates' inspired palinode leads to the conversation in the last half of the *Phaedrus* about the speeches of the first half, and the dialogue as a whole concludes with Socrates' and Phaedrus' plans to return to the city to speak to others.

Allowing the events of the *Phaedrus* to unfold in this chapter, we shall begin with Socrates' meeting Phaedrus and agreeing to accompany him to the countryside to hear a speech of the rhetorician Lysias' that Phaedrus has with him, a speech that tries to persuade a youth that it is to his advantage to accept a sexual relationship with a non-lover rather than a lover.[11] The dialogue therefore begins with a striking contrast

---

[10] Hackforth, *Plato's Phaedrus*, 72; see Percival Frutiger, *Les Mythes de Platon: Etude philosophique et litteraire* (Paris: Librairie Felix Alcan, 1930), 223; Paul Friedlander, *Plato: An Introduction*, vol. 1, trans. Hans Meyerhoff (Princeton: Princeton University Press, 1958), 171–210, esp. 207–08; Nicholson, who also gives a helpful discussion of scholarly treatment of myth in Plato, *Plato's Phaedrus*, 24–34; and Nussbaum, *The Fragility of Goodness*, 225. Others see myths for Plato as "metaphors [that] illuminate issues about life in this world." Cobb, *The Symposium and the Phaedrus*, 143; see also Griswold, *Self-Knowledge*, 141–51.

[11] Whether the speech attributed to Lysias in the *Phaedrus* is written by Lysias or by Plato himself has been "an age-long dispute," as Hackforth notes. Hackforth himself takes the view that Plato wrote the speech as a clever parody that exaggerates the shortcomings of Lysias and the rhetoric of his day. *Plato's Phaedrus*, 16–18.

between its setting, especially the physical beauties of the countryside, and the cold, calculating rhetoric of Lysias' speech. The difference between the beautiful and the useful or the good that we saw in *Symposium*'s encomia to Love thus appears from the outset in the *Phaedrus*. When Socrates offers a speech with the same thesis as Lycias' speech, he shows that the "non-lover" speaker himself is torn by his pretense of self-sufficiency and his eager pursuit, by his own interest and what subordinates him to another. He too, like the mad lover whom he criticizes, is "beside himself" (see 234d). He is a reflection of Phaedrus, who both looks to his health and preservation and also delights in sharing speeches in a beautiful setting with Socrates. And even Socrates cannot understand himself simply as "partaking in a divine lot," as a gentle and simple being whose self-knowledge is God-knowledge through a recollection of the Ideas. Art, which operates through calculation or reasoning, and which Socrates contrasts with madness at the beginning of his recantation (244d and 245a), hides this complexity from us, just as the artisans whom Socrates describes in his *Apology* think they know all things on the basis of the knowledge their arts give them (*Apology* 22d).

After exploring the problems with understanding the soul as a non-lover, which emerge in the dialogue's first two speeches, we will turn to Socrates' recantation, his great praise of Love, which paradoxically shows the problems in trying to understand the soul as erotic. There Socrates gives "self-motion" – not love – as the being and definition of soul. Whereas Socrates' "non-lover" speech insists that non-loving is a disguise of a lover, the palinode recognizes the truth in the non-lover disguise. The lover and beloved whom Socrates describes as friends and who can see themselves in each other share the same type of human soul. Their love is a version of self-love. Socrates nevertheless indicates in his myth about the soul, as we shall see, the complexity of any one human being, as well as the human capacity for choice. It is precisely because the soul is not completely absorbed by the same universal truths accessible to all that the role of speech is not merely reminding but also generation. Like Diotima, the *Phaedrus* turns to the political life.

The problems that emerge in the palinode lead to the conversation in the last half of the dialogue, where Socrates directly faces the challenge of contemporary rhetoric that Lysias' speech poses. But while rhetoric is prone to the despotic and self-interested manipulation of others that we see in the rhetoric of the non-lover, rhetoric indicates the necessity of adjusting speeches to the souls of one's listeners. This is essential to the genuine art of rhetoric that Socrates proposes. The true rhetorician finds in the diverse human beings he encounters different human types, and hence those unlike himself, who provide both limits to his rhetoric – he must fit his speeches to the souls of his addressees – as well as fertile grounds that can receive and nurture what he is able to give. Socrates' description of the genuine art of rhetoric in the *Phaedrus* both narrows what Diotima presents as possible for the lover and expands its reach. Whereas the lover she describes generates that with which his soul is pregnant when he comes into the presence of beauty, the genuine rhetorician whom Socrates describes in the *Phaedrus* generates only what is appropriate to others. His offspring therefore are not wholly his own, but he plays a part in different ways in the education of different types of human beings.

If one's generation comes to fruition in diverse ways over time, it is appropriate that the *Phaedrus* conclude with a criticism of writing, especially for its permanence and rigidity – for its always repeating the same thing. By the end of the dialogue, Socrates defends only that writer "who writes knowing where the truth lies, able to assist in cross-examination of what he has written, and able to show that his writings are of little worth" (278d). In other words, he defends only a writing that incorporates into itself a criticism of writing, that mocks its own illusion of wholeness by making explicit the imperfection of its arguments, and is therefore written in such a way that it assists in its own cross-examination, but only assists. That is, if a writing came from the genuine art of rhetoric, if could be understood only through the interpretation and therewith the contribution of its readers. Like the task of the genuine rhetorician, such writing would be no "small work" (269c and 272b).

THE SETTING

Although the dramatic date of the *Phaedrus* is uncertain, the presence of Lysias in Athens indicates that it occurs a number of years after the *Symposium*, after Lysias moves to Athens from southern Italy. The difficulty in placing the date arises from the fact that historical sources also reveal that Phaedrus – along with Eryximachus – was exiled from Athens between 415 and 404 BCE as a result of charges of impiety. Yet the dialogue could not have occurred after 404, inasmuch as Socrates refers to Lysias' brother Polemarchus, a member of the democratic party in Athens killed by the Thirty Tyrants in 404, as if he were alive (257b). The dialogue would have had to occur when Phaedrus was in exile. The *Phaedrus* thus replaces the actual history of Phaedrus' impious deeds and their consequences.[12] Socrates' correction or recantation of his own impious speech is at the same time a correction of Phaedrus, who admires Lysias' speech with the same thesis. And by the end of the dialogue, Phaedrus is moved to join Socrates in prayer (279c). By this means, Plato continues his defense of Socrates against the charges of the city, by showing Socrates' attempt to stem corruption and impiety.

Consistent with Phaedrus' alleged impiety, Plato presents him in this dialogue as a skeptic concerning tales about the gods. Phaedrus expresses surprise, for example, that Socrates might believe the story of Boreas' abduction of Oreithyia, daughter of a legendary Athenian king, as she played with a companion along the river Illisus. Phaedrus' surprise suggests that he is one of those described by Socrates who explain the myths in terms of natural occurrences – how, for example, Oreithyia was simply hurled by a strong north wind to the rocks below. Socrates contrasts himself with such men, for since he has not yet been able to know himself, as the writing on the temple at Delphi commands, he has no leisure for such sophistries and so accepts what is conventionally held about such things (229c–e; cf. *Clouds* 374–407). Socrates does not even know, he admits, "whether he is a wild beast more complex and furious than Typhon, or a gentler and simpler animal sharing by nature in a divine and un-Typhonic lot" (230a).

Typhon was a monster of Greek myth, with one hundred heads in the form of snakes, whom Zeus subdued to establish the rule of the Olympian gods (see Hesiod, *Theogony* 820–85). Socrates does not simply dismiss the tales of the gods while he pursues self-knowledge, nor does he simply follow them in a conventional way. Rather, for him, the tales indicate the beastly and divine in light of which he tries to understand himself.[13] Socrates thus manifests neither the pious belief Phaedrus disdains nor the sophistical tendencies to which Phaedrus is attracted, but rather turns to myths for help in understanding himself.

---

[12] See K. J. Dover, *Lysias and the Corpus Lysiacum* (Berkeley: University of California Press, 1968), 31 and 38; Hackforth, *Plato's Phaedrus*, 8 and 13; and Nussbaum, *The Fragility of Goodness*, 212–13.

[13] See Griswold, *Self-Knowledge*, 147; Ronna Burger, *Plato's Phaedrus: A Defense of a Philosophic Art of Writing* (Tuscaloosa, AL: University of Alabama Press, 1980), 14; Anne Lebeck, "The Central Myth of Plato's *Phaedrus*," *Greek, Roman, and Byzantine Studies* 13 (1972): 282 n. 31; and G. R. F. Ferrari, *Listening to the Cicadas* (Cambridge, UK: Cambridge University Press, 1987), 11.

Myths should nevertheless not serve as the last resort when reason fails, for they might simplify the truth. The alternatives that Socrates presents here at least suggest a stark contrast between beast and divine that abstracts from Diotima's efforts in the *Symposium* to present what binds the whole together.[14] They also leave no place for the one like Socrates who is perplexed about himself. Such wonder on the part of Typhon would mean that he is gentler than he appears, and on the part of a gentler, simpler animal that he is less simple than he would otherwise be. Socrates' question does not exhaust or close his inquiry, but rather keeps it alive.

Although Socrates' pursuit of self-knowledge leaves him no leisure for rationalizing myths, he does have time to spend with those in the city and to accompany Phaedrus to hear Lysias' speech (230d–e; 227b). In fact, Phaedrus tells Socrates that he is "just the person to hear a speech that is somehow or other erotic" (227c), no doubt remembering Socrates' claim in the *Symposium* that he "knows nothing except matters of love" (177d–e). And yet Phaedrus seems to renege on his promise to let Socrates hear Lysias' speech (227c): he knows only its "meaning" or "intent," not its words, he claims. Socrates knows better: Phaedrus is playing coy, and is ready to practice on Socrates. Socrates suspects even further that Phaedrus has with him Lysias' speech itself, which he has taken on his walk to memorize. Socrates is not willing to hear Phaedrus' summary when "Lysias himself is present" (228a–e). Socrates refuses to depend on an interpreter, since an alternative is available. Nor is he content with a summary; he wants to hear the "words." Phaedrus uses *rhēmata* for the speech's words, which is etymologically related to "rhetoric." The "meaning" or "intent" is no substitute for the latter.

So too does Socrates praise the appearance of the setting to which they have come, calling Phaedrus' attention to its beauties – "the spreading and lofty plane tree," "the flowering and fragrance of the willow," "the coolness of the stream," "the charm of the breeze," "the echo of the cicadas," and the comfort of the grass (230b–c). Socrates twice uses a form of the adjective *pangkalos* ("all beautiful") to describe the place where they sit for Phaedrus' reading of Lysias' speech (230b and c). It might seem to romantics the perfect setting for a lover to woo a beloved, but neither Socrates nor Phaedrus are wooing each

[14] Seth Benardete, *The Rhetoric of Morality and Philosophy: Plato's Gorgias and Phaedrus* (Chicago: The University of Chicago Press, 1991 127–28. See Nussbaum, *The Fragility of Goodness*, 223; Griswold, *Self-Knowledge*, 41–42.

other, at least in any conventional sense. In fact, Phaedrus is reading to Socrates a speech written by someone else and addressed to someone else. That speech makes a case for a non-lover's superiority to a lover, and it appeals to self-interest rather than to love. While Plato emphasizes the details of the setting in this dialogue perhaps more than in any other dialogue he wrote, there seems a glaring lack of fit between the setting and its initial topic, at least if Phaedrus has understood it correctly. Plato encourages us to suspect that there is some error or mistake here, and that it involves self-forgetting.

NON-LOVERS (LYSIAS' SPEECH AND SOCRATES' FIRST SPEECH)

Lysias' speech resembles a love speech: addressing a youth, its speaker urges him to accept his sexual advances. But the clever thing about it, Phaedrus claims, is that its speaker claims he is not a lover. This is why, presumably, Phaedrus describes it to Socrates as only somehow or other erotic (227c). In fact, the speech argues that it is in the interest of its addressee to form a relationship with a non-lover rather than a lover. The speaker woos, not in the name of love but in the name of self-interest. He is self-interested, and he asks his addressee to be self-interested as well. The relationship he urges is one that accommodates the interests of both. He wants sex, and he will provide benefits in return. In arguing that non-lovers are more beneficial to young men than lovers, Lysias' speech captures the utilitarianism of Phaedrus' praise of Love in the *Symposium*: if Love is good because it is useful to beloveds and to cities, as Phaedrus argues there, "non-love" might appeal to him as even more useful, if a clever rhetorician succeeded in presenting it that way.

In arguing against an affair with a lover, the speaker points out that the desire of the lover eventually ceases, as the youth's bloom fades in time. Because the lover has acted contrary to his interests in benefitting the youth, the speech's argument goes, the lover will regret the favors he bestowed. Love is an unfortunate betrayal of human self-interest. This view of the lover is consistent with Pausanias' portrayal in the *Symposium*: entreating his beloved, promising everything, sleeping in doorways, generally acting like a slave, and shaming his friends as a consequence (*Symposium* 183a–b; see also *Lysis* 205c–d). Alcibiades is dismayed when he starts resembling such a lover in his relationship with Socrates (*Symposium* 217b–d and 219e), and Pausanias is led to imagine a "heavenly" lover as an alternative, who is in a position to offer as much, if not more, than he requires of his beloved (*Symposium* 184c ff.; cf. 218c). And now Lysias invents a "non-lover" and a "clever" rhetoric through which he might obtain the sexual favors desired by the lover while avoiding such servile abasement. Because he bestows benefits on his youth only after deliberation about what is best for himself, he has no regrets when his desire ceases. He urges nothing special about his addressee that moves him to approach him, and in time he will have the same relationship with someone else. Nor is there anything that distinguishes him from others, except his lack of love for his addressee. His speech could be given by any non-lover to anyone from whom he wants sex. He is a cool customer, and if his addressee can be a cool customer too, their relationship will flourish. The deeper appeal of the non-lover for Phaedrus is not that of the benefits he provides for the one who offers him sex. Rather it is his self-sufficiency, his freedom from passion and the subservience that it produces, that attracts Phaedrus, just as in his speech in the *Symposium* he finds the "virtue" of the beloved more admirable than that of the lover because the latter is "god-inspired" (*Symposium* 180b).

When Socrates later takes his turn at a speech with a similar thesis, he prefaces it with a description of its speaker: a lover disguises himself as a non-lover in order to make his case to the boy he loves (237b). Lysias' speech offers no such explanation of itself. Is its speaker the non-lover he pretends to be? Or is he, like the speaker of Socrates' speech, a lover in disguise? And if he is a lover, is his disguise intentional? That is, does he intend to deceive his addressee? Or is he deceived about himself? Before he finishes speaking, the speaker insists that his addressee gratify no non-lover but himself, for favors spread are not so highly prized. It is not merely that an exclusive relationship with his youth gives him more opportunity for sex at his convenience; rather the favors are "worth" more to him if they are his alone (234b–c). Showing signs of jealousy, the cool non-lover is not as immune to the entanglements of love as he pretends to be. When Phaedrus describes Lysias' speech as "somehow or other" erotic (227a), he too, like its non-lover speaker, may say more than he intends, for he uses an idiom that means literally, "I do not know how." Phaedrus does not know how Lysias' speech is erotic. Impressed by its arguments in favor of the non-lover, Phaedrus knows only the speech's words, not its meaning or intent (see 228d). The speech's obscurity is underlined by its conclusion: the speaker ends with an invitation to his addressee to ask questions. But there is no speaker to answer them. Lysias is present, as Socrates says (228e), but only in the written words that merely repeat themselves.

Lysias' intention in writing the speech is as ambiguous as that of its speaker. Did Lysias write the speech for himself to deliver to a youth? Is he the non-lover speaker? And if so, was Phaedrus its addressee? After all, Phaedrus admits to Socrates that Lysias had been feasting him with words since dawn, and it is not clear whether others are present (227 and b). Or did Lysias write the speech for Phaedrus (or some other) to deliver to a youth, just as the historical Lysias wrote defense speeches for accused men to deliver in Athenian courts? Phaedrus, the dialogue reveals, has taken the speech on his walk in order to practice it (228b and d). That is, might Phaedrus identify with the speaker rather than with the addressee? Or was the speech composed not for purposes of seduction but simply as a "clever" rhetorical piece, written for the pleasure or admiration of its listener?[15] This surely is one effect it has on Phaedrus, as Socrates suggests when he recognizes Phaedrus' enthusiasm (227c). Socrates describes himself as "a lover of speeches," even "sick over hearing speeches," and so revels with Phaedrus as they enjoy speeches together (228b–c). The delight in speeches that he and Phaedrus share, as Socrates presents it here, appears to be disinterested, and finds no place in the world of the speech in which they delight. Phaedrus seems to take pleasure in something for its own sake, even to share that pleasure with someone else. Like a non-lover, Phaedrus considers his own good, and yet he is pleased to meet Socrates and to deliver the speech to him. And Socrates, for his part, proclaims his enthusiasm – he is "beside himself" in hearing Phaedrus read the speech[16] – although it is not for the speech itself but from his sight of Phaedrus, who like beauty itself as Socrates later describes it (250d) "beams" or "shines" as he reads the speech (234d). He consequently joins Phaedrus in "Dionysian revelry" (234d). The understanding of human beings and their relationships expressed in Lysias' speech does not explain the very two who are reading and hearing it.

Because Socrates claims that his enthusiasm does not come from hearing the speech but from looking at Phaedrus, Phaedrus perceives an insult to both Lysias and himself, insofar as he is delighted by Lysias' speech. He accuses Socrates of joking at their expense (234d).

---

[15] Nicholson, *Plato's Phaedrus*, 41.

[16] The word that Socrates uses here (*ekplagēnai*) means literally being "knocked outside" himself. This is the same verb that Socrates uses later in the palinode of the lover and then of his beloved (250a and 255b). The English idioms "to be beside oneself" and "out of one's mind" capture the meaning of the Greek expression and its connection to madness.

Continuing the banter, Socrates "perceives that his breast is full" and that he is inspired by he knows not whom, with a speech on the same subject, "different and no worse" than Lysias' (235c). Phaedrus' desire to hear Socrates' speech overcomes at least for the moment his defensiveness, when Socrates claims he is unwilling to attempt to surpass Lysias' wisdom. Just as Phaedrus earlier pretends not to want to deliver Lysias' speech, and Socrates reveals his pretense, Phaedrus now does the same when Socrates takes his turn at "playing coy": "if I don't know Socrates I have forgotten myself," Phaedrus says, echoing Socrates' earlier words (236c). Phaedrus calls attention to his relative youth and strength and their solitary location, but forces Socrates to speak only by swearing that he will never again show or report to Socrates another speech of anyone unless Socrates comply. Socrates of course yields (236d–e; see *Republic* 327c–328b).

This exchange suggests that there is a greater opportunity for reconciliation with Socrates for Phaedrus than for Alcibiades (*Symposium* 213d). Whereas Alcibiades fears growing old listening to Socrates' speeches and flees (*Symposium* 216a–b), Phaedrus does not hesitate to sit with Socrates for the greater part of the day in the countryside delivering speeches and conversing. "What else would one live for?" he later asks (258e). But then Phaedrus is aware of the part that he himself plays in the speeches – an awareness that Socrates encourages by reminding him that he was the *Symposium*'s "father of the *logos*" (242a–b).

Phaedrus readily agrees to Socrates' desire to deliver his speech with his head covered lest he become ashamed when looking at Phaedrus (237a; see also *Symposium* 199b). Phaedrus wants only to hear the speech, and does not care whether he sees the speaker. For Phaedrus, Socrates' speech might as well be a writing, disembodied. Socrates, after all, claims that his inspired speech is not his (235c–d). Socrates may be just the person to hear an erotic speech, but Phaedrus is just the one to read aloud the speech of a non-lover, especially when we cannot be sure whether the speaker is a lover pretending to be a non-lover. Thus when Socrates proceeds to present to him the speech of such a man – even to make explicit his pretense – he offers Phaedrus a chance to see himself, in a way that Lysias' speech does not. Socrates later claims that the speech is "of Phaedrus," or "from Phaedrus" (243e–244a).[17] Because Socrates covers his head while he

---

[17] Burger argues that "Socrates must make himself into an image which Phaedrus will follow because he sees something of himself in it" *Plato's Phaedrus*, 8. See also Griswold, *Self-Knowledge*, 28–29; and Benardete, *The Rhetoric of Morality and Philosophy*, 119.

delivers the speech, Phaedrus will have no distractions from the words of the speech, as Socrates did when seeing the delight on Phaedrus' face.

Socrates' speech differs from Lysias' not only by introducing its speaker as a lover in disguise. It begins with reflections on how deliberations should begin: one must know what one is deliberating about so that by having agreement "at the beginning" of the inquiry, the speaker and addressee will not come to disagreement in the end – with both themselves and with each other. The speaker will therefore define love. He offers two "ruling and leading ideas" in each of us, acquired opinion aiming at the best, and a natural desire for pleasure. When the former holds sway, it is called "moderation"; when the latter, it is called "hubris." Since desires are many, so too are the forms of hubris. Love is that form that desires the beauty of bodies. The lover lacks the moderating effect of opinion that presumably characterizes the non-lover in his pursuit of beauty (237b–238c).

Although Socrates presents his speech as having the same thesis as Lysias' (235e–236a), the lover he describes differs considerably. The lover in Lysias' speech, for example, harms his beloved by praising him excessively, for he does everything to please the one he loves. The lover in Socrates' speech, in contrast, tries to please himself, as he is by definition ruled by his desire for pleasure. Because what does not resist him is pleasant, the argument goes, the lover attempts to keep his beloved inferior to himself, making him a weakling, in mind and body, and depriving him of other associates and possessions. Whereas Lysias presents the lover as slave to his beloved, his property suffering as a result of his love (which is why he repents when his desire ceases), in Socrates' speech it is the beloved who is the slave, and it is his property that suffers as a result (cf. 240a with 231a). In "contriving that his beloved look to him for everything" (239b), the lover who in Lysias' speech is a slave becomes in Socrates' speech a master. Socrates' speech describes his stance toward his beloved as that of a wolf toward a lamb (241c). In attempting to conceal his dependence or need, he disguises himself as a non-lover. He does not run away from his servility, as Alcibiades does, but stays around to control and to rule.

The lover in Lysias' speech ceases loving his beloved when the bloom of his beloved fades. He breaks off his past association when a new beloved demands that he do so. The lover in Socrates' speech, in contrast, simply ceases loving. He changes, Socrates says, to another ruler in himself, intelligence and moderation in the place of love and madness. He has become a non-lover, who stops pursuing. The moderation of this non-lover is not simply a restraint on his desire as he pursues sex, as Socrates' earlier definitions suggest; rather, it seems to suppress his desire. But just as Lysias' non-lover reveals his jealousy, so too does this new non-lover wear a mask: he does not go near his former beloved, Socrates says, lest he become a lover again. He is only a lover pretending to be a non-lover, and in the end running away protects his presumed self-sufficiency better than his despotism does. He follows Alcibiades after all. His beloved now pursues him, expecting return for his favors, but the beloved is no longer speaking to the same man (241a–b). "Not knowing from the beginning" that his senseless lover would become a "sensible non-lover" (see 241b–c), the beloved learns too late (see Aeschylus, *Agamemnon* 250–51 and Sophocles, *Antigone* 1270). So too does the lover, who has disguised himself as a non-lover in order to woo, and who now has nothing to say in favor of his non-lover's suit, for his appearance of moderation requires his retreat. His "agreed upon" definitions rule out any other understanding of love, and he has only opinion, which aims at the best by restraining desire, to fall back on. He is a tragic figure, whose means of pursuit guarantees his failure. He leaves himself nothing to say in his behalf.

Because Socrates' speech focuses only on the deficiencies of the lover, even if it culminates in the lover's adopting a non-lover disguise, Phaedrus supposes that Socrates has broken off his speech "in the middle" (241e). Socrates tells him that the case for the non-lover can be made "in one word": all the goods contrary to what we reproached in the lover should be attributed to him (241e). Of course, if someone is attentive to another, fostering virtue and wisdom (239a–b), that person might more appropriately be described as a lover. It will soon turn out that Socrates has more to say about such a person, and will do so in another speech about love.[18] Just as Phaedrus does not know in what way Lysias' speech is erotic, he also does not know in what way Socrates' speech is in the middle, for he expects to hear about the non-lover when in fact he needs to hear about a different sort of lover.

The world of Socrates' speech allows little room for the divine. The speaker points out that the lover does not hesitate to break his oaths and promises to his beloved, and that when the betrayed beloved calls upon the gods, he gets no response (241a–b). Inasmuch as Socrates' first speech explains love without recourse to the divine, it is analogous to the rationalization of the Boreas myth, which replaces the love of a god

[18] Griswold, *Self-Knowledge*, 70.

for a maiden with the violence of nature (the destructive North Wind). In fact, love is no less violent in Socrates' speech than is a wolf toward a lamb. Socrates seems to be "rationalizing," after all, for the lover he describes is not moved by anything divine, but is only in the grip of a passion harmful to himself and the one he loves.

Whereas the gods make no appearance in Socrates' speech, Socrates claims that he is inspired all the while he is speaking. He interrupts his speech to ask Phaedrus to confirm that he appears inspired, and tells him not to wonder if the nymphs to whom Phaedrus has exposed him capture him (238c–d). Socrates' speech leaves no room for the experience he has of giving the speech. By alluding to his inspiration and to his uncontrollably poetic language, Socrates seems to question whether he is "beside himself" again (see 234d). Once Socrates stops speaking to "avert the attack" of the nymphs (238d), he appears to be attacked from several other directions. His "customary daemonic sign," which opposes him whenever he is about to do something he should not (see *Apology* 40a), now comes to him and prevents him from going back to the city before making expiation for his impious speech about Love. So too does his "prophetic soul" disturb him as he delivers his speech. But now he perceives his "error," for he "was sinning against the gods" (242b–e), he admits, using the word Aristotle was to apply to tragic figures (Aristotle, *Poetics* 1453a10). He will therefore take as his model the poet Stesichorus: like Homer, he was blinded after speaking ill of Helen, but regained his sight by composing a palinode that claimed that Helen did not go to Troy (243a–b). Socrates presents a barrage of appeals to non-rational experiences to explain why he is recanting his criticism of love. Finally, he finds himself ashamed before a lover of gentle and noble character, who in listening to Lysias' and Socrates' speeches would suppose he was hearing people "brought up among sailors" (243c). He seems to have struck a chord in Phaedrus, who agrees with an oath to Zeus (243d), and insists that he will compel Lysias to write a recantation too.

Where is the boy to whom I was speaking, Socrates asks, for he must hear Socrates' recantation before he gratifies a non-lover. "Here he is beside you," Phaedrus responds, "very near, always present, whenever you wish" (243e). Some scholars see in this evidence that Socrates and Phaedrus are lover and beloved, or at least on route to becoming so.[19] But Socrates consistently pairs Phaedrus with Lysias (or with his lover

---

[19] For example, Herman L. Sinaiko, *Love, Knowledge, and Discourse in Plato: Dialogue and Dialectic in Phaedrus, Republic, Parmenides* (Chicago: University of Chicago Press, 1965), 109.

Eryximachus, whom we meet in the *Symposium*) (e.g., 236b; 257b; 278b; and 268a). In looking for the "boy" to whom he had been speaking, Socrates seems to be adopting a role again, now that of a lover rather than of a non-lover. The latter role Socrates never recants, at least explicitly, as he does the first. Phaedrus, for his part, may quickly embrace the role of the boy who is the palinode's addressee, because he thinks of himself as one to whom others offer benefits. In the palinode, however, the beloved whom Socrates describes becomes a lover in response to his lover's love. It would be to Phaedrus' credit if his role as the palinode's addressee were a better fit for him, or at least could become one, than is that either that of Lysias' calculating and self-interested seducer or that of the addressee whose advantage he urges.

Socrates claims to have the presence of mind that Stesichorus and Homer lack, for he "will be wiser than they" by recanting before he is blinded (243b). He learns from their experience so that he can avert what they suffer. He is also wiser in another way. Stesichorus may save Helen from blame, but hardly Love, for in his revised version of the story, the devastating Trojan war is fought over an image of Helen that the gods substitute for Helen herself.[20] Both Achaeans and Trojans alike die in the pursuit of a beautiful illusion. Destruction still comes from Love, even if the lover pursues only a phantom. Socrates' palinode will transcend this tragic view of human life that Stesichorus manifests, and that we have seen in the *Phaedrus* in praise of a non-lover. And Phaedrus is pleased to stay for another speech, his love of speeches supported by the heat of the noonday sun, which makes it too hot for him to walk back to the city (242a). Even the "oppressions" of nature have their benefits for us, if we put our opportunities to good use.

SOULS AND THEIR FALL

The non-lover who speaks in Lysias' speech attempts to play it safe, as he deliberates about his own good and tries to secure it through his clever rhetoric. And Socrates' speech explicitly contrasts the "intelligence and moderation" of the non-lover with "the love and madness" experienced by the lover (241a). "Moderation" (*sōphrosunē*), literally means being "safe" or "secure" (*sōs*) "in one's mind" (*phrēn*) (see

---

[20] Only a fragment of Stesichorus' palinode has survived. Euripides based his play *Helen* on the alternative account. While Helen waits out the Trojan War in Egypt, the Greeks and the Trojans fight over a phantom of Helen that the gods put in her place.

Aristotle, *NE* 1140b12–13). While the control that the non-lovers achieve is not what they want it to be, inasmuch as the one in Lysias' speech manifests jealousy and the other flees in Socrates' speech lest he succumb to love, there could be no greater threat to human control than Socrates' insistence at the beginning of the palinode that the greatest goods come to human beings from madness, at least when it comes from the gods (244a). His praise of madness brings to the forefront both what most appalls the non-lover, as revealed in the non-lover's criticisms of the lover, and also what his own lack of self-knowledge threatens, for his love makes him "beside himself" without his knowing it.

Socrates gives as examples of madness prophecy, purification from pollution, poetic inspiration, and finally love, demoting the self-control sought by the non-lover to inferior and unsuccessful attempts to achieve by reason and art the goods that come through madness. Through "bird-augury," humans attempt to predict the future "through reasoning" about the flights and cries of birds (244c–d), and the poetry of the one who derives his competence "from art" comes to nothing in comparison with the poetry of madmen (245a). Socrates supports his position that the greatest benefits come through god-given madness by appealing to the authority of the ancients and the names they gave to prophecy and bird-augury. They gave prophecy (*mantikē*) the name of "madness" (*manikē*), whereas the moderns lost sight of the connection and added a "t" to its name. As to bird-augury (*oiōnistikē*), Socrates traces its etymology to understanding (*oiēisis*), intelligence (*nous*), and information (*historia*). Thus its ancient name indicates its inferiority to god-inspired prophecy; not aware of these connections the moderns change the spelling of the art so that it refers to birds (*oiōnoi*) (244a–d).

Socrates' fanciful and absurd etymologies provide comic relief from his praise of god-given madness in a way that Aristophanes interrupts the solemn entrance of the divine Clouds with Strepsiades' low and vulgar remarks (*Clouds* 293ff.). Moreover, the inspired prophet, poet, and lover would not be aware of their same counterparts. It takes Socrates to contrast their madness with these "inferior" skills. The madmen praised in the palinode could not themselves deliver the palinode.[21] As Socrates

---

[21] Griswold notes that "the speech about love is not mad in the same sense love is." This is one of the ways in which Griswold understands what he calls "the self-qualification of the myth" of the palinode – that Socrates gives an account of things in the palinode that according to the palinode "no human soul could possibly know." *Self-Knowledge*, 151–56. See also Joseph Cropsey, *Political Philosophy and the Issues of Politics* (Chicago: University of Chicago Press, 1977), 245.

turns from madness to his "demonstration" or "proof" that love, in particular, is sent by the gods for our greatest good fortune, he notes that "it will be distrusted by the clever, and trusted by the wise" (245b–c). Reason must be supplemented in some way by trust, and not replaced by madness.

Socrates' "demonstration" begins with the soul's immortality. Only something self-moving, he argues, can be the beginning of motion; otherwise its motion would originate in another. Moreover, something self-moving could itself have no beginning, which would require a cause outside itself, in which case it would not be self-moving. Nor could its motion ever cease, inasmuch as it would have no cause other than itself that could withdraw. Since that which moves itself is eternal, having neither a beginning nor an end to its motion, whoever says that self-motion is the "being and definition (*logos*) of soul will not be ashamed" (245e). One could not ask of the soul that Socrates describes here, what Socrates asks of Phaedrus at the beginning of this dialogue – where it is going and where it comes from (227a). If Socrates' demonstration of the soul stopped here, the soul would be a non-lover, moved by nothing outside itself.[22] Socrates says that we understand the soul by seeing "how it acts" (*erga*) and "how it is acted upon" (*pathē*) (245c). As self-motion, however, the soul acts upon itself, and is acted upon by itself. Its action and its being acted upon are one and the same.

When Socrates observes that whoever gives self-motion as "the being and definition" of soul "will not be ashamed" (245e), however, we should remember that he has already acknowledged his shame at his speech about the non-lover. His recantation proceeds at least in part from this shame. Very quickly, Socrates expands the soul's reach: the soul both moves and even "takes care of" all that is soulless, or all body (245e and 246b).[23] And its wings carry the soul upward, where it is nurtured by "the beautiful, the wise, the good, and all such things" (246d–e). The movements and cares of soul are manifold, connected to what is both below it and above it.

When Socrates moves from his demonstration of the soul as a self-moving eternal being to his image of the soul, he moves to a plurality of

---

[22] Griswold also connects self-motion, inasmuch as it suggests self-sufficiency, with the non-lover. *Self-Knowledge*, 86.

[23] How does soul do such a double duty? Why does that which is self-moving move other things? And why do souls join bodies (see *Republic* 616a)? See Burger: "Socrates does not take up the problem of the self-moving that is simultaneously responsible for moving something else," *Plato's* Phaedrus, 51.

souls. With the image of the soul as charioteer and horses, there is differentiation into kinds, including divine souls and those that are not divine.[24] As Socrates' tale develops, the heavens themselves are filled with activity. Zeus is the "great leader" of an army of souls organized into squadrons each led in turn by one of the gods. Souls are thus not only divided into divine and those that are not, but divine souls themselves are differentiated, Zeus playing a leading role, with other gods leading other souls. Following the traditional number of gods in the Greek pantheon, Socrates designates twelve, although there are only eleven squadrons of souls in the heavens, inasmuch as Hestia stays in "the home of the gods" (247a). There are many blessed sights and pathways within the heavens, "along which the race of happy gods passes to and fro, each one of them doing his own thing, and whoever wishes and is able follows" (247a). But the ultimate toil and contest lie before souls when they proceed upward to the rim outside the heavens ("the hyperuranian place"), where they are nourished on "what is visible to the mind alone," such as justice, moderation, and knowledge itself (247c–d).

   In this description of the souls' movement in the heavens, there are two sorts of motion. There is the movement within the heavens, which is idiosyncratic, inasmuch as each god does "his own thing," and other souls follow according to their wishes and abilities. There is also the ascent to the place outside the heavens. Since in this account, the souls' "human" lives depend on the latter (they fall to the earth and join bodies when their wings break in their struggle to ascend), the former motion seems hardly necessary to the story Socrates tells. Yet it is the former motion that might more easily be described as self-motion, as it seems to depend on the souls themselves. Their motion upward, toward the hyperuranian beings on which they are nourished, in contrast, depends on need and what satisfies it. To ascend is to have a goal outside oneself, and therefore not to be entirely self-moving. Griswold observes that "it is not clear how eros and self-motion are to be connected, especially since erotic motion seems to be caused by the object of desire."[25]

   Time after time, in the palinode, Socrates' presentation of soul reveals this ambiguity. When divine souls complete their ascent, stand

---

[24] Socrates' move from one soul to many exploits the ambiguity of the Greek word "all" (*pas*) in the proof that "all soul is immortal." The word translated as "all" also means "every." Nichols, *Plato Phaedrus*, 49 n. 86.

[25] Griswold, *Self-Knowledge*, 80; see also 86, and Burger, *Plato's* Phaedrus, 82.

on the back of heaven, and behold the beings, they do so until "the rotation [of heaven] carries them around" (247c–d). The circular motion is not that of soul, but of the heavens, which carries these divine souls along with it. Socrates' language emphasizes the difference between the self-motion of the soul and its nourishment by those things "visible to the mind alone," for it is the motion of the heavens that moves the souls as they behold the truth.

In the *Republic*'s theology, Socrates assimilates the gods to the ideas that the philosophers are said to behold (e.g., *Republic* 486d): he describes the gods as unchanging, perfect, and motionless (*Republic* 380d–e; see 485b). There he bypasses the question of the *Euthyphro* in a way the *Phaedrus* does not: is the holy holy because the gods love it, or do the gods love it because it is holy (*Euthyphro* 10a)? The *Republic*'s "gods," assimilated to the ideas, do not love; they are the holy. So too the beings beheld by souls outside the heavens do not love. It is in relation to those beings, Socrates says, that "the god is divine" (249c).[26] In terms of the *Euthyphro*, the gods love the holy because it is holy. And yet if the gods in the palinode are self-moving, as the definition of soul suggests, their motion toward the beings they behold lies within themselves, and those beings are holy because they are loved.

Consider also Socrates' references to "the home" of the gods. The wings of the soul carry it upward to "where the race of the gods have their home" (246d), Socrates explains, but after the gods feast on the beings they "sink down again into the heavens" and return "home" where the charioteers feed and rest their horses (247e). This "home" is presumably the one Socrates refers to earlier, when he explains that Hestia does not have her own squadron in the heavens, for she "stays in the home of the gods" (247a). If the gods love the holy because it is holy, their home would be the hyperuranian place, to which "the wing carries the soul upward" (246d–e). Whereas if the holy is holy because the gods love it, their home would be with Hestia.

A similar question arises about the army of souls in the heavens of whom Zeus is the leader, and which consists of squadrons each led by one of the gods. Why is one soul in one squadron, another in another? Different types of souls follow different gods in the heavens, as becomes clear when Socrates describes the souls on earth, once they fall from the

---

[26] Emphasizing this side of Socrates' treatment of the divine in the palinode, Nicholson argues that it is to "to the vision of true being that the gods owe their divinity." *Plato's Phaedrus*, 124; see also 180.

heavens and are united with bodies. A follower of Zeus is philosophic, for example, while a follower of Hera is kingly (253a–b). But it is not clear whether Zeus, who arranges the army in the heavens, assigns different types of souls to their appropriate god (in the way the *Republic*'s rulers assign different soul types to the appropriate classes in the city, *Republic* 415b–c), or whether souls become different types as a result of their assignation. Does a soul follow Hera because it is kingly, or does it become kingly because it follows Hera? The question remains open. It is a question that affects our earthly lives as well, when the question of choice arises for embodied souls.

The fall to the earth occurs during the ascent to the rim outside the heavens. The divine souls, whose horses and charioteer are all good and of noble descent, proceed without difficulty to feast on the beings there, while other souls proceed with difficulty, weighed down by their unruly horses, and struggling due to the charioteer's lack of skill. They see the beings outside the heavens only imperfectly, viewing some things but not others, and eventually break their wings in the struggle and fall to the earth. The motion that is required to attain a vision of the beings disrupts that vision. "Human beings" as we know them are born as a consequence.

The lives we live – from that of philosopher and lover of beauty to tyrant – depend on the different visions of the beings we have attained in our former lives (246e–248e). The palinode thus adds a second way of classifying soul types to the division that derives from the different god each followed in the heavenly army. The two different classifications of human types reflect the split we have seen in the divine – between the soul as self-moving – since the souls follow their gods as they wish and are able – and the soul as moved toward the truth that nourishes it. Because some fallen souls have seen some of the beings, Socrates explains, and because others have seen others, and for different periods of time, the result is different types of human soul. Since Socrates does not give us a definite number of beings in his account, and since he introduces the issue of the duration of the visions different souls attain, there are in principle an infinite number of human types, with varying similarities and differences, although Socrates lists nine, with each having different human manifestations within it. The statesman, the household manager, and the moneymaker, for example, all constitute one type. Only the tyrant occupies a class of his own, the lowest type of human being (258d–e).

Once souls fall from the heavens, Socrates continues, they enter into ten thousand year cycles of human birth and death, each life followed by reward and punishment based on the justice of their lives on earth, and finally by their choice of new lives and rebirth (248e–249b). The self-motion of soul, qualified to be sure, comes into play when human beings live justly or unjustly in their embodied lives, and in their choice of new lives at the time of rebirth. Some souls descend so low as to choose lives of beasts, but only those that have seen something of the beings outside the heavens can have a human life, for "a human being must understand what is spoken in relation to its class [or idea], that which is collected together from many perceptions by reasoning." This is the recollection of the beings we once saw above the heavens, Socrates says (249b–c; also 249e–250a). For the first time, speaking or reasoning enters Socrates' account of the soul in the palinode. Before birth, the "mind" is nourished by the beings above the heavens (247c–d), but there is no speech either among the divine or other souls. Socrates reverses Aristophanes' account in the *Symposium*, where gods speak, and human beings remain mute (*Symposium* 190c–d and 192d). But since Socrates' palinode, a recantation of his criticism of love, involves the madness experienced by the lover when he recollects true beauty as a result of beholding beauty here (249d),[27] Socrates' more complete development of the place of speech in human life awaits his discussion with Phaedrus after the palinode.

Socrates' account of recollection here hardly produces a view of universal man, as Kierkegaard's Climacus derives from Socrates' theory of recollection. Even if self-knowledge consisted in truths seen before birth, self-knowledge would differ from individual to individual, because human beings have not had the same vision or experiences. They have seen only some of the beings in their former lives, for

---

[27] Although this is not the only time in the Platonic corpus that Plato's Socrates explains the "doctrine of recollection," this is the only time in which he connects this account of knowledge with our experience of love. See Klein's account of recollection and memory in the Platonic corpus in *A Commentary on Plato's Meno* (Chapel Hill, NC: University of North Carolina Press, 1965), 108–72. Curiously enough, Klein does not mention Love in his discussion of memory and recollection in the *Phaedrus*, 151–52. In the other accounts of recollection in the Platonic corpus, the issue is not love, and its worth, but the possibility of knowledge (*Meno*) or the immortality of the soul (*Phaedo*). Socrates nevertheless underlines the absence of love from his presentation in these dialogues. In the *Meno*, he deals with Meno's "contentious" proposition that learning is impossible by eliciting a mathematical theorem from a slave boy rather than offering (he says) "an image of beauty" (*Meno*, 80c and 80e ff.). In the *Phaedo*, as I discuss in Chapter 1, Socrates includes in his examples of how one thing can remind us of another the example of a lover who is reminded of his beloved by his beloved's cloak or lyre (*Phaedo* 73d).

example, and not very clearly as they struggle to ascend. To know the truth, then, one must go beyond oneself. It is therefore not the case that according to the theory of recollection, at least as it is presented in the *Phaedrus*, that each human being has the truth within himself and so needs only to be reminded of it. Should we acquire the truth, it would come to us in part from outside ourselves. It is not surprising that Climacus refers to the *Meno*, and not to the *Phaedrus*, when he explains the doctrine of recollection in the process of setting up his foil for the god as teacher, and only later refers to the *Phaedrus* for Socrates' perplexity about himself.

Moreover, since self-motion defines soul, self-knowledge cannot be simply what one attains when one recollects the beings seen above the heavens. Self-motion means that self-knowledge cannot be simply God-knowledge, to use Climacus' language. Nussbaum recognizes the irreducible individuality that follows from the palinode's presentation of soul as self-motion, but removes the paradox by downplaying the "recollection" side of the teaching. Thus her formulation moves Plato in a Kantian direction: "[in the palinode] love's value is closely linked to the fact that this unique person is valued, throughout, as a separate being with his or her own self-moving soul."[28]

Griswold, for his part, reconciles self-motion with love by subordinating the former to the latter: "at [the] highest level, the value of the goal desired by the soul derives both from the goal and from the soul. The soul desires Being because Being nourishes it, and Being is desirable because it is intrinsically nourishing." There is "a natural fit" for Plato, he says "between soul and Truth." Love of the forms, or the "ideas, he writes, "is self-fulfillment."[29] Griswold's understanding of Plato thus escapes the paradox that Climacus attributes to Socrates' pursuit of knowledge, but in the opposite direction from Nussbaum. Socrates speaks of self-motion, he suggests, to indicate "that the locus of activity and life is in the soul (the beings are, by contrast, lifeless)." Self-motion means that the soul moves toward what nourishes it, that the soul is, in other words, erotic. Griswold also argues that the language of self-motion "points to the soul's capacity, indeed its freedom, to recover what it naturally desires or to move away from it." The former

---

[28] Nussbaum, *The Fragility of Goodness*, 218.
[29] Griswold, *Self-Knowledge*, 110–11, 113–14. See also Friedlander, "The central point of the myth is again the necessary correlation between soul and *Eidos* [the Idea], just as it is the focal point of all of Plato's philosophy." *Plato: An Introduction*, 193.

movement is erotic, the latter obstructs our pursuit of the good that is true human fulfillment. Self-motion, insofar as it differs from erotic motion, is error. When Griswold writes that "the change from horizontal to vertical motion comes through self-knowledge,"[30] he in effect accepts Climacus' initial formulation of the Socratic position on recollection. To know oneself is to recollect the beings. Self-knowledge, could it be achieved by human beings, would be God-knowledge.

For Nussbaum, the truth as a problem disappears; for Griswold, self-motion as a problem does so. Burger's formulation of the "tension between the stable identity of the beings and the ever-moving motion of soul" comes closer to Kierkegaard's understanding.[31] Only because Socrates remains distinct from the beings that he recollects does self-knowledge become a question for him. By the same token, to give a love speech or to woo a beloved means that one is not simply a lover. One also wants to be loved in return. If a lover were in no way aware of this, a non-lover disguise would never enter his mind. Although Socrates does not remember where he heard his first speech on love, or how it came to him, he knows that it is not his own (235c–d). He knows enough to raise the question of where his first speech comes from. So too Socrates may be beside himself as he looks at Phaedrus (234d), but he can also be aware of it, and even acknowledge it. When he says that he is beside himself, he recalls himself to himself. He is not simply moved toward what he loves. The soul is not simply erotic. Even in his praise of love, Socrates defines the soul as self-motion; otherwise he would have left no room for his own speech.

LOVERS AND THEIR ASCENT

Like Diotima, Socrates describes the lover's ascent from the beauty that he sees in his beloved to beauty itself, but he presents the soul's ascent and longing as more complex than she does. Nor is its path as smooth. The hyperuranian beings include not only beauty but also other beings such as moderation, justice, knowledge, and prudence (247d and 250d; cf. *Symposium* 211b and e). But these latter do not shine as brightly here as does beauty, Socrates says. Moreover, our visions of the beings were

---

[30] Griswold, *Self-Knowledge*, 110–11. But see his qualifications, 227.

[31] Burger, *Plato's* Phaedrus, 89. See Benardete's observation on the *Phaedrus*: "The universality of knowledge and the individuality of self-knowledge seem not to consist with one another." *The Rhetoric of Morality and Philosophy*, 104.

brief or long ago, and we have experiences here that maim our souls. Because beauty is "the most manifest and loveliest" of the things we once saw, its images are our readiest access to our former lives (250a–d). "Carried swiftly from here to beauty itself" at the sight of his beloved, the lover feels awe and reverence. If lovers did not "fear a reputation (*doxan*) for madness they would sacrifice to their darling as if he were an idol or a god" (250e–251a). Their fear of a reputation for madness indicates that they are not simply mad.

While opinion holds the lover back from treating his beloved as a god, his unruly black horse pushes him in another direction, thrusting him toward his beloved for the purpose of sex. Since at the sight of his beloved, a lover's "memory is carried toward the nature of beauty and he sees it once more together with moderation" (254b), he pulls back on his reins, and the lover retreats. The black horse angrily accuses the charioteer and white horse, as Socrates tells the tale, of deserting their post and not keeping their agreements (254d). After several such approaches to the beloved, the black horse is finally tamed, and the soul of the lover follows his darling in awe and fear (254e). Although the soul is pulled by its parts in different directions, the soul recollects moderation along with beauty, and its charioteer is eventually able to master his unruly horse. Socrates' account thus incorporates the soul's self-motion into its earthly life, while it places the virtue that Socrates' earlier speech attributes to the non-lover (moderation) in the service of love. Moderation, or self-control, plays no similar role in Diotima's account of the soul's ascent in the *Symposium*.[32] It is Alcibiades who identifies self-control as Socrates' virtue, while understanding his eroticism as a mask that hides a self-sufficient non-lover. He senses something in Socrates that Diotima misses in her account of Love and that Socrates now attempts to reflect in his own presentation of love, even if it requires an image of the soul that suggests its monstrous character, part human (the charioteer) and part beast (two horses, one of them especially ugly, and with a snub nose like Socrates [cf. 253e with *Theaetetus* 143e]).

Without the urging of his black horse, the lover would not approach the beloved at all, nor would he return once he retreated. Moreover,

---

[32] Moderation is used only once by Diotima, not when describing the ascent toward the beautiful but when explaining the various offspring of lovers of the beautiful – such as poets, craftsmen, and those concerned with families and cities, who generate moderation and justice (*Symposium* 209a–b). Moderation in Diotima's account characterizes not love or the lover but the political life he establishes and nurtures.

while the beloved reminds the lover of beauty, it is his black horse who reminds him of courage and justice, if only by way of reproach. And whereas one can remind of beauty without speaking, the black horse needs speech to rebuke on behalf of courage and justice. The black horse appears to be the element of the soul most associated with speech. When the charioteer pulls back from the beloved, the "words" the black horse would deliver to the beloved are not spoken (254d; see also 254e). When Socrates says that the black horse "mentions" the delights of sexual pleasures to his charioteer and yokemate, he uses a word that literally means "reminds" (254a). Curiously, the black horse is able to remind them of what none of the three has ever experienced.

The recollection from the past that the experience of love elicits is not simply of the beings the lover once imperfectly beheld but of the god in the heavens whom he once followed. This occurs because of the factor that Socrates now introduces: in love we seek a soul of the same sort as our own, understood in terms of the god our soul once followed in the heavens. Zeus followers love other Zeus followers, for example, and therefore seek a beloved with a philosophic nature and capable of leadership, while followers of Hera seek one of a kingly nature like themselves. Once he finds a suitable beloved, the lover attempts "to make him as like as possible to *their* god" (emphasis mine) (253a–b). The lover's "formation" of his beloved brings his beloved to his own. The "free [or liberal] love" that Socrates told Phaedrus his palinode would present in contrast to his first speech (243c) finds limit and support in the character that lover and beloved share.

Moved to make his beloved as like as possible to their god, the lover tries to learn from wherever he can "the nature of his god," Socrates continues, and inspired by his beloved the lover himself draws to his god "through memory." He takes up the character and practices of his god to the extent it is possible for a human being (252e–253a). His movement toward his beloved is at the same time a movement toward his god, which in turn informs his movement toward his beloved. The lover's desire to help his beloved become as much like their god as possible, leads the lover also to become as much like their god as possible. Seeking self-knowledge arises from love. And it aims at improving another. To put what Socrates is describing in the language of teaching, the lover desires to teach and is consequently moved to learn. As Diotima told Socrates in the *Symposium*, "when a lover meets a beautiful and naturally gifted soul, he "becomes resourceful in speeches about virtue – and of what sort the good man must be and what he must practice – and he tries to educate him" (*Symposium* 209b–c). Socrates adds to Diotima's account that the "resources" that the lover seeks for his beloved are resources for the lover as well.

As Socrates explains the effect of the lover on the beloved, he reveals an even greater bond and reciprocity between them. As the lover and beloved spend time together, the stream of particles from the beautiful beloved flows not merely to the lover's soul but overflows from his soul back to the beloved. The stream of love acts like an echo rebounding off surfaces to return to its point of origin (254c). The beloved's sight of his own beauty, now reflected by his lover, functions for him as it does for the lover, and he loves in return, even though he thinks his condition to be one of "friendship." So too "he sees himself in his lover as in a mirror, but he does not know it," Socrates observes (255d–e). Love changes the lover, and changes the beloved in turn.[33] As they realize the practices of their god, their relationship leads to the betterment of each. The word that Socrates uses for the beloved's "love in return," *anterōs*, is a word that more obviously refers to "rivalry in love" for another's affection.[34] The rivals for the favors of a youth, who motivate the first two speeches of the *Phaedrus*, have been superseded by this pair of lover and beloved.

Socrates says that "if the better sides of lover and beloved conquer," they will achieve a well-ordered life and philosophy. They then live as friends as they "journey together" in the heavens (255b and 256a–e). There is no simple return, then, to the previous condition, at least for this pair of human beings, whose original fall gave them the opportunity to attain self-knowledge through their love of the other, and whose achievement is both rewarded and maintained in Socrates' myth by their continued being together after death. As in traditional comedies, the tale ends in a kind of marriage. Socrates even suggests at one point that love ceases and gives way to friendship, when he says that lover and beloved "live as friends both during their love and when they have passed beyond it" (256d; see also *Symposium* 209c).

The motion of the soul is therefore not entirely self-motion, for it requires another. Of all the tales and arguments that we find in the Platonic corpus, the palinode is the only one in which the life of

---

[33] For a good statement of the reciprocity involved in this relationship, see Lebeck, who explains how first the beloved leads the lover to the god, and then the lover does so for the beloved in turn. "The Central Myth," 278.

[34] While *anterōs* occurs only here in extant classical Greek literature, *anterastēs*, "rival in love," is quite common. See, for example, Plato, *Lovers* 132c and 133b; *Republic* 521b; Aristophanes, *Knights* 733; and Aristotle, *Rhetoric* 1388a15.

immortality that it foresees is enriched by the continued "journeying together" of friends. As suggested by this myth of their immortality, in which lover and beloved remain together after death, love is for a particular human being, and not simply the good or beautiful qualities shared with others. To this extent, Nussbaum is correct: "The focus on character takes away much of love's replaceability; the focus on history removes the rest."[35] The focus on character and history to which Nussbaum refers follows from the palinode's presentation of self-motion as the definition of soul, which means that the other who arouses our love cannot be reduced to an image of the beings (i.e., the qualities he shares with others), as Vlastos maintains.[36] By the same token, the lover himself is not simply erotic. If love were "the being and definition of soul," love of another would lead to self-forgetting rather than self-knowledge, and lover and beloved would disappear into the good qualities they share. Or, as Griswold says, reminding us of the side of the palinode that Nussbaum neglects, "the suppression of the subject . . . is

---

[35] Nussbaum, *The Fragility of Goodness*, 218. Although Griswold sides with Vlastos (although with some qualifications) against Nussbaum, he nevertheless observes that the lover and beloved of the palinode "do *seem* attached to each other as individuals, perhaps because they have had the experience, which they have not shared with others, of helping each learn over a lifetime," *Self-Knowledge*, 129. For his reservations on Vlastos' position, see *Self-Knowledge*, 128–29 and "The Politics of Self-Knowledge: Liberal Variations on the *Phaedrus*," in *Understanding the Phaedrus*, ed. Livio Rossetti (Sankt Augustin: Academia Verlag, 1992), 179 n. 17.

[36] Vlastos, "The Individual as an Object of Love in Plato," 31–32. F. C. White responds to Vlastos with respect to the *Phaedrus* in particular, arguing that "the beloved resembles Beauty so plainly as fully to justify his being loved for his own sake," "Love and the Individual in Plato's *Phaedrus*," *Classical Quarterly* 40 (1990): 401. Santas observes that "the best lover in the *Phaedrus* never severs himself completely . . . , it seems, from a particular beautiful person," for he prizes him "for being a particularly good image of divine Beauty," "Passionate Platonic Love in the *Phaedrus*," 112. Griswold, consistent with his view of self-knowledge as knowledge of the beings, as I discuss above, writes that although "a soul is held to be worthy of love in virtue of the lovable qualities it exhibits, . . . Plato's point [is] that the 'transcendent' nature of these qualities rescues value for the soul rather than deprives it of value," "The Politics of Self-Knowledge," 179; see also *Self-Knowledge*, 128–29. So too James M. Rhodes argues against Vlastos that he "fails to understand that the identity of the individual is to be an image of the divine." "Platonic *Philia* and Political Order," in *Friendship and Politics: Essays in Political Thought*, ed. John von Heyking and Richard Avramenko (Notre Dame IN: Notre Dame University Press, 2008). Sinaiko distinguishes three levels in "the object of every human love": the unique individual, the generic class to which the object belongs, and transcendent Being. *Love, Knowledge, and Discourse*, 86. Such formulations attempt to give their due to both sides of the Vlastos–Nussbaum divide in their interpretation of Plato, although they do not treat the problem on which Kierkegaard focuses in the *Fragments*.

its perfection."[37] But, as Socrates says in his playful exchange with Phaedrus earlier, "If I fail to know Phaedrus, I have forgotten myself, but neither of these is the case" (228a). Socrates does not forget himself in his knowledge of the other (see also *Apology* 17a).

While the lover's recollection of beauty (along with moderation [254b]) plays a major role in the lover's attraction to the beloved, Socrates says little about any relation between the recollection of beauty and that of any of the other "lovely beings" with which the mind is nourished (250d–e). Moreover, the relation between the palinode's two classifica- tions of soul types – the one based on the god that souls followed in the heavens, the other on their different visions of the beings above the heavens before falling to the earth – remains an unexplored question in the background of Socrates' tale of human life. Even if lover and beloved become as much as possible like the god they once followed, is this the best they are able to become? They have followed the same god, in terms of the myth, but they have not necessarily seen the same visions in the heavens. This difference might provide the basis of a deeper relation – as they might have more to give to each other if the other were capable of receiving it. Socrates, however, does not discuss any such exchanges. And although each sees himself in the other, they do not know what is hap- pening to them. As Socrates says of the beloved, for example, when the beloved sees himself in his lover, he does not know it (255d). Even if they know themselves as a result of their loving another, they do not know that they know themselves. While Socrates refers to them as friends, he leaves undeveloped what friendship is, or what its relation to love is. There appears to be little speech between the lover and beloved whom Socrates describes in the palinode, although he insists that being able to under- stand speech is the mark of a human life (249b). Socrates does mention that the beloved, moved by his lover's good will, admits him to "speech and association" (255b), but he tells us nothing about their "speech." The word for "conversing" (*dialegesthai*) never occurs in the palinode. When Socrates gives the details of the "capture of the beloved," it is the black horse who has the most to say, and his speech must be curbed (254a ff.). In the palinode, Socrates associates recollection primarily with looking, not with questioning as he does in the *Meno*. And although the philos- opher is among the group of human types who have "seen most" of the hyperuranian beings in their lives before birth (248d), by the end of the palinode he associates the philosophic lover and beloved not with any

[37] Griswold, *Self-Knowledge*, 104.

recollection or knowledge they share but with the "ordered life" made possible by the better parts of the soul "conquering" (256a).

To the philosophic lover and beloved, Socrates contrasts a pair of lovers who are moved by love of honor (256b). In the list of nine soul types, lawful kings, statesmen, and poets, for example, who in Diotima's speech all desire to be remembered by their communities (*Symposium* 208d and 209d), fall in different classes, but there are no lovers of honor as such in Socrates' list (248c–d). Nor did Socrates associate love of honor with any particular god whom souls follow in the heavens (252c and 253a–b). Presumably love of honor is found in all types, just as are love, recollection, and speech. Socrates now distinguishes lovers of honor from philosophic lovers not as different types of soul, but by the extent to which their black horses get their way. The relationship of the lovers of honor, Socrates relates, is not free from enmity and discord, although they believe that they "have exchanged the greatest pledges of fidelity [i.e., claims of being worthy of trust]" (256d).[38] By implication, it is not this couple but the philosophic pair who have indeed exchanged "the greatest pledges." Whatever they know of the other, and however much the other is like himself, knowledge does not replace the need for trust.

Socrates gives us no indication of the cause of the discord of the pair who love honor, or even any hint that it has to do with their love of honor. In fact, their love of honor seems superfluous in Socrates' account of them, unless it is seen in their supposition that theirs are the "greatest" pledges of fidelity – that is, that theirs is the highest love. Socrates' mentioning the lovers of honor, however, recalls his earlier description of the white horse as "a lover of honor" (253d). The white horse in Socrates' description of love supports the charioteer in his struggle with the black horse, but offers no direction of his own to the soul. Earlier, Socrates mentions, almost in passing, that the lover is restrained in his worship of his beloved for fear of acquiring a reputation for madness (251a). Now, as he draws his palinode to a close, Socrates' reference to lovers of honor reveals that there is an aspect of the human condition that his account of fallen souls leaves undeveloped. Although Socrates says that lover and beloved become friends (256a–b), he says nothing about their becoming citizens or in any way

[38] "Exchanged" is my translation of "given and received." The souls in the heavens, prior to the fall to the earth, were said to simply "receive" what was fitting when they gazed upon truth (247d).

serving the city. Phaedrus, who had argued in the *Symposium* that cities should arrange lover and beloved together in battle to ensure their noble deeds (*Symposium* 178c–179a), should know that the palinode, as he claims of Socrates' first speech, is not yet finished (241d).

Socrates has improved the comic presentation of the human condition that Aristophanes gives in the *Symposium*, to be sure. Consistent with Diotima's identification of Love as the link between gods and humans, Socrates has explained how our love of another is elevated by our memory of the divine and serves the education of both lover and beloved. But his speech is still incomplete. Socrates says as much himself in the prayer to Love with which he concludes his palinode.

PRAYER TO LOVE

At the end of the palinode, Socrates prays to Love. Whether this determines that he believes that Love is a god, rather than merely something divine (242e), we cannot know for sure. At the beginning of the palinode itself, Socrates describes love as a kind of madness given to us by the gods for our greatest benefit, and therefore not himself a god (245b–c; see also 252b–c). Since Love is not mentioned among the Olympian gods who lead squadrons in the army of souls in the myth, there is no "erotic type," just different ways in which different types of souls experience love. As in Aristophanes' *Symposium* tale, love appears explicitly only after the "fall" and is born of poverty or need. And as in Diotima's lessons, love links us to the divine once we assume our mortal forms. Again, Love seems to be born of Resource as well as Poverty.

Socrates first prays for himself: "Forgive my former speech and favor this one, do not take from me the erotic art you gave me, nor maim me through anger, but grant that even more than now I be honored by the beautiful" (257a). Whereas Socrates begins the palinode with the claim that the madness of love is given by the gods for our great good fortune (245b–c), and even contrasts the kinds of madness with inferior arts (245a; see also 244a–d), he now prays at the end to preserve his erotic art. While Socrates elsewhere speaks of his knowledge of erotic matters (*Symposium* 177e; see also *Lysis* 204c), he does not elsewhere admit his possession of an erotic "art." Inasmuch as arts are rational, and can give accounts (*logoi*) of themselves (see *Gorgias* 456a), they seem to be the opposite of madness, which is unintelligible (*aphrōn*; see 265e). There is something paradoxical about speaking of an "art" as a gift from a god, for if arts are intelligible and can be explained, they come "from us," and they can be taught to others. Socrates does not explain what his erotic art is. We might call the lover's educating his beloved in the likeness of their god a result of an "erotic art," but Socrates does not do so. We have no reason to suppose that a mad lover could give the account of his condition that Socrates does any more than could a beloved who "does not know what he is suffering," and "is unable to say its cause" (255d). Moreover, art seems to reach beyond the individual case in a way that the lover's education in the palinode does not (see Aristotle, *NE* 1180b10–28). So too does Socrates pray to be honored by the beautiful. He speaks of the beautiful from whom he desires honor in the plural. In expressing this prayer, Socrates not only raises the question of who the beautiful are from whom he desires honor (see *Protagoras* 209c–d and *Theaetetus* 185e), but he points beyond the world of the palinode to the community in which such honor is awarded.

Having prayed for himself, Socrates prays for Lysias and Phaedrus, whom he now refers to as Lysias' lover. After the palinode, the beloved's non-lover disguise is no longer credible. Socrates asks Love not to blame either him or Phaedrus if they said anything harsh against Love in their former speech, but to blame Lysias, "the father of the speech," and to turn Lysias toward philosophy so that "his lover" no longer vacillates but "turns his life simply toward Love with philosophic speeches" (257b). Socrates calls Lysias "the father" of the speech that Socrates himself gave on the same theme, using the expression that Eryximachus applies to Phaedrus in the *Symposium* (177d). Whereas Phaedrus receives this appellation because he proposes the encomia to Love, Lysias does so because he prompts a speech that competes with his own. Speeches have different kinds of causes, as the *Phaedrus* dramatizes earlier when Socrates elicits Phaedrus' reading of the speech Lysias wrote, and Phaedrus causes Socrates to deliver the speech with which "[his] breast is full" (235c). Socrates concludes the palinode with the thought that the causes of generation are complex, that one birth leads to another, and that one does not generate alone. In the palinode, lover and beloved do not seem to generate anything outside themselves. In the latter half of the *Phaedrus*, however, Socrates does not forget Diotima's lessons about generation or the relation between generation and happiness and the way in which generation connects us to others. Not only does Socrates turn to the statesmen's love of honor and desire to leave their writings behind so that they will be remembered, but with the palinode's presentation of the soul in the background, he is able to expand Diotima's account to include the dialectician–rhetorician who generates speeches in the souls of others, which generate other speeches in turn (258a ff. and 276e–277a).

CONTEMPORARY RHETORIC AND POLITICS

When Socrates stops speaking, Phaedrus wonders at the beauty of Socrates' speech, specifically that he made his speech so much "more beautiful" than his previous one. Phaedrus "shrinks in hesitation, lest Lysias appear rather low" should Lysias be willing to compete (257c). Many scholars find Phaedrus' response shallow, and trace the dialogue's descent from the heights of love to the discussion of rhetoric to Phaedrus. Rhodes writes that Phaedrus "has understood nothing," and that "the discussion of writing and speaking that Phaedrus initiates is a descent from real philosophy, via erotic madness, to a subphilosophic rational sobriety."[39] Griswold agrees that the dialogue has "tumbl[ed] down . . . to the more familiar earth – to the level of Phaedrus," and points out that Phaedrus "ignores *what* is said in the speech" (emphasis Griswold's).[40] Similarly, Geier observes that "Phaedrus is still very mindful of the *authors* of each speech," whereas Socrates is trying to draw his attention "to something broader and higher (emphasis Geier's)."[41]

Phaedrus' response here, however, is one that Socrates himself provokes in his concluding prayer to love. When he asks that Lysias desist from his speeches against love and turn to philosophy, so that Phaedrus will do so as well, he picks up on his earlier advice that Lysias "write" a recantation as quickly as possible (243d). It is Socrates who refers to Lysias both as he moves toward his palinode and brings it to a conclusion.[42] He discourses about the soul's pre-existence, its ten-thousand-year cycles of birth and death (248e), and the "being that truly is" (247c), but he does not forget Lysias or where Phaedrus has come from when they met or that he will be going back to Lysias. Moreover, Phaedrus' response indicates that Socrates has had an effect, for he now judges a speech in terms of beauty rather than of utility or cleverness. When he admits its greater beauty than Socrates' first speech, we can assume he is

---

[39] Rhodes, *Eros, Wisdom, and Silence* (Columbia, MO: University of Missouri Press, 2003), 519–20.

[40] Griswold, *Self-Knowledge*, 157–58.

[41] Geier, *Plato's Erotic Thought*, 182. See also Ferrari, *Listening to the Cicadas*, 28; and Tejera, *Plato's Dialogues One by One*, 46.

[42] As does Plato in his dialogue, which in effect begins with Lysias' speech and ends with a message for Lysias.

thinking as well of its greater beauty than Lysias' speech, and perhaps of any speech that Lysias could ever write. He fears that Lysias will make a poor showing in his eyes if he competes. He cares for Lysias and does not want him to be humiliated. He is no longer willing to "compel" another speech – something Socrates had trusted he would do "as long as [he] is who [he] is" (243e).

Perhaps trying to avert attention from Lysias' inability to compete, Phaedrus observes that a statesman (or politician) recently reproached Lysias for writing speeches. The "love of honor" that will hold Lysias back, as Phaedrus conjectures, is shame at being called a speech writer (257c). Of course the reproach of the statesman had not dimmed Phaedrus' enthusiasm for Lysias' speech earlier in the day. His desire to protect Lysias, if only from a poor showing in competition with Socrates, seems to lead him to consider the opinions of the city. While Phaedrus argues in the *Symposium* that the lover's and beloved's shame and ambition in the eyes of the other indirectly benefit their cities (*Symposium* 178c–e), he now imagines that Lysias' shame before his city itself might act as a restraint on his actions. And with the concern for reputation comes the concern for memory over time. In a way, Phaedrus makes the movement toward community that we have seen in Socrates' *Symposium* speech, and that Plato is now reproducing in the *Phaedrus* itself.

When Phaedrus notes that even those with the greatest power and the most revered in their cities are ashamed to write speeches lest they be called sophists by posterity (257d; see *Protagoras* 312a and *Meno*, 91b–c), he uses "city" for the first time in the dialogue.[43] Whereas Socrates places statesmen third in his list of types of souls in the palinode (248d), statesmen now provide a standard for praise and blame. The palinode says little of our lives in cities, as it connects our mortal lives with our existence before birth and after death. Socrates' uninterrupted monologue now gives way to conversation between Socrates and Phaedrus that prepares their return to the city.

Socrates disagrees with Phaedrus that statesmen disdain speech writing, for they themselves, he says, "love writing and leaving behind writings" (257e). Socrates reminds us of Diotima's teaching, as he applies the verb for loving to statesmen's love of writing, and connects love with generation and with the desire to leave something of oneself

---

[43] When Socrates earlier asked Phaedrus whether Lysias was in town, he used the word *astu* rather than *polis* (227b). *Astu* refers to the town, as opposed to the country, rather than to the city as a political unit.

behind – namely, laws. Love is not exhausted by the private relationship between lover and beloved. Statesmen desire to be remembered in their cities, even to gain immortality as writers (258c). Diotima also speaks of statesmen's desire for immortality, not only their love of "immortal renown" but also of the laws as their "offspring" (*Symposium* 208d–e, and 209d). But she does not refer to the laws as "writings." By doing so, Socrates emphasizes their enduring character.

Statesmen so love writing, according to Socrates, that whenever they write a speech they refer at the beginning to those who give them their approval. That is, when something a statesman proposes is passed by the council or the people, the document begins by stating that the law in question "has seemed best" to the approving body. But if the statesman's speech (his proposal for a law) is not approved, and he is not considered worthy of being a "speech writer," he and his companions lament. By looking to what statesmen do rather than to what they say, Socrates is able to conclude that they could hardly consider "speech writing" in all cases to be a term of reproach (258a–b). Socrates proposes that they investigate when writing is shameful and when not, and hence when it is beautiful and when not (258d). Socrates soon expands the question from beautiful writing to beautiful speech, and Phaedrus expresses his enthusiasm for having such a discussion.

What else would one live for, Phaedrus asks, but such pleasures without pains, in contrast to bodily pleasures, which are connected with previous pain and justly called slavish (258e)? He is still attracted by the unmixed good represented by the non-lover (see 240a–b). Phaedrus' enthusiasm does not this time arouse its like in Socrates, who proceeds to rebuke his desire with the story of the cicadas, who are now "singing" and "conversing" in the tree overhead. "When the Muses were born and song appeared, there were some human beings who became so overcome with pleasure that they neglected food and drink in order to sing, and died without noticing it." Seeking the pleasures without pains that Phaedrus desires, they pay the consequences that mortal beings must (see *Symposium* 191a–b). These human beings, Socrates continues, were allowed to return as cicadas, endowed by the Muses with the privilege of "being able to sing without food or drink until they die" (259c) – the very thing they did previously that led to their deaths.[44] Socrates no longer says that they "converse" as well as sing.

---

[44] Socrates says that the cicadas "do not need (*deisthai*) sustenance" (259c). His use of this verb echoes his recent question to Phaedrus, "do we need (*deometha*) to examine Lysias

In order to have the cicadas give a good report of them to the Muses, Socrates warns Phaedrus, they must not be lulled to sleep at noonday by their humming, as if they were slaves, but spend the time conversing. What offers pleasures without pain is not conversation in the noonday heat, as Phaedrus thinks, for that requires resistance to the lull of the cicadas and to the attraction of dozing, but rather slavish slumber (see *Apology* 40b–c). There is no escape to any Isles of the Blessed (see *Symposium* 180b), at least not without the loss of self-awareness, as in the case of those who became cicadas, who die without noticing it, and who continue singing until they die again, without engaging in the more difficult task of conversing.[45] Phaedrus has tried to convert Socrates' proposed conversation into the painless pleasures of the *Symposium* speeches he fathered (see *Symposium* 176c–d). But this time Socrates corrects him. Socrates himself has become "the father of the speech." It will be a conversation rather than a monologue.

Socrates begins the discussion of speech by asking whether the rhetorician must know the truth about what he speaks, if his speech is to be noble (or beautiful). It is said, Phaedrus answers, that rhetoricians need not learn what is just, good, and noble, but only what seems so to the multitude. Socrates responds with the example of a man who, from ignorance of the differences between an ass and a horse, praises an ass for possessing all the fine qualities of a horse, and consequently sells it to someone equally ignorant (259e–260b). Phaedrus is ready to dismiss their situation as ridiculous, but his dismissal is hasty. An ignorant seller might succeed in making a sale to an ignorant buyer – as Lysias himself may have sold Phaedrus a lover disguised with all the fine qualities of a non-lover. Moreover, even if the truth were necessary to success, is the truth sufficient? Socrates proceeds to argue on behalf of rhetoric that once one acquires the truth one must still learn rhetoric in order to persuade (260d).

Rhetoric is "a soul-leading through speeches, not only in law courts and other public assemblies, but also in private ones," Socrates offers. It is the same in small and great matters (261a–b). Socrates' choice of "soul-leading" for defining rhetoric – rather than the more usual "persuasion," for example (see 270b; 271a; *Gorgias* 453a; and Aristotle, *Rhetoric* 327c) – recalls his tale of the gods who lead souls in the heavens.

---

and whoever else has ever written or will write anything?" (258d). Unlike the cicadas, Socrates and Phaedrus have needs, which result in discussion.

[45] Ferrari, *Listening to the Cicadas*, 28; Geier, *Plato's Erotic Thought*, 183–84; and Griswold, *Self-Knowledge*, 165.

Whereas Socrates does not explain how gods exert their leadership on other souls, Socrates' definition of rhetoric indicates that it is through speech that soul-leading occurs here.[46] Rhetoricians accomplish through speech what the gods accomplish mysteriously.[47] Rhetoric's ability to "lead souls" through speech suggests its power and danger as well as its potential for good. The gods' lead, in the palinode, brought souls to the place of truth.

Socrates turns to the danger of rhetoric when he proceeds to argue that knowing the truth is necessary to detect the deceptions of others as well as to deceive. Since deception occurs in presenting one thing as another when the differences between them are small, to avoid being deceived one "must therefore distinguish precisely the similarity and dissimilarity of beings" (261e–262c). This skill, however, is also useful in deceiving others, for making the same things appear at one time just and at others times unjust in law courts, and in public assemblies at one time good, at other times bad (261c–d; see *Gorgias* 452e). Just as Socrates rescued love from its degrading presentation in Lysias' speech, he must also rescue speech from the corruption of contemporary rhetoricians and statesmen.

When Socrates turns to a third example of rhetoric, one that he says occurs in private settings, we expect him to exemplify it with encomia such as he and Phaedrus hear and deliver in the *Symposium* concerning the beautiful or noble and the ugly or shameful (*Symposium* 198d), or with the love speeches just delivered. The latter speeches demonstrate that rhetoric can make one thing (for example, love) appear at one time shameful or ugly, and at another time beautiful or noble, or at least directed to what is so (see Aristotle, *Rhetoric* 1358b). For a rhetoric that occurs in private places, however, Socrates refers to "the Eleatic Palamedes," who makes the same things appear like and unlike, one and many, at rest and in motion (261d–e). Whether Socrates has in mind Zeno, an Eleatic philosopher who is known for "demonstrating" just such opposites,[48] or his teacher Parmenides, also

---

[46] Joseph Cropsey argues that the latter half of the *Phaedrus* is a "terrestrialization" of the palinode. *Political Philosophy*, 251.

[47] While the noun *psuchagogia* does not occur elsewhere in extant classical Greek literature, the adjectival form, *psuchagogos*, is used by Greek tragedians to refer to raising souls from the dead – for example, Aeschylus, *Persians* 687 and Euripides, *Alcestis* 1128.

[48] See *Parmenides* 127e. Robin Waterfield notes that "antilogic has a history in Greek philosophy," and that Zeno of Elea "probably invented it, to refute views contrary to Parmenides' metaphysical monism." "Introduction to the *Euthydemus*," in *Early Socratic Dialogues*, trans. and intro. Trevor J. Saunders, Iain Lane, Donald Watt, and Robin Waterfield (London: The Penguin Group, 1987), 299.

from Elea,[49] Socrates slips in a philosopher among the rhetoricians, a philosopher whose "rhetorical" exercise depends not on arguing one thing "at one time, and oppose it at another" – as a politician might support one thing at one time and oppose it at another – but on showing that opposite propositions are equally valid. If all things are one – as Parmenides is famous for maintaining (e.g., *Parmenides* 180c) – and the multiplicity we perceive in the world does not exist – then nothing can be said of anything, for speech connects one thing with another. No proposition would be more valid than any other, and speech might make, for example, something appear both like and unlike, one and many, and at rest and in motion.

Eleatic philosophy therefore produces the same result as do Heraclitus and those who say that all things are in motion (see *Theaetetus* 183a). From this perspective, there is nothing that one cannot deconstruct, once one has been taught rhetoric, and philosophy is the most fundamental form of rhetoric. Eleatic rhetoric may seem to belong to private settings, but it supports the public rhetoric of the day. Indeed, if nothing can withstand refutation, then one is justified in speaking of the same things as just at one time and as unjust at another, or at one time as good and at another time as bad. By including Eleatic philosophy among the forms of rhetoric, Socrates suggests its connection with the rhetoric that makes the weaker argument the stronger in law courts and public assemblies. Socrates' attempt to find a way between the advocates of rest and those of motion (see *Parmenides* 128e–130b and *Theaetetus* 180e–181b) is necessary for a new kind of political life as well as for philosophy.

Socrates proposes that they examine Lysias' speech and those of Socrates as examples, and Phaedrus agrees that their discussion has been "abstract" or "bare" (262c). Although Love belongs to the "disputed" class of things, Lysias does not define it at the outset of his speech, Socrates and Phaedrus agree. Consequently, his speech lacks "clearness" or "consistency" (263a–e and 265d). So too are its parts thrown together randomly, with no necessity for the second to come second, and so on. Thus it lacks what Socrates calls "speech writing" or "logographic necessity," whereby a writer constructs his speech as if it were a living animal, with all its parts written appropriately to each other and to the whole (264c). Speeches without logographic necessity lack coherence or wholeness. In advocating defining one's terms at the outset, Socrates implies that the whole is present from the beginning,

---

[49] In the *Parmenides*, Plato shows us Parmenides using this method on his own monism.

which in fact it would have to be for a speech that has logographic necessity. In light of the end, a speaker would know where he is going, or the whole in light of which he organizes the parts of his speech. His speech would have a kind of self-motion, for its parts flow from and are therefore determined by itself. Nothing extraneous, nothing from the outside, would intrude to effect a change of direction.

Socrates' speech, the two interlocutors agree, fares better by the tests of defining and logographic necessity. Indeed, Socrates describes his two speeches as if they together form a whole, as a pair stemming from a single division of madness into two kinds, one coming from human diseases, the other from a divine release from customary habits. The love described in his first speech exemplifies the former, and the love described in the palinode the latter (265a–b). Socrates' account of his two speeches, however, accords them more consistency than they have. In Socrates' first speech, love results not from a division of madness but from a division of hubris (237d–238c). Moreover, in looking back at his speeches, Socrates ignores the fact that his first is spoken by a lover who disguises himself as a non-lover, and that his second appears as a recantation to avoid the wrath of the gods.[50] Socrates' recollection of his speeches thus abstracts them from the circumstances that account for their being delivered and the purposes they serve. When Phaedrus reminds him that unlike Lysias he defined love at the outset, Socrates takes no credit: how much more artful about speeches than Lysias are the nymphs and Pan, son of Hermes, he exclaims (263d). The monster to whom he attributes his speech's unity, half-goat, half-human, himself lacks parts that "fit together with a view to one another and to the whole." His very name may mean "all," but it is not clear if he is a "whole" (see *Theaetetus* 204b ff).[51] Logographic necessity is an artifice, and cannot alone prevent the destructive effects of Eleatic rhetoric, which in revealing contradictions undermines wholes.

This is confirmed by Socrates' explanation of the two principles that he sees in the structure of his speech, collection and division. Collection, literally, "leading together" (266b), "sees together many scattered particulars . . . , so that by defining one makes clear what one wishes to

---

[50] Griswold, *Self-Knowledge*, 179. He observes also that Socrates' "schema altogether omits the pivotal interlude that joins the two speeches," 179.

[51] Although the god's name is commonly understood as derived from the verb *paein*, "to pasture," Socrates connects the name "Pan" with "all" in the *Cratylus* (408c; see also *Homeric Hymn to Pan*, 47).

teach, just as Love was recently defined, whether well or badly" (265d). What, then, determines whether defining is done well or badly? Although Socrates' first speech defines love at the beginning, and thereby gains "clearness and consistency," it is in error about love, as Socrates later proclaims. In fact, it is because Socrates' two speeches about love are able to take such opposing views that Phaedrus is able to locate love in the class of disputable things (263c; see also 265a). Definition and logographic necessity, and the resulting consistency, are not enough. There is a difference for good reason between the class of "disputed" things, in which Socrates includes love, along with the just and the good, and the undisputed class, which Socrates exemplifies with iron and silver (263a; see Aristotle, *NE* 1094b14–19). The word translated as "disputed" (*amphisbētēsimos*) could also be translated as "disputable" or "ambiguous." Definition abstracts from and thus covers the "ambiguity." It is an answer that obscures the question. It is a "determination,"[52] and thereby makes a whole of something only by cutting it off from other things to which it is related. As Socrates' disguised lover says at the beginning of his speech, if we do not agree on a "definition" of love at the outset, speaker and addressee will end up "agreeing neither with themselves nor with each other" (237c–d). His purpose in defining is agreement, not truth.[53] Perhaps this is why Socrates uses the verb to force or to compel when he asks whether Lysias defined love at the beginning of his speech: did Lysias, he asks Phaedrus, "compel us to suppose that love were some one thing that he himself wished?" (263d).

Socrates illustrates the principle of division with reference to a butcher, who prepares an animal for cooking by dividing it by its natural joints (265e). A butcher, however, is dealing with a dead animal (or one that will soon be dead), not the "living animal" that Socrates says a properly written speech should resemble (264c).[54] By the time the butcher does his job, the once living being is no more than the sum of its

---

[52] The Greek word for definition is *horos*, a word that also refers to the boundary stone that separates one's property from that of others. To define is, literally, to recognize or place boundaries.

[53] Sinaiko, *Love, Knowledge, and Discourse*, 32–33, and 42, and Griswold, *Self-Knowledge*, 177–78.

[54] In the *Statesman*, the Eleatic Stranger compares the division by natural joints to that of someone preparing an animal for "sacrifice" (*Statesman* 287c). In light of the relation to the divine, it seems, wholeness is sacrificed. On the other hand, we should remember how in Aristophanes' speech in the *Symposium*, the gods themselves acknowledge that their division of the circle-beings calls for some repair (*Symposium* 191b).

parts. Its unifying principle, its soul, and the cause of its motion (245e and 246c), has disappeared. Division, Socrates implies, loses sight of the whole with which it is dealing, for it reduces the whole that it divides to the sum of parts. Division is as problematic as collection or definition. Socrates gives his division of madness in his speech about love as an example of division. Whereas madness is being *aphrōn*, or outside one's mind (265e), the principles of collection and division enable him "to speak (*legein*) and think (*phronein*)" (literally, to use one's mind [*phrēn*]) (266b). By his choice of words, Socrates suggests both that the processes of collection and division to which he is subscribing save him from madness and also that an incommensurability exists between our minds and the world it takes as its object, which includes the *aphrōn*, or what may not be amenable to thought. Indeed, we have seen Socrates also suggest this possibility when he traces the inspiration for his speech to the nymphs and Pan. His speech not only has multiple sources but one of them is made up of contradictory parts.

Because these processes enable him to speak and to think, Socrates claims, he is "a lover of these divisions and collections." If he thinks that anyone is able to see "natural" collections and divisions, he pursues him "following in his footsteps as if a god's" (266b). Socrates quotes the words Homer ascribes to Odysseus, when he follows the immortal nymph Calypso to her cave. For Odysseus, Calypso (whose name in Greek means "I shall hide" or "deceive") is a temptation, who lures him with the offer of immortality to stay with her on her island "far away from the cities of human beings" (*Odyssey* 5.101) rather than returning home. Odysseus follows her to her cave, but homecoming lies in the other direction. Only with divine intervention is Calypso made to serve his homecoming by helping him build a raft to leave her island (*Odyssey* 164–69 and 233 ff.). For Odysseus, then, Calypso is like the cicadas whom Socrates describes earlier, whom we must resist in order to reap the rewards they have in store. Given the problems with collection and division discussed eaither, Socrates' implicit analogy between their practitioner and a deceptive nymph is appropriate. Perhaps Socrates can use these processes of collection and division, which like the deceptive Calypso, can be made to help him toward his end. What is required for Socrates to return home, after following in Phaedrus' footsteps into the countryside, tempted by what Socrates himself, referring to Lysias' speech, called "a drug" or "a poison" (230d–e)?[55]

---

[55] Cf. Griswold, *Self-Knowledge*, 281 n. 31.

With his description of the principles of collection and division, which he now calls "dialectic," Socrates claims to have described "the art of words" for which they are searching (266c). The word translated as "dialectic" is from the verb that ordinarily means "to converse." Socrates uses it when he spoke of what he and Phaedrus should do to resist the cicadas (259a), and Phaedrus uses it to describe Socrates' preferred way of speaking in the *Symposium* (194d). Dialectic now appears not as conversation in the ordinary sense, in which at least two individuals engage, and with which Phaedrus associates Socrates, but as a method of defining and classifying.[56] It is not clear that this dialectic requires an interlocutor, although Socrates says that he would follow in the footsteps of anyone who possesses this ability, as if he sought to learn from him. Socrates has pursued on behalf of the rhetoricians the argument that whoever knows the truth still requires rhetoric (260d). But rhetoric has collapsed into dialectic, the art of words for which they are looking, understood as collection and division, and learning the truth into dialectic so understood. Phaedrus still thinks that something eludes them, and refers Socrates to "the books" about rhetoric (266c–d). Socrates agress to examine them. Perhaps the books will teach him something about what remains, just as the deceptive Calypso helps Odysseus to his homecoming.

Although it is Phaedrus who brings up the books written on rhetoric, Socrates is so well-versed in them that he is able to list their individual recommendations. He begins with the parts of a speech that are described in the books, such as introduction, narrative, witnesses, proofs, and confirmations, and concludes with "the end of speeches," about which all agree although they use different names, such as recapitulation or summary (267d–e). The rhetoricians of the day, it seems, are no strangers to the concept of logographic necessity, even though Socrates does not find it in Lysias' speech. But they also remind Socrates and Phaedrus of the larger context of speech, such as the speaker's intention and the effects it has on its hearers. They write of speeches that arouse pity for old age or poverty, for example, and that provoke anger or soothe their audiences. Speeches have effects, and speakers intend to produce them. The dialectical principles of collection and division abstract from the speaker and his addressee, and the

---

[56] For a useful recent discussion of the scholarship on dialectic in the *Phaedrus* and its relation to Plato's treatment of dialectic in his work as a whole, see Nicholson, *Plato's Phaedrus*, 56–74.

books of the day bring both back into the picture. Socrates refers to their authors by name, as he lists their individual contributions.

What "power" does this rhetoric have, Socrates asks Phaedrus? "A very forceful one," Phaedrus responds (268a). "Power," however, is ambiguous, as Socrates argues in another Platonic dialogue with two of the very rhetoricians he mentions here. With Gorgias and Polus, Socrates inquires whether a rhetoric without knowledge of what is good could give power to its practitioner if power is the ability to benefit oneself (*Gorgias* 466b ff.). Here, however, Socrates does not proceed directly to what is missing from the rhetorician's conception of power – an understanding of what is good – but appeals to those with skills whom Phaedrus respects, beginning with the doctors. Acumenus, whose advice about exercise Phaedrus is following when he meets Socrates, and Eryximachus, his lover whom we meet in the *Symposium*, would tell a would-be doctor, Phaedrus himself answers, that he must know not merely what drugs and medical procedures produce what effects, but to whom, when, and for how long to prescribe them (268a–c). The doctor's knowledge must include what is good for the particular human beings he treats, and not only drugs and other procedures and their effects. The example is a good one for Phaedrus, who would know from experience of his lover–physician's particular care of him.[57] It is thus Phaedrus – having been reminded of Eryximachus' care – who introduces the concern on which Socrates will base his later argument for the superiority of speaking to writing: whereas writing says the same things to everyone, the one who possesses the genuine art of rhetoric will know what speeches should be given to which types of souls.

Socrates then turns to the tragedians. Should a man who knows how to compose pity-provoking or tearful speeches, and threatening and fearful ones, whenever he wishes be called a tragedian (268c–d)? Socrates thus suggests that poetry, like medicine, is defined in relation to its effect on others and asks poets once again to give an account of their compositions (see *Apology* 22b–c). Since there are no tragedians present, Phaedrus speaks for them, as he had for the doctors. An answer paralleling the one Phaedrus gave in the case of the doctor would be: the tragic poet knows not only how to make speeches that arouse pity and fear, but also whom he should affect, when, and for how long. But tragedy, unlike medicine, is public, directed not to one human being at

---

[57] Socrates emphasizes the personal connection between Eryximachus and Phaedrus when he refers to Eryximachus as "your companion" (268a).

a time but to many. Phaedrus therefore turns to Socrates' discussion of logographic necessity for an answer: tragedians must also know how to arrange their passion-arousing speeches in a manner "appropriate to one another and to the whole" (268d; see 264c). By implication, some speeches are appropriate to everyone, at least if properly arranged into a whole with a view to their effects on their audiences. And logographic necessity is now defined by a purpose outside the speech itself.

Although Socrates does not dispute Phaedrus' answer on behalf of the tragedians, he disagrees with Phaedrus' supposing that they would "ridicule" the pretender to the art (268d). Socrates offers the way in which musicians would respond to would-be musicians as a model for how those who know should treat those who do not know. If musicians encounter someone who thinks that merely knowing how to strike the highest and lowest chord gives him knowledge of harmony, they would not abuse him "roughly," but "being musical," would tell him "gently" that he does not know what he thinks he knows (268d–e). Proper speech is based not simply on the addressee of the speech and on the demands of the composition but also on the character – and the knowledge – of the speaker (see Aristotle, *Rhetoric* 1356a1–4). "Being musical," and "knowing harmony," musicians know what is lacking in the boastful individual they encounter, and are able to be gentle in their response to him (see *Apology* 25e–26a). Using them as a model, tragedians should not ridicule those in error, as Phaedrus thought they would, but should try to teach them that they do not know what they claim to know. If reformed tragedians were gentler toward error than were the tragedians for whom Phaedrus spoke, and attempted to show those in error that they are not as resourceful as they suppose, learning might divert tragic doom. So too if learning were possible, ridicule might give way to a laughter that could reform, precisely because it saw the resources for change. Socrates' addressing the poets here is therefore consistent with his response to them in the *Symposium*, but here that response is only preliminary to his elaboration of a genuine art of rhetoric. Socrates includes the poets among the recipients of the message that he asks Phaedrus to carry back to the city for Lysias. He includes legislators as well (278c). In the *Phaedrus*, Socrates not only envisions a reformed poetry, but he tries to find a way to reach those like Alcibiades as well.

Socrates' examples from medicine, tragedy, and music prepare for his turning to those claiming to be rhetoricians on the basis of the skills taught in the books of rhetoric. Although he conjures doctors to speak to would-be doctors, and tragedians to speak to would-be tragedians,

Socrates turns to statesmen to speak to would-be rhetoricians. Rhetoric is not an independent art. Just as Phaedrus looked to the authority of an anonymous statesman who abused Lysias for being a speech writer, so Socrates turns to statesmen to act as the judges of rhetoricians (see Aristotle, *NE* 1094b1–4). By bringing forward statesmen as the judges of the claimants to rhetoric, Socrates indicates that rhetoric must be judged with respect to standards outside itself. The statesmen whom Socrates mentions, however, do not live up to their promise as judges of rhetoric.

There is Pericles, renowned for his ability to make speeches (see e.g., Thucydides 2.65.1 and 9), and Adrastus, legendary king of Argos, whom Socrates calls "mellifluous" (269a). They are rhetoricians themselves. They speak to the claimants of rhetoric of the need "to use [the devices in the books of rhetoric] persuasively and to put the whole together" (269c). Since persuasion and composition were the very things we heard Socrates report as found in the books of rhetoric, these statesmen do not seem to have anything to add. Pericles probably was "the most perfect of all in rhetoric" (269d–e), Socrates continues, in effect calling the man revered as the greatest statesman in antiquity a "speech writer" (Thucydides 2.65.10; cf. 256c and *Menexenus* 236b). Not only rhetoric, Socrates now admits, but all the arts that are great require "idle chatter and talk about what's above," which produce "high-mindedness" and "perfect accomplishment." Pericles' association with Anaxagoras gave him such an art. Being filled with such talk, and "attaining the nature of mind and mindlessness," Pericles "dragged" what is fitting from Anaxagoras to the art of speeches (270a). If Phaedrus understands Socrates to be mocking, he does not accuse him here, as he has earlier (234d and 264e).[58] Socrates' use of *adoleschia*, translated as "idle chatter," is a phrase with which Aristophanes mocks Socrates' activity in the *Clouds* (*Clouds* 1480).[59]

In other dialogues, Socrates questions Pericles' ability as a statesman – precisely because his inability to teach others the knowledge or art he

---

[58] For different readings of this passage, see Hackforth, *Plato's Phaedrus*, 150; W. H. Thompson, *The Phaedrus of Plato, with English Notes and Dissertations* (London: Whittaker and Co., 1868), 121; Geier, *Plato's Erotic Thought*, 194; and Griswold, *Self-Knowledge*, 183 and 189.

[59] Socrates himself remembers this portrayal in the *Phaedo*, when discussing the soul's immortality on the day of his execution he mentions that no comic poet could say that he is now engaged in "idle chatter" (*Phaedo* 70b–c). Plato uses "idle chatter" or "idle chatterer" in a derogatory way at *Republic* 489a, *Theaetetus* 195b, and *Parmenides* 135d; see also *Statesman* 299b; and *Republic* 489c. Aristophanes portrays Socrates in the *Clouds* as engaged in talk about "what's above," *Clouds* 228; see also 490 and *Apology* 18b.

possesses calls into question his possession of any such knowledge or art.[60] Whatever "knack" Pericles possesses, he is not a teacher. Socrates also questions Anaxagoras and his teaching about "mind" in other dialogues. In the *Gorgias*, for example, when the rhetorician Polus praises rhetoric for endowing its possessor with power in his city to do whatever he wants, Socrates traces his views to the influence of Anaxagoras. Polus is unable to make correct distinctions between things such as the pleasant and the good, Socrates explains to him, for according to Anaxagoras "all things are mixed together" (*Gorgias* 465d; see also *Apology* 26d). Consistent with this, Socrates in the *Phaedrus* attributes to Anaxagoras a teaching about "mindlessness" as well as "mind," an addition that can be found in none of the extant sources.

In the *Phaedo*, Socrates recounts his early experience of hearing that Anaxagoras teaches that mind arranges or orders all things. He supposes that all things consequently would be arranged for the best, and that he has found a teacher "to his mind" (*Phaedo* 97c–d). He loses hope, however, when he discovers that Anaxagoras explains the world in terms only of material causation, with no consideration given to why it is good for things to be the way they are (98b–e). Anaxagoras is clearly more to Pericles' liking or "mind" than to that of Socrates. Statesmen such as Pericles arrange things, imitating mind, if indeed one can be mindful without being mindful about the good. They are more like the would-be doctor, who knows which drugs produce which effects but gives them to patients with no understanding of the patient and hence of what is good for him. A city inspired by Anaxagoras-educated statesmen or rhetoricians represents mind divorced from good. Like the Eleatic Palamedes who undermines the distinction between just and unjust, good and bad, by making things appear as their opposites, Anaxagoras provides a natural or philosophic foundation for the Athenian imperialism that Pericles promoted. Given Anaxagoras' finding only material explanations as the causes of things, rhetoric appealing to what is just or good could be only a mask for appeals to force. When Socrates criticizes Pericles for his failure to educate his two sons in the *Protagoras*, Alcibiades, of whom Pericles was uncle and

---

[60] *Gorgias* 515b–516b; *Protagoras* 319e–320a; and *Meno* 91a and 94b. Tejera attempts to reconcile Socrates' criticism of Pericles with his apparent praise of him here by distinguishing Pericles as statesman, in which capacity Socrates thinks he is deficient, from Pericles as rhetorician. *Plato's Dialogues One by One*, 51.

guardian, is also present (*Protagoras* 319e–320a). Pericles, Socrates implies, fails as well to give Alcibiades a proper education.[61] With Alcibiades and the expedition to Sicily, Athenian imperialism recoils upon itself.

Plato thus situates the genuine art of rhetoric that Socrates develops in the *Phaedrus* as an alternative to the teachings of both the philosopher whose art of contradiction demonstrates the devastating power of words and the one whose materialistic explanations underlie his appeal to mind. That art of rhetoric provides an alternative as well to the rhetoric connected with imperialistic politics that Eleatic philosophy and Anaxagoras support. This genuine art of rhetoric is not to be found with Pericles. For that we must return to the example of the doctor who responded to the would-be doctor and whose knowledge of each individual whom he treats serves as a model.

A GENUINE ART OF RHETORIC

When Phaedrus asks Socrates for further explanation of the rhetorical art, Socrates says that the rhetorician, like the doctor, "must divide nature, that of the body in the one, that of the soul in the other, ... by applying drugs and nourishment in the one case to produce health and strength, and speeches and lawful practices in the other to transmit whatever persuasion he wishes and virtue" (270b). The parallel is not exact. Whereas the doctor's art is bound to the good of his patient, in the "art" of rhetoric there is an element of freedom. The rhetorician transmits not only virtue but "whatever persuasion he wishes." The phrase Socrates uses here echoes Polus' praise in the *Gorgias* of one who has power in his city to do "whatever he wishes" (*Gorgias* 466c ff.). And we saw in the palinode that souls follow gods in the heavens "as they are able and *wish* to do so" (emphasis mine) (247a). Socrates immediately qualifies his statement that the rhetorician "transmits persuasion" when he says that he "*attempts* to produce persuasion" (271a; emphasis mine; see also Aristotle, *Rhetoric* 1355b). The power and freedom of the rhetorician are limited by that of the addressee, who may or may not be persuaded. Even

---

[61] This is confirmed when Socrates mentions that Pericles sent Alcibiades' younger brother Cleinias, of whom Pericles was also the guardian, to be educated in a different household, lest he be corrupted by Alcibiades (*Protagoras* 320a). Pericles was "at a loss," Socrates says, as to what to do with Cleinias. We can assume that Pericles, and not only Pericles, was "at a loss" about what to do with Alcibiades as well.

when Alcibiades experiences the "compulsion" of Socrates' speeches, he is able to run away, *as if* from Sirens (*Symposium* 216a; emphasis mine; see also *Republic* 327c). When Socrates proceeds to describe the true rhetorician's understanding of the soul, he mentions that he must know both "what it does" and "how it is affected" – that is, its actions as well as its sufferings (271a; see also 245c).

The goal of the rhetorician, however, is not only persuasion, but virtue. If Socrates' definition of the soul as self-moving in the palinode can be considered a concession to the truth in Polus' position, Socrates nevertheless insists on the soul's upward motion. The greater respect that he shows for Gorgias than for Polus in the *Gorgias* (e.g., *Gorgias* 448d–e) is related to Gorgias' admission that if a student comes to him without a knowledge of justice, he will teach it to him as well as rhetoric (*Gorgias* 460a–b; cf. *Meno* 95c). However much Gorgias' admission may be due to shame (see *Gorgias* 461b–c), it manifests a sense of the soul's aspirations (see 247d). Following his reference to virtue as a goal of the art of rhetoric, Socrates observes that one cannot know the nature of the soul without also knowing the nature of the whole (270c).[62] The twofold goal of rhetoric follows from the soul's self-motion as well as its upward ascent to the beings.

Socrates explains that the rhetorician must understand whether soul is simple or complex, and if the latter, see its many forms, explaining in each case how they act and how they are acted upon. The means by which souls act and are acted upon are speeches, however mediated by body. Speeches connect souls to each other. After dividing the forms of soul, the rhetorician must also divide speeches into forms appropriate to each form of soul. Then, when he encounters someone, he must be able "to demonstrate to himself" that a human being of a particular nature is "now present in deed." Finally, he must know when to speak and when to keep silent, and the times for the different sorts of speeches appropriate to different souls (270e–272b). "Not impossible, but no small work," Phaedrus volunteers, echoing the warning of Socrates' Pericles to would-be rhetoricians (272b and 269c). Indeed, Socrates' account of the "long and rough road" that the rhetorician must take

---

[62] Socrates' remark could be translated to mean that to know the soul one must know it as a whole. If this were the case, Socrates would suggest the soul's self-motion rather than its belonging to a larger whole. Scholars are divided in their reading of this passage. I agree with Griswold that the ambiguity is intentional, *Self-Knowledge*, 190. See also Burger, *Plato's* Phaedrus, 85.

sounds like the "completely divine and long discourse" about the soul that Socrates suggests that no human being can give (246a). Socrates seems to propose that the would-be rhetorician undertake a task he has already proclaimed as impossible for a human being.

Moreover, in the palinode each human being seems limited to understanding a soul like his own, which he comes to know through love, by "seeking within himself" for the characters and pursuits of the god whom he shares with his beloved. Even the philosophic lover and beloved are satisfied and complete through their relation with each other; in terms of Socrates' image, they have no need for anyone besides each other in order to become winged. Why, then, would anyone, in terms of the palinode's tale of human life, seek to know someone different from himself?[63] And how, from this perspective, would knowing what is different be possible? How can the rhetorician understand all types of human soul and the speeches appropriate to each? Do we not need a more comprehensive palinode, a longer and rougher path, as Socrates now suggests?

This revisiting of the palinode is prepared by the very existence of that speech, inasmuch as its author knew enough about human beings to incorporate a variety of types into his myth. And when he distinguishes his human discourse about the soul from a divine one, he acknowledges his own ignorance of the divine in a way that those described in the palinode do not. Whereas Socrates' more human discourse is aware of its necessary recourse to images, for example, the lover does not understand that his beloved is only an image of beauty when he wants to worship him as a god, nor does the beloved understand that it is his own image that he sees in the lover. Nor could Socrates' question whether he is more furious and complex than

---

[63] Hackforth understands the rhetorician and his addressee in terms of the lover and beloved of the palinode: Socrates' descriptions of both expresses "the same fundamental thought": "The association of two kindred souls, the one guiding and the other guided, in the pursuit of truth, beauty, and goodness, is the means to the highest human felicity." *Plato's Phaedrus*, 164. But while the lover and beloved can be understood as "kindred" – insofar as they follow the same god in the heavens – the rhetorician is able to give appropriate speeches to all human types. Although Cropsey points out the wider range of the verbal *psychagogia* than of the erotic, he also sees a "plain consistency" between Socrates' arguments about the lover and the rhetorician. *Political Philosophy*, 232. This is one of the ways in which Cropsey understands the description of rhetoric in the second half of the dialogue to be a "terrestrialization" of the myth in the palinode, 251. For parallels between the lover and beloved of the palinode, and the dialectician–rhetorician and his addressee, see also C. J. Rowe, *Plato: Phaedrus*, with trans. and commentary (Warminster: Aris and Phillips, 1986), 9; Lebeck, "The Central Myth," 287–88 ; Griswold, *Self-Knowledge*, 130 and 214; and Nicholson, *Plato's* Phaedrus, 66.

Typhon or whether he "shares in" a divine lot (230a) arise as a question for the lover in the palinode. The lover "shares in" the divine, Socrates says, when he grasps his god through memory (253a). So too would his beloved, formed by him as an image of their god. Socrates, in contrast, confronts what he does not know about himself. He cannot fit himself into any class. That the truth about any classification of human types can be only partial is implied by the need in the palinode for two different classifications of souls that do not easily correspond to each other: lover and beloved follow the same god as they make their way within the heavens, but there is no reason to suppose that their success in the ascent to the rim of the heavens is identical.

Just as Socrates confronts the unknown in himself, he converses with diverse human beings, who are both like and unlike himself, as in the case of Phaedrus. Socrates' dialectician–rhetorician is not therefore simply modeled on the lover of the palinode in his relation to his beloved; he is also modeled on Socrates in his relationship with his interlocutors. Socrates has prepared us for this: rhetoric deals with likes *and* unlikes, we remember from Socrates' earlier description of three kinds of rhetoric (261b ff.). Having delivered the palinode, Socrates is remembering himself again. The long and rough road is the only one appropriate to a human being. Only the divine souls in the myth, after all, have an easy time. As gods, they have no need of persuading others, or even of speech, and they act and are acted upon (for example, when they see the hyperuranian beings they are "carried around" by the rotation of the heavens [247c–d]) in silence. The genuine art of rhetoric that Socrates presents in the *Phaedrus* is a human task. Dialectic understood as division and collection is crucial, just as is Calypso to Odysseus' homecoming, but neither provides the impetus for moving forward. Dialectic's divisions must look to soul types and speeches, and its collections "bring" or "lead together" souls and speeches. Dialectic finds its limit and purpose in the human beings whom the rhetorician encounters. Unlike the lover in the palinode, the rhetorician does not simply see himself in others, for he encounters different types of human souls. That is why he has something to say to them, and they to him. Socrates prefers the city to the countryside, inasmuch as human beings are willing to teach him in contrast to country places and trees (230d). By bringing together souls and appropriate speeches, the rhetorician also brings himself together with his addressee, for they share the speeches that he makes to him.

Although Phaedrus has nothing more to say on behalf of the rhetoric of the day, Socrates makes one last plea in its defense, for "it is said that it is just for even the wolf to have his say," Socrates insists (272c). The case Socrates makes for the wolf involves a position that Socrates earlier includes among the contributions of contemporary rhetoric – the view that "probabilities (*ta eikota*) are to be honored more than truth," a position he associates with Tisias (267a). After all, people will believe what is probable rather than what is true, especially when the truth happens to be improbable. If a courageous weakling, for example, attacked and robbed a strong coward, and the coward brought him to court, the truth would not persuade (273b–c). It is not probable that a weak individual would assault a strong one, nor that a strong individual would yield to a weak one. Consequently, according to Tisias, the strong coward should claim he was assaulted by several, whereas the courageous weakling should prove that only the two were present – and hence he could not have attacked the strong man as claimed.

To his credit, Phaedrus is unimpressed. When Socrates responds to Tisias that one should strive to please not one's fellow slaves but one's good masters, the gods, Phaedrus' reaction shows none of the skepticism that appears earlier in his attitude toward myth: "What you have spoken, Socrates, is all beautiful (*pangkalōs*), if only one were able to do it" (274a), Phaedrus says, echoing Socrates' description of the natural beauties of the setting (230b and c), but speaking now of Socrates' own words. Presumably, however, the appeal to the probable although untrue case would win in court, precisely because of its likeness to what is true for the most part. As a general rule, a weakling would not assault a strong man, nor would a strong man yield to a weak one. The general rule does not do justice to the exceptions, the particular cases that cannot be reduced to the class to which they belong. So too do the particular human beings whom the rhetorician encounters belong to any given human type only for the most part, for there are different ways of classifying human types, as Socrates indicates in the palinode. Socrates himself, whom Alcibiades refers to as "strange," literally, "out of place" (*atopos*) (*Symposium* 221d), and who claims he is unknown even to himself, most obviously falls outside the general rule. But in the *Phaedrus*, even when he is most impressed with how strange Socrates acts, Phaedrus says only that Socrates is "most out of place" (230c), just as the oracle at Delphi says only that no one is wiser than Socrates, not that Socrates is wise (*Apology* 21a).

Law courts or public assemblies are nevertheless not places for exceptions to prevail, at least not generally so; nor do laws take the exceptions into account but are "written" with a view to what applies

"for the most part" (*Statesman* 295a–b). It is no accident, given his
awareness of the danger of prosecution he is incurring (see *Gorgias*
486a–b and 511a–b), that Socrates illustrates probability with Tisias'
example from a lawcourt. And he begins his *Apology* by claiming he is
out of place in court (specifically, "a stranger" to its manner of speech,
Apology 17d). Unable to understand himself wholly as a member of a
class, he knows that the probable is not always the true, and that a
genuine art of rhetoric must direct itself to that difference, just as it
directs itself to the souls of its individual addressees.

In looking to the natures or characters of the particular human beings
he encounters, and finding the speeches appropriate to each, the
rhetorician Socrates describes differs from that of the "Eleatic
Palamedes," whose speech reveals the same things as opposites, and
thereby dissolves any individual differences between things. And unlike
Anaxagoras, whose materialism in effect collapses persuasion into
force, Socrates' "soul-leading" brings to life, and is therefore successful
only with the concurrence of its addressee. Socratic rhetoric is therefore
antithetical to any politics of empire based on power. It is not clear,
however, that a rhetoric so addressed to individuals can have any
broader political scope. Griswold concludes that it cannot. On the basis
of the palinode's description of the lover and beloved, Socrates' description of the dialectician and his student, and the implication that the
true art of rhetoric is "effective with individual souls rather than masses
of people," he writes: "The message of the *Phaedrus* is clear: philosophy
is a form of private eros, and it is essentially nobler and higher than the
political concerns and the public rhetoric of the polis."[64] Socrates'
resurrection of Tisias for one more defense of contemporary rhetoric,
his comparison of him to a wolf, and his associating probability rather
than truth with political life all appear to support this conclusion.

Socrates concludes his discussion with Phaedrus, however, by
returning to the question of writing, and therewith to political life. Laws,
we remember, are writings, which are not addressed to particular types
of human beings but to everyone in the city (257e–258b). Writings,

---

[64] Griswold, *Self-Knowledge*, 133. Griswold argues on the basis of the *Phaedrus* that the
best practical political community for Plato is a liberal one, which recognizes that the
process of developing a soul's virtue is a private one and therefore permits liberty "to
discuss, to question, to have students of one's own choice, to wander outside the city's
walls, and to do so in the company of some politically doubtful souls." "The Politics of
Self-Knowledge: Liberal Variations on the *Phaedrus*," in *Understanding the Phaedrus*,
ed. Livio Rossetti (Sankt Augustin: Academia Verlag, 1992), 184 and 181.

which might be read by anyone who picks them up, and especially laws that apply to all the citizens, do not seem to fall within the scope of the genuine art of rhetoric that Socrates describes. And yet Socrates speculates at his trial that he might have persuaded his judges of his innocence, if he had more time in court, if, for example, Athenians had "a law, as other human beings do," that requires not just one day for capital cases but many (*Apology* 37a–b; see also *Laws*, 719c–e). Even when facing death from the city, Socrates holds out hope of political reform that could take such cases as his into account. And in the *Phaedrus*, Socrates acknowledges that his task of knowing himself comes from the temple of Delphi. It is a command, displayed in public, a writing, that says the same thing to every human being who can read its letters.

WRITING

Having described the genuine art of rhetoric as speech directed to the particular souls of its addressees, Socrates returns to the question of writing, "its propriety and impropriety, and when it is done nobly (or beautifully) and when not" (274b). Socrates begins his discussion by telling a tale of two gods, the Egyptian god Theuth, a great inventor – of numbers, arithmetic, geometry, and astronomy, of draughts and dice, and especially of letters (*grammata*) (274d) – and of the god Thamus, ruler of Egypt. The gods themselves in Socrates' tale discuss the benefits and harmful effects of writing, taking different sides on this issue. Defending his inventions before Thamus, Theuth explains that writing will make the Egyptians wiser and improve their memories, "for it is a drug of memory and wisdom I discovered." Thamus claims to the contrary that letters cause those who use them to trust external marks, and neglect their own memories. Picking up on Theuth's reference to a drug (*pharmakon*), which in Greek means poison as well, Thamus responds that writing is a poison that produces forgetfulness (cf. 274e and 275a).[65] Writing makes us "seem to know many things when we are ignorant," or "seem to be wise" when

---

[65] Thus when Socrates refers to Lysias' writing as a "drug" (*pharmakon*) with which Phaedrus is able to lead him around, his use of *pharmakon* is ominous, for it connects the written word with death. So too in recounting the story of Oreithyia's abduction by Boreas, Socrates mentions that she was playing at the time with a companion named Pharmakeia (229c). *Pharmakon* is the word that Plato uses to refer to the poison with which Socrates was executed (*Phaedo* 57a–b; 63d–e; and 115a–117e). For discussion, see Cropsey, *Political Philosophy*, 238–39.

we are not, Thamus warns (274e–275b). Socrates may call the gods good "masters" (see 274a), but this one does not want his subjects to be "slaves," and supports "human wisdom," as Socrates recounts discovering it in the *Apology*.

Socrates continues to elaborate Thamus' argument against writing in his own name. Writing is like the paintings of figures who seem to be alive, but "if one asks them something they stand in solemn silence." So too writing, Socrates says, appears to have intelligence, but when questioned about what it says, it always repeats the same thing (275d). Writing may be a poison because like the humming of the cicadas it distracts us from the questioning that keeps the argument alive. Lysias' writing seems to have diverted Phaedrus' attention away from any questions about its understanding of love when Socrates finds him taking it on his walk in order to memorize it. Had he not met Socrates, he would have been repeating Lysias' speech over and over to engrave it on his memory, becoming like the bronze maiden on Midas' tomb, who repeats the same verse "written" on the tomb over and over (264d).[66]

Moreover, once written, a work rolls about alike among those who understand and those for whom it is not fitting, Socrates says, and knows not to whom to speak and to whom to be silent. Writing thus falls short of the true art of speaking that Socrates describes to Phaedrus, because it cannot direct itself toward particular addressees but says the same things to everyone. Finally, writing falls short of the spoken word since it is unable to defend or protect itself, its author not being present. The *Phaedrus* itself demonstrates this last criticism of writing, for we saw Phaedrus fail to defend Lysias' writing against Socrates' criticisms in the absence of its author (cf. 228e).

This last criticism of writing, however, opens up a possible defense against Socrates' most important critiques. A writing may be abused when its author is not present to defend it precisely because it does not say the same things to everyone. An author needs to be present to defend his speech, because different interpretations are possible. A speech does not speak for itself. Socrates' speech in the *Symposium* about Diotima's lessons in love, although not a writing, is a monologue, directed to a large group, and therefore has some of the characteristics Socrates attributes to writing (see *Protagoras* 329a).

---

[66] Lebeck refers to Phaedrus' relation to the written speech of Lysias as "an object lesson of this tale [i.e., Thamus' argument about writing]," "The Central Myth," 286.

But that speech responds at different times to previous speakers.[67] More generally, one teaching can respond to partial views in different ways: for example, Socrates' presentation of Love as an intermediary between human and divine in the *Symposium* corrects the view that severs any connection and one that collapses any difference. The same speech can address even opposite positions at once. We are left with the possibility of another recantation – of one of the criticisms of writing. It is the Platonic dialogue. Socrates' own recounting of Diotima's lessons, which corrects different perspectives while leading them to a view that they can all share, serves as its model. Socrates' speech in this case is appropriate to all the previous speakers, as they have revealed themselves in their encomia.

The concept of logographic necessity plays a crucial role in a defense of writing: we can ask of a writing, as Socrates asks Phaedrus about Lysias' speech, whether there is some logographic necessity for its parts, how they fit together with a view to one another and to the whole (264a). The *Phaedrus* even forces us to raise this question of itself, insofar as Plato gives it the appearance of two quite disparate parts.[68] Only if we ask how the parts of the *Phaedrus* fit together, and thus look to their place in the whole, will we understand the dialogue. Through its logographic necessity, a written work may answer the questions we ask, at least metaphorically. Because of the very monstrous structure of the *Phaedrus*, scholars have been conversing with the dialogue and with one another for more than two thousand years. All the more would a written work compel us to ask it questions about the relation of its parts to one another and to the whole – and guide to our doing so – if it were a drama whose parts include characters who speak and act in particular contexts. Some writings may indeed be willing to converse with us.

Like a Platonic dialogue, Socrates' tale of Theuth and Thamus involves characters who present different perspectives about what benefits human beings, who engage each other in dialogue, and give reasons for their positions. Plato calls attention to Socrates' poetic

---

[67] For example, to Phaedrus, 208d (cf. 179b–180a); to Pausanias, 209b–c (cf. 184e); to Eryximachus, 203a (cf. 188c–d); to Aristophanes, 205e and 211d (cf. 191b); and to Agathon, 199b ff.
[68] Ferrari captures this aspect of the *Phaedrus* when he describes it as "a dialogue, which, taken as a whole, is *deliberately* disunified in its structure – more exactly, attains organic unity only on a second order, by jarring its readers and urging them thereby to reconstitute the living creature from its scattered limbs" (emphasis mine). *Listening to the Cicadas*, 53.

activity when Phaedrus observes that Socrates "easily composes (*poieis*) speeches about Egypt or any place [he] wishes" (275b). Although Socrates claims that one should be concerned only with whether Thamus' words are true, and not with "who is speaking them and where he comes from" (275c), if these issues made no difference Socrates would have no reason to tell the story rather than simply present Thamus' argument against writing. Moreover, in the story itself, Thamus himself understands Theuth's argument in favor of his writing in light of its source: Theuth is partial to writing, he claims, because it is his invention or discovery (275a).

Thamus therefore inadvertently endorses our understanding his criticism of writing in light of its source. Socrates' and Phaedrus' discussion of writing, we remember, arose from a disagreement among statesmen over whether writing is shameful or noble. Whereas a statesman criticized Lysias as a speech writer, as Phaedrus reports, statesmen generally, Socrates points out, delight in leaving behind their own writings in the form of laws, to attain immortality in the city, supposing that they can become "equal to the gods" (257e–258d). The disagreement between the gods over the benefits of writing, in contrast, gives no consideration to laws, "written speeches," as Socrates calls them earlier (258b), or the benefits for political communities that might flow from them. Nor does Thamus' criticism of letters as "external marks" that take the place of the memory of individuals suggest to either of them that written documents such as laws, works of poets, or public speeches might provide a community with an identity or continuity from one generation to another. There is something to be said for writings, even in their repeating always one and the same thing. That this is not only a political concern is suggested by Socrates' description of "the word *written* with knowledge in the soul of the learner" (276a; emphasis mine). Even with respect to the word in the soul, Socrates has recourse to the image of writing, with its suggestion of permanence. It is this word that the true rhetorician plants in fitting souls, which when nurtured "bears fruit" from which come other seeds in other souls, "capable of continuing this forever." Because of this the rhetorician becomes "as happy as possible for a human being" (277a). Thamus may be a king, but he is a god-king, whose rule is not threatened by his mortality, or by the need to rely on general rules or probabilities that apply only for the most part. Neither Theuth nor Thamus need strive to be "equal to gods." They are gods. We must consider who is speaking and where he comes from.

Because Socrates does not give due consideration to where the argument against writing comes from when he develops Thamus' criticism of writing, as his rebuke to Phaedrus warns us, Plato allows us to do so. Socrates does not, however, forget about laws – or poetry – when he sends Phaedrus with a message back to the city not only "for Lysias and whoever composes speeches" but also "for Homer and whoever composes poetry, and for Solon and whoever writes writings named laws" (278c). Those to whom Phaedrus should deliver Socrates' message represent the leaders of the city, those "responsible for shaping the opinions of the political community."[69] They also represent those who in the name of the city brought charges against Socrates: Meletus "on behalf of the poets," Anytus "on behalf of the craftsmen and statesmen," and Lycon "on behalf of the rhetoricians" (*Apology* 23e). At the end of the *Phaedrus*, it seems, Socrates is trying to reach not only the future leaders of the city but those who might be his future accusers.

The message that Socrates gives Phaedrus to deliver to rhetoricians, poets, and legislators is that "anyone who writes knowing where the truth lies, able to assist in cross-examination of what he has written, and being able to show that his writings are of little worth," should not be named after his writings but after what he takes most seriously. He should not be called "wise," Socrates says, for that applies only to the god, but rather he should be called a philosopher (278d). The poets and lawgivers described by Diotima who give birth out of a love of the beautiful (*Symposium* 209a) must recognize what is superior to their own offspring, the truth that their productions only more or less reflect. They must be able to question their speeches, works of poetry, and laws, just as they accept that they themselves are not wise. Writing is not shameful, then, when the writer understands and can in fact demonstrate the meaning of human wisdom as knowledge of ignorance. Socrates in the end defends the writings of poets as well as statesmen who understand that their writings hold at best for the most part, and who can incorporate this limitation in their writings, for example, by writing dialogues that leave questions, or laws that leave room for application to individual cases that arise in time.

As is appropriate, Socrates gives Phaedrus only a summary to carry back, what Phaedrus thought he had of Lysias' speech, the "meaning," or "intent" rather than "the words" (228d). We are given no reason in the *Phaedrus* to suppose that this is enough to persuade. For that result,

[69] Burger, *Plato's* Phaedrus, 9.

the entire conversation might be necessary, and Socrates knows that Phaedrus requires a lot of practice even for the repetition of Lysias' speech, and that he requires that Lysias' speech be written in order to memorize it. Again, as in the case of his reaching Alcibiades, Socrates requires Plato. And he requires writing, which might compensate for the limitations of human memory.

Phaedrus agrees that the message Socrates reports is a worthy one (278d). Whereas Phaedrus did not inquire about Socrates' plans when they met as Socrates did of his (227), he now recognizes that Socrates will be returning to the city, and that Socrates too has connections with others. What message will Socrates bring to his companion, "Isocrates the beautiful" (278e), Phaedrus asks. Plato – or history for that matter – has not recorded any connection between Socrates and Isocrates, a prominent teacher of rhetoric and speech writer. Socrates does not object to Phaedrus' association of himself with Isocrates, however, and in fact enters into its spirit. Isocrates is "still young," he says, and "prophesies" that inasmuch as Isocrates "has some philosophy by nature in his mind," "a divine impulse will lead him to greater things." This is Socrates' message for his "darling Isocrates," while Phaedrus should bring the other to his "darling Lysias" (279b). Using the common term for a beloved, Socrates suggests that both he and Phaedrus are lovers, alike in that but with different objects of their love (see *Gorgias* 481d).

Since it is "a divine impulse" that will lead Isocrates to greater things, and not Socrates himself, Socrates acknowledges the limits of any "soul-leading" rhetoric he may possess. He seems more aware of his limits now than when he approaches the young Alcibiades with the offer to help him toward greater things (*Alcibiades I* 105e–106e). Socrates will carry a message to Isocrates, but its effect depends on whether he gives it to a fitting soul. By the time Plato wrote the *Phaedrus*, Isocrates was no longer "young," and had in fact become a rival teacher and a critic of Plato's.[70]

---

[70] For a discussion, see G .J. De Vries, *A Commentary on the Phaedrus of Plato* (Amsterdam: Adolf M. Hakkert, 1969), 15–18, and Burger, "Isocrates the Beautiful," in *Plato's Phaedrus*, 115–26. Commentators are divided concerning the thrust of this reference to Isocrates. Some suppose that Plato does hope for Isocrates to fulfill the potential Socrates attributes to him, while others read it as an ironic criticism of Isocrates on Plato's part. For the former, see Hackforth, *Plato's Phaedrus*, 167–68. For the latter, see Cobb, *The Symposium and the Phaedrus*, 169; Arieti, *Interpreting Plato*, 198 and Rowe, *Plato: Phaedrus*, 215–16. Malcolm Brown and James Coulter argue that Socrates' first speech in the *Phaedrus* presents the mentality and perspective of the "rhetorical sophistical culture" represented by Isocrates. "The Middle Speech of Plato's *Phaedrus*," *Journal of the History of Philosophy* 9 (1971): 405.

From the perspective of hindsight, Socrates' prophecy for Isocrates indicates the imperfection of his understanding of the souls of others, for he expects in this case more than is warranted. Socrates' "prophecy" does not come to fruition. Our knowledge of the souls of others remains imperfect, and the words Socrates uses to Isocrates are less fitting for him than for another, perhaps for Plato himself.[71] Perhaps, too, Socrates' mistake about Isocrates illustrates how love, as Socrates describes it in the palinode, leads the lover to see more in his beloved than is really there (251a), or Theuth is led to exaggerate the benefits of writing because he lacks distance from his own invention (275a). Another defense of writing appears, for the spoken word is limited by the capacity of its speaker to judge what is appropriate and its addressee to make use of it.[72] Although a writing might fall into the hands of those who do not understand it and who consequently abuse it, it might also fall into the hands of someone who can understand it. If the conversation between Socrates and Phaedrus took place only beside the river Illissus, it would be available only to Phaedrus and to those with whom he is willing and able to share it. Because it was written down by Plato, it is available to us.

Socrates concludes that writing is defensible if it is viewed by its author as playful rather than serious. Such a writer resembles a farmer who sows seeds for play in a window box, where they become beautiful in eight days. The more serious farmer, in contrast, sows his seeds in more fitting ground and watches them mature in eight months. Beauty comes quickly, maturation slowly. Writing can create something beautiful – it can be taken in by a single glance (at least in theory), because it can have a beginning, a middle, and an end. For this reason, writing can, as conversations do not, offer us a whole. Platonic writings, however, dramatize conversations, about which we can ask, as Socrates did of Phaedrus, where they are coming from and where they are going. They have intentions and purposes that underlie and are manifest in their appearances, and this complexity makes them more than a beautiful whole. Like Socrates and Phaedrus, who carry messages to others, Platonic writings speak to us. They are not self-sufficient. Rather, they are like the soul whose being and definition may be self-motion but whose flight metaphorically manifests its openness to a world beyond. Plato's writings are serious business,

---

[71] This is Cropsey's suggestion, *Political Philosophy*, 247.
[72] Burger points out that in speaking to all, and not to a particular addressee, writing has a potential for objectivity that the spoken word does not, *Plato's* Phaedrus, 97.

precisely because by their very playfulness they leave much of the work to us. Perhaps this is why Socrates concludes his "defense" of writing by echoing the last words of Aristophanes' *Thesmophorizusae*: "we have played in due measure," he tells Phaedrus (278b and *Thesmophorizusae* 1227; see also *Clouds* 1510). Although Socrates has just contrasted the playful written word with the serious spoken one, he now acknowledges that his own spoken words are playful (see also 262d, 265c, and 265d) and perhaps only preliminary to the serious work of writing that Plato himself was to undertake.

Like the women maddened by Dionysus in Euripides *Bacchae*, Socrates has "celebrated Dionysus" (234d and *Bacchae* 726) together with Phaedrus in the countryside outside the city. But they are able to return to the city without the tragic results of Euripides' play. Plato's poetry has greater affinity with comedy than with tragedy. Truth emerges not from the dissolution of boundaries, the primordial unity that Nietzsche says tragedy reveals in *The Birth of Tragedy*, but from responding to the differences about which Socrates learns through his conversations with people in the city. Nietzsche was right that Dionysus finds his greatest challenge in Socrates.

PRAYER TO PAN

Just as Socrates concludes the palinode with a prayer to Love, before leaving with Phaedrus to return to the city he prays to Pan and the gods of the place. Because of Pan's goat-like lower half, Socrates associates him with tragedy (*Cratylus* 408c), literally, "goat-song" (from the goat skins worn by the satyrs, who were the first choruses in tragedy). In Greek myth, while Pan is ugly to look at, he himself is not "typhonic." He does not require conquest by the Olympians, as did Typhon. His disparate elements do not drive him mad. He is a piper, but his piping does not compete with the Olympians, as did that of Marsyas, to whom Alcibiades likens Socrates in the *Symposium* (*Symposium* 215c). In fact, although Pan's appearance at birth frightens his nurse, he delights "all" the immortals. According to the Homeric hymn, that is why he is called "pan" (*Homeric Hymn to Pan* 38–47). He might just as well be a god of comedy as of tragedy.

Socrates prays that he become beautiful within, that his external things be friendly to his inner ones, that he consider the wise rich, and that he have no more gold than a moderate person can bear (279 b–c). In his prayer, Socrates recognizes that what belongs to him includes both "inner" and "outer" things, that something exists for him apart from his inner being – for example, his appearance, his possessions, his relationships – that are his as well. And he prays for friendship between the possibly disparate things that constitute him. Consistent with his acknowledging his complexity, he also prays that only those things are his that are good for him. In the palinode's myth, a human being finds what is good for himself through loving another, and his beloved finds what is good for himself through his loving in return. Socrates says when delivering that speech that they become friends (e. g., 255b). If Socrates is praying for a friend, inasmuch as a friend is a route to one's own good, their friendship cannot be based simply on the sight of beauty, as is love in the palinode, for if Socrates is beautiful, it is "within," as he prays himself to become. It must be based on conversation (see *Charmides* 154e). The prayer at the end of the *Phaedrus* provides a transition to the *Lysis*, where Socrates tells a group of young men that he has since his youth been desirous of finding a good friend, even "erotically inclined" toward acquiring friends (*Lysis* 211d–e). Some scholars point out the importance of friendship in the *Phaedrus*, but say little about its meaning, or how love becomes friendship, or indeed what is the difference between the two.[73] Nor could they do so, for the *Phaedrus* does not explore the question, "what is a friend," which Socrates asks only in the *Lysis*. Socrates concludes his prayer by asking Phaedrus whether his prayer "is in need of anything else" (279c). Socrates' prayer, as is the *Phaedrus*, is in need of the *Lysis*.

Phaedrus mentions nothing that Socrates' prayer needs, but he does ask that Socrates include him in his prayer. Phaedrus would like to be included, he says, because "friends have all things in common." Socrates does not respond to Phaedrus' wish. After all, he has not yet said what a friend is. The last words of the dialogue are Socrates' "let us go." Unlike the end of the *Symposium*, where Aristodemus only follows Socrates, here the two, Socrates and Phaedrus, go together to the city, each with his own mission (see *Symposium* 174b). The motion of neither

---

[73] Cobb, *The Symposium and the Phaedrus*, 154, 168–70; Nicholson, *Plato's* Phaedrus, 205; Rhodes makes the promising suggestion in his analysis of the *Phaedrus* that love is a response to beauty, which becomes a response to the good as it develops into friendship. "Platonic *Philia* and Political Order," 44–45. Once the palinode is over, with the exception of Socrates' concluding prayer and Phaedrus' response, the words for friendship and its derivatives occur only when Socrates addresses Phaedrus, and not in their discussion.

is simply self-motion; they move together, and are moved by each other. They share the motion of friends. They journey together back to the city, but they have different messages for different beloveds. Whether they are to be called friends depends on an answer to the question, what is the friend? Since this is a question that Socrates raises directly in the *Lysis*, we will now turn to this dialogue.

4

Who Is a Friend? (*The Lysis*)

Some years after Socrates leaves Agathon's dinner party with Aristodemus in tow, and a few years after Socrates follows Phaedrus outside the city walls to hear Lysias' speech, Socrates discusses friendship with two young boys at a palaestra.[1] He admits to them and the others present that ever since he was young he desired to acquire friends, but he is so far from succeeding that he does not even know how one becomes the friend of another (211d–212b).[2] If we can take Socrates at his word, he counts neither Aristodemus nor Phaedrus as a friend. When Phaedrus asks to be included in Socrates' prayer at the end of the dialogue bearing his name, because "the things of friends are common," Socrates says only "let us go [back to the city]" (279c). Socrates' response can be contrasted with his remark at the end of the *Lysis* that he considers himself and his two young interlocutors to be friends (223b). At the end of the *Lysis*, it appears that "three go together," and Socrates corrupts a Homeric dictum once again (see *Symposium* 174b and 174d).

---

[1] It is possible to date the *Lysis* around the same time or shortly after the *Euthydemus*, inasmuch as the character Ctseippus occupies a similar role in both dialogues. Moreover, he is shown to learn how to argue from the sophists in the latter dialogue, whereas he is said in the *Lysis* to have taught Menexenus skill at argument (211b–c). See Catherine H. Zuckert's discussion of the *Lysis*. *Plato's Philosophers* (forthcoming University of Chicago Press, 2009).

[2] References in parentheses in this chapter, unless otherwise noted, are to Plato's *Lysis*. I have used the translation of David Bolotin, *Plato's Dialogue on Friendship: A New Interpretation of the Lysis, with a New Translation* (Ithaca: Cornell University Press, 1977), although I have made changes from time to time. I have adapted the argument in this chapter from my article "Friendship and Community in Plato's *Lysis*," *The Review of Politics* 68, no. 1 (Winter 2006): 1–19. Copyright © 2006 University of Notre Dame. Reprinted with the permission of Cambridge University Press.

Even if Socrates has found friends by the end of the *Lysis*, they have not been able to discover what a friend is. The *Lysis* is one of Plato's *aporetic* dialogues, which end in perplexity (*aporia*) about the question discussed. Scholars have long held that Plato wrote his *aporetic* dialogues early when he was most influenced by Socrates' manner of questioning everything, and that he only later developed the philosophic positions we most associate with him.[3] More recently, scholars have read the *Lysis* as a rich exploration of the problems and potentials of friendship.[4] In one of the most weighty commentaries on the *Lysis*, David Bolotin argues that the teaching of the dialogue involves the inherent difficulties in friendship.[5] He points out that Socrates' last words of the dialogue, "we have not yet been able to discover what a friend is," might also be translated as "we have not yet been able to discover *that* a friend is (or exists)."[6] "While appearing to desire or even to love each other," Bolotin argues, friends desire only their own good: each is a friend to himself, for each friend loves primarily his own good, and the other as a means to his fulfillment.[7]

---

[3] See, for example, Paul Friedlander, *Plato: The Dialogues, First Period*, vol. 2, trans. Hans Meyerhoff (New York: Random House, 1964), 102–04; W. K. C. Guthrie, *History of Greek Philosophy*, Vol. IV (Cambridge, UK: Cambridge University Press, 1975), 143; and Price, *Love and Friendship in Plato and Aristotle*, 12–14. Although he accepts assumptions about Platonic development, Laszlo Versenyi argues that the *Lysis* contains an understanding of love that is "essentially complete," but it is Socrates', not Plato's, and that beyond which Socrates, unlike Plato, would not want to go. "Plato's *Lysis*," *Phronesis* (1975) 18: 186–87. Geier also finds a "Socratic" rather than a Platonic understanding of friendship in the *Lysis*. *Plato's Erotic Thought*, 142.

[4] Among interpretations that find teachings in the *Lysis* about friendship in spite of its *aporetic* character are Francisco J. Gonzalez, "Plato's *Lysis*: An Enactment of Philosophical Kinship," *Ancient Philosophy* 12 (1995): 69–90; James Hadon, "Friendship in Plato's *Lysis*," *Review of Metaphysics* 37 (December 1983), 327–56, esp. 354–56; T. Brian Mooney, "Plato's Theory of Love in the *Lysis*: A Defence," *Irish Philosophical Journal* 7 (1990): 131–59; Lorraine Smith Pangle, *Aristotle and the Philosophy of Friendship* (Cambridge: Cambridge University Press, 2003), 20–36, esp. 34–36; Rhodes, "Platonic *Philia* and Political Order," esp. 43–44; Scott, *Plato's Socrates as Educator*, esp. 76–79; Aristide Tessitore, "Plato's *Lysis*: An Introduction to Philosophic Friendship," *The Southern Journal of Philosophy* 28, no. 1 (1990): 115–32; Zuckert, *Plato's Philosophers*; and Davis, *The Autobiography of Philosophy*, 67–81.

[5] Bolotin, *Plato's Dialogue on Friendship*, esp. 176; Stewart Umphrey, "Eros and Thumos," *Interpretation* 10, no. 2 and no. 3 (May and September 1982), 355–422, esp. 379–81; and Bolotin, "Response to Umphrey," *Interpretation* 10, no. 2 and no. 3 (May and September, 1982), esp. 424.

[6] Bolotin, *Plato's Dialogue on Friendship*, 61 n. 86.

[7] Bolotin, *Plato's Dialogue on Friendship*, 139. Bolotin does qualify his argument by maintaining that friendship is a deceptive whole "at least to the extent that it is love of opposites." But the one reciprocal friendship that Bolotin does not find deceptive – between two more or less self-sufficient beings – is rare, he argues, if it exists at all, and

Although we may be mistaken when we hold ordinary human relations dear, Bolotin argues, there is a higher satisfaction open to human beings – that of philosophy – which means literally "friend" of wisdom. Philosophy, an individual's pursuit of his true good, should therefore take precedence over mutual friendship. Thus Bolotin claims that it is to Socrates' credit that he "resists the charm of acknowledged reciprocal friendship."[8] By implication from Bolotin's interpretation, Platonic political philosophy presents a conflict between the philosophic quest and the goods that most people hold dear, with no obvious meeting point between them. And although Plato sheds light on the satisfaction open to individuals, he has little positive to offer in the *Lysis* concerning reciprocal human relationships. By this reading, a rather harsh teaching lurks in the *Lysis*.

My analysis of Plato's *Lysis*, in contrast, argues that Plato has a more positive understanding of the possibilities and benefits of human association. In this chapter, I trace Plato's teaching about the friend by examining the dialogue's dramatic setting, the major definitions of the friend that are discussed, and, finally, the significance of the friendship between Lysis and Menexenus and of the dialogue's concluding *aporia*. Far from replacing friendship with philosophy as the truly satisfying human activity, or turning to the philosopher's relation to wisdom as the exemplar of friendship, I argue that we must understand philosophy as an experience analogous to friendship. Inasmuch as friendship is reciprocal, it requires that our friend love us in return, that he concur or be willing – something that our friend can give or withhold. Our friend belongs to us, but is not entirely our own. Friends do not become one in the manner desired by the lovers of Aristophanes' speech in the *Symposium* (192e). Friends thus have an experience of themselves as not wholly their own (for they belong to another), and of another as their own. So too the knowledge the philosopher seeks is both his own and elusive. If the truth were in no way our own, we would remain forever alienated from it, and philosophy would not be possible. If the truth were in no way other, we would from the outset have it within ourselves, and philosophy would not be necessary. Friendship serves as a standard for philosophy insofar as friends remain separate, while they belong

---

is friendship only "in a limited sense," 194–95. In any case, it could not apply to needy human beings. I discuss Bolotin's position on this "friendship" later in this chapter in the section "Who Might Friends Be?"

[8] Bolotin, *Plato's Dialogue on Friendship*, 187.

together. Of course, the relation between the philosopher and the truth he pursues is not reciprocal. But that is precisely why philosophy must understand itself as a friend of wisdom. Otherwise, philosophy would collapse into *erotosophia* (*erōs* for wisdom), with the potential alienation and despotism that the *Phaedrus'* early speeches about love reveal. And the *Symposium* and the *Phaedrus* would not lead us to the *Lysis*.[9]

In the *Republic*, Socrates proposes common wives and children in the political community he describes, claiming that he is following "the proverb that friends have all things in common" (*Republic* 419a–420b; 423e). Citizens will then be able to speak as it were with one voice, saying "mine" of all in the city and "not mine" of foreigners. This makes for a well-governed community, Socrates observes, for there is no greater good for a city than "what binds it together and makes it one" (*Republic* 462a–d). Aristotle objects in his *Politics* that such unity is the ruin of a city. The understanding of friendship on which the community of wives and children is based, he claims, assimilates friendship to the view of love that Plato gives to Aristophanes in the *Symposium*, where lovers desire to grow together. If this actually happened, Aristotle observes, either one or both of the lovers would disappear (*Politics* 1262b10–14). The view of friends that emerges in my analysis of the *Lysis*, in contrast, who in effect say both "mine" and "not mine" of each another, provides a model for a political community that answers Aristotle's criticism of the *Republic*.[10]

JOINING THE GROUP

While the *Symposium* is narrated by Apollodorus, and the *Phaedrus* is dramatic rather than narrated, the *Lysis* is narrated by Socrates himself. Of these three dialogues on love and friendship, it is the only one that Plato's Socrates chooses to tell. We learn from Apollodorus, who heard

[9] In arguing that the *Lysis*, dramatically later in Socrates' life, indicates a more developed and more positive vision than either the *Symposium* or the *Phaedrus*, I am indebted to the pioneering work of Catherine H. Zuckert on the significance of the dramatic dates of Plato's dialogues, and in particular for the argument that the dramatically later *Lysis* presents Plato's more developed understanding of love and friendship than the dramatically earlier *Symposium* and *Phaedrus*.

[10] Darrell Dobbs argues, contra Aristotle, that the guardian in the *Republic*'s city says "mine" and "not mine" not of distinct things (for example, citizens and foreigners) but of the very ones he loves. "Communism," *The Journal of Politics* 62 (2000), 499. If Dobbs is correct, the discussion of friendship in the *Lysis*, as I interpret it, is not so much a correction of the *Republic*'s but a development of it.

about the *Symposium*'s dinner party from Aristodemus, who was there, that Socrates confirmed some of the details Aristodemus gave (*Symposium* 173b), but apparently he does not fill in anything that Aristodemus missed (e.g., *Symposium* 180c and 223c). In the *Phaedrus*, Socrates agrees to deliver a message to Isocrates, but it does not involve telling him about the conversation he had with Phaedrus (*Phaedrus* 278b–279b). In the *Lysis*, in contrast, Socrates tells the tale.

Whereas Plato gives us considerable detail about the circumstances surrounding some of his other narrated dialogues, he leaves us entirely in the dark about Socrates' narration of the *Lysis*. Socrates makes no allusion to his listener(s), for example, nor does he ever address him or them directly, so we do not even know whether he is speaking to a single individual or to a group. Nor do we know where or when the narration took place.[11] No particular circumstances prevent us from supposing that Socrates is speaking directly to us.

Although Plato tells us nothing of the circumstances of Socrates' narration of the *Lysis*, Socrates gives his listener(s) considerable detail about those surrounding the dialogue itself. Socrates informs us that he meets a group of young men, including Hippothales, Ctesippus, and their other comrades, who ask him where he is coming from and where he is heading, and invite him to join their group.[12] Hippothales' question to Socrates echoes Socrates' questions to Phaedrus – where are you coming from and where are you going? (cf. 203a with *Phaedrus* 227). Here it is others who inquire of Socrates' doings, and ask him to join their group. Socrates was going, he relates, from the Academy to the Lyceum, from one palaestra to another, making his way "along the road outside the wall and close under the wall itself" (203a). When he eventually accepts the young men's invitation, they go to another

---

[11] Socrates' narration of the *Protagoras* and the *Euthydemus*, for example, includes a dramatic prologue between Socrates and his addressee. *Protagoras* 309a–310a and *Euthydemus* 271a–272e. Socrates narrates two other dialogues, the *Republic* and the *Charmides*, soon after they take place. *Republic* 327a and *Charmides* 153a. Of the six dialogues that Socrates narrates, only the *Lovers* is like the *Lysis* in giving us no information about the narration itself.

[12] Socrates relates that he met Hippothales, "son of Hieronymous," and Ctesippus "of Paeania" – that is, he identifies the former by his patronymic and the latter by his deme. Inasmuch as the former designation is an older, more aristocratic one, and the latter a more democratic one (based on Solon's division of Athens into demes), one cannot infer anything about Socrates' listener(s) by how he identifies for him or them the people whom he meets. By the same token, however, Socrates does demonstrate his respect for both the old and the new.

palaestra near the wall, near the place they happen to meet. Unlike the settings of both the *Symposium* and *Phaedrus*, that of the *Lysis* is a perfectly customary one for Socrates.[13] And whereas the *Symposium* occurs in the city, at Agathon's house, and the *Phaedrus* outside the city in the country, the *Lysis'* conversation takes place near the walls of the city, in-between the settings of the other two dialogues, right on the city's boundary.

When Hippothales invites Socrates to the palaestra, where he and many others, beautiful ones, pass their time for the most part by talking (204a), Socrates is cautious: before he accepts Hippothales' invitation he wants "to hear first on what terms I'm to enter and who the beautiful one is." Although Hippothales mentions that many spend time there, Socrates inquires only of one. Hippothales' reference to many, he appears to suspect, veils an interest in one. But why would Socrates care to know such personal matters before agreeing to engage in discussion? And, even more puzzling, why does Socrates inquire into the terms upon which he will enter the palaestra? Isn't the prospect of conversation sufficient to move him to stay (see *Republic* 328a–b)?

One boy seems beautiful to one person, another to another, Hippothales tells Socrates. Instead of singling out a beautiful boy, he again refers to many. Hippothales keeps losing Lysis, whom we eventually learn is his favorite, and himself in a crowd. Just as he will do when he enters the palaestra (207b), Hippothales screens himself behind others who stand between him and his beloved. But Socrates will not let him hide (cf. 210e–211a). When Socrates insists that Hippothales tell him which boy seems beautiful to him, the lover blushes. His blush confirms what Socrates' question implies – Hippothales is in love. At the same time his blush reveals his secret, it also reveals that it is a secret: had he not been trying to conceal his love he would not have blushed at Socrates' question.

When Hippothales blushes, Socrates observes that Hippothales is already far gone in love, for "it has been somehow given me by god quickly to recognize a lover and a beloved" (204b–c), and Hippothales blushes "still more" (204c). Hippothales' reticence before Socrates is surprising, Ctesippus points out, since Hippothales has in fact deafened their ears by singing praises to his beloved. He also finds it notable that Hippothales "has nothing private to say" of his darling, nothing more than "the whole city sings" about Lysis' renowned family and ancestors (205c–d). Hippothales speaks not to Lysis but to Ctesippus,

---

[13] For example, the *Charmides*, the *Lovers*, and the *Euthydemus* are each set in a palaestra.

and apparently to anyone who will listen about his beloved. His all-consuming desire leads him to say just what everyone else, even the whole city, says. And he speaks about the public deeds of Lysis' family rather than about Lysis himself. This lover's speech is neither to Lysis, nor about Lysis, nor uniquely his own. The private discourse that Ctesippus supposes important in love eludes Hippothales' speech and makes him ridiculous.[14]

Socrates heaps more ridicule upon Hippothales, for while he thinks he is praising his beloved, Socrates claims, he is really praising himself. The more admirable his beloved, Socrates explains, the greater prize he will attain, and the more is he to be congratulated. All the more ridiculous will he be, Socrates continues, if his beloved escapes, for the greater loss he will seem to suffer. Moreover, his praise will make his beloved more difficult to capture, for it will fill him "with proud thoughts and bragging." Hippothales obviously needs help, for the means he uses to obtain his heart's desire make it more difficult for him to do so. Tragically, his devices frustrate his goals. But just as Socrates knows enough to avert the consequences of his error in the *Phaedrus* – for he recants his speech about love before he is blinded (*Phaedrus* 243a–b) – Hippothales knows enough to ask for help (206b–c).

Socrates' observations about Hippothales' condition give the lover an opening: he wants Socrates to advise him about how he might win Lysis' love. Although Socrates claims merely to be able to recognize lovers and beloveds, Hippothales' request assumes that Socrates can provide help in his winning the love of his beloved. Perhaps he has heard of Socrates' erotic art (*Phaedrus* 257a), and knows that arts do not merely provide knowledge. When Socrates uses the arts as models for justice in the *Republic*, they appear as skills that bring together what is fitting (literally, what comes together, *prosēkon*). The medical art, for example, gives appropriate drugs, foods, and drinks to bodies, the art of cooking appropriate seasonings to meats (*Republic* 332c). The artisans of this discussion in the *Republic* are kinds of matchmakers. As matchmakers of the fitting, they bring together "what comes together," almost as if the fitting required fitting, or as if the lovers in Aristophanes' speech in the *Symposium* required rhetoric to persuade each other to embrace. Our commonplace experience of the arts thus reproduces the paradox in

---

[14] It is not clear that Hippothales has even had "private" discourse with Lysis. Socrates' request that he demonstrate what he thinks a lover should say about his beloved "*to him* and others" (emphasis mine) suggests his awareness of this situation (205a).

Diotima's description of the daemonic in the *Symposium* as a joining that seems either unnecessary for what comes together or fits, or impossible for what does not. Plato moves from Socrates' knowledge of erotic matters in the *Symposium* (177d–e), which is implicitly linked to Diotima's lessons and her appeal to the experience of philosophy to explain love's intermediate status, to Socrates' erotic art in the *Phaedrus*, and now to a request in effect that Socrates act as matchmaker. As his erotic expertise becomes more paradoxical, Socrates more clearly acknowledges its divine source.

When Hippothales asks Socrates to advise him how he might become dear (*prosphilēs*) to Lysis (206c), he supposes that he wants Lysis' love in return, but his word choice may say more than he knows, since *prosphilēs* contains the Greek for friend, *philos*. Perhaps his intimation of a desire for a friend influences Socrates' agreement to Hippothales' request. When Socrates later acknowledges that he does not yet know how one becomes the friend of another (212a), he is addressing the lover's implicit concern, not simply changing the discussion from love to friendship. Had the rhetorician Lysias been given the task of helping Hippothales win Lysis, he might have given him the written speech he gave to Phaedrus, at least before he heard Socrates' message. Socrates, for his part, might have given Hippothales the palinode – his corrected version of the lover's speech to his darling. But Socrates now proposes instead that he himself give a demonstration of how a lover should speak to his beloved, for it would not be easy to say how to do it, Socrates admits. His demonstration consists not of delivering a speech but of engaging the favorite in conversation: if Lysis would converse with him, Socrates says to the lover, "I could display for you what conversation you should have with him" (206c). Socrates will play the part of a lover to provide Hippothales an example of how to woo.

Hippothales' erotic attraction thus provides the frame of the *Lysis'* discussion, which turns into an inquiry into what a friend is. If we ask of Socrates' discussion with Lysis the question that Hippothales asked of Socrates when he first saw him – where are you coming from and where are you going (203a–b) – the frame provides an initial answer. The discussion comes out of Hippothales' desire for Lysis and its goal is to satisfy that desire. Lysis is, in a way, set up: when Socrates meets him and raises a question about the friend, Lysis thinks he is engaging in a discussion for one purpose, whereas Socrates and others have agreed on another before meeting him (see also *Charmides* 155b and e). Even near the end of the *Lysis*, Socrates reminds us of the discussion's ulterior purpose, when he relates the hidden lover's delight at a definition of a friend favorable to his relationship with Lysis (222b). Socrates' interlocutors may not be aware that Hippothales is watching, but Socrates has his eye on him. Indeed, is Socrates himself merely a disinterested go-between? Socrates is famous for his own pursuit of beautiful young men (see, e.g., *Charmides* 153d and *Alcibiades I* 103a–b). Perhaps the lover himself is Socrates' excuse for speaking with the beautiful boy, using Hippothales as a way to Lysis as Hippothales is using Socrates.

Socrates' demonstration of how to win a beloved, it turns out, consists in humbling him by refuting him (210e). Instead of being puffed up by his lover's praise, the youth will be more aware of his own defects and needs, and as a consequence more amenable to his lover's advances. The way to speak to a beloved is nothing other than the refutations of others for which Socrates is famous. Refutation need not be only a matter of competition, as Alcibiades understands it (see *Protagoras* 336d–e), or an attempt to discover the truth, as Socrates often presents it (see *Apology* 21b ff.), but might be the work of a lover, who humbles his beloved instead of conferring the praise that lovers typically do. If his refutation produces *aporia*, or an awareness of perplexity that he and his interlocutor share, as happens in the *Lysis*, his "wooing" might lead to further conversation rather than to the self-contradiction and silence of the "non-lover" whom we meet in the *Phaedrus*. In this way, a Socratic refutation constitutes a more effective courtship than even the palinode in the *Phaedrus*, which, although it praises love for bringing the greatest benefits to humanity, does not necessarily lead its addressee to question his understanding of himself. He is still being "wooed." After all, the beloved in Socrates' account there is moved by his own beauty that he sees reflected in his lover (*Phaedrus* 255d). He does not, in other words, see himself as needy. To be sure, Socratic refutations, as Socrates recounts in the *Apology*, provoked hostility that led to the city's charges against him (*Apology* 21c–d). Here, in the *Lysis*, Socrates demonstrates another possibility: Socrates leads Lysis to admit that he is in need of a teacher because he is not wise (210d).

While Socrates now has a reason to speak to Lysis – in order to demonstrate to a lover how to capture his beloved – he still lacks a reason that he can present to Lysis. Just as Hippothales would like Socrates to help bring him and Lysis together, Socrates asks Hippothales to get Lysis to converse with him (206c). Socrates, the matchmaker, seems to require a matchmaker. Socrates' request, however, requires that Hippothales have had some previous contact with Lysis, so that he can provide an introduction for Socrates. The plan would therefore fail at the outset were it not for a fact that Hippothales reveals: since Lysis is "exceedingly fond of listening," he will join the group if Socrates starts a discussion (206c–d). Although listening is not the same as conversing, it is a good start.

Although Lysis does desire to join the group, it turns out that he shrinks from doing so.[15] Help comes in the form of Lysis' friend Menexenus, who does not shrink from joining Socrates' group, and thus draws Lysis himself in (207a–b). Even one exceedingly fond of listening requires an excuse, or at least an intermediary, to pursue what he desires. The bolder Menexenus joins Socrates' group, leaving a game he is playing with other boys "in the middle" (207b). And now he is Lysis' intermediary to Socrates. Menexenus seems to belong in the middle of things, even if his name means, literally, "remains a stranger."

When Socrates spots Lysis among the other boys, he recounts that "he stood out by his appearance as someone worth being spoken of not only for being beautiful but because he was beautiful and good" (207a). Hippothales had spoken of Lysis only as beautiful. How does one stand out "by one's appearance" as good as well as beautiful? The terms "beautiful and good" are often coupled in Greek as a term of praise. Bolotin points out that the pair "was commonly thought of as a single notion."[16] What we think of as one, in this case, however, is really two, as we saw in Socrates' account in the *Symposium* of his conversations with Diotima. Because the beautiful seems to have no end beyond itself, Socrates cannot say what the lover gains when he attains the beautiful. We love the beautiful for itself, not because it is useful to us. Diotima must substitute the good for the beautiful as the object of love in order to show its use. In contrast to the beautiful, we ask of the good its end or its use. The good is good for something. Although Socrates has no way to answer Diotima's question about beauty, he "has a good way" to answer her question about what the lover of the good gains when he attains his object – he becomes happy (*Symposium* 204d–205a). To ask

---

[15] Plato uses the verb *oknein*, "to shrink," only one other time in the *Lysis*: Ctesippus claims that Hippothales "shrinks" from telling Socrates the name of his beloved (204c). We soon see him shrink from Lysis as well when he screens himself behind those listening to Socrates' conversation with Lysis. In shrinking, Hippothales and Lysis are alike, but they are alike in such a way that their similarity keeps them apart.

[16] Bolotin, *Plato's Dialogue on Friendship*, 54 n. 19.

about the good is to remember oneself, as Socrates does when he questions Diotima about the use of love.

When Socrates attributes both beauty and goodness to Hippothales' beloved, he thus exposes a tension in love. We may think that we love what we love solely for its own sake, but we also love it as a means to something else, for the sake of our own good, our own happiness. Hippothales thought he was praising Lysis, Socrates said, but he was praising himself. And he would like to capture his beloved, or to make him his own. If there is no good outside the beautiful, the lover both forgets about his own good in his love of the beautiful and also finds no limit to his own good in that of his beloved. Both the lover's slavery to his beloved and his despotic treatment of him, revealed in Lysias' speech and in Socrates' first speech in the *Phaedrus*, emerge in Hippothales' relation to Lysis, for he both makes a fool of himself in his pursuit and is willing to deceive him in order to capture him. Socrates' turn from love to friendship in the *Lysis* is another correction, another palinode. It will explore the possibility of a greater accommodation between the beautiful and the good, or between our self-forgetting and our self-love. After all, Lysis, after whom the dialogue is named, is described by Socrates as beautiful and good. And if Socrates cannot yet know whether Lysis is good as well as beautiful, we have already seen Socrates' uncanny ability to see into those he meets. Besides, Socrates intends to engage Lysis in conversation (see *Charmides* 154b–e).

GETTING ACQUAINTED

When Menexenus and then Lysis join Socrates and his new companions after they enter the palaestra, Socrates turns first to Menexenus, asking him about their relative ages, birth, beauty, and wealth.[17] In response to Socrates' questions, Menexenus admits that he and Lysis dispute as to which is the older and which is more nobly born. As to whether they dispute about which of them is the more beautiful, the two boys merely laugh when Socrates asks (207c). Whatever difference in beauty separates them, their laughter is shared. With respect to their relative wealth, Socrates does not have to ask, he says, since friends hold

---

[17] This brief exchange between Socrates and Menexenus is not often discussed in the literature on the *Lysis*. Friedlander ignores its existence, for example, when he observes that "Socrates will talk first with Lysis and then with Menexenus." *Plato: The Dialogues, First Period*, 93. Bolotin and Geier are exceptions. *Plato's Dialogue on Friendship*, 80–81, and *Plato's Erotic Thought*, 87–90.

possessions in common, and the boys admit they are friends (207c). Their sharing is consistent with the differences between them, which Socrates' questions highlight.

Socrates moves to question the boys about their relative justice and wisdom, he tells his listener(s), but Menexenus is called away. Since they are only "in the middle" (207d), as Socrates points out in his narration of events, we must wonder where the discussion is going, and why Socrates asks these young friends to compare themselves with each other. It is possible that Socrates' questions could come between these friends, for they reveal the boys' "spirit of rivalry."[18] Friends' reflecting on and speaking about their relationship, however, does not necessarily have negative consequences. Indeed, the boys' responses to Socrates' questions point to the complex bonds that hold friends together, bonds that include agreement about some things as well as dispute about others. If the boys dispute over their relative ages and birth, they cannot be so far apart in age or birth that their quarreling makes no sense. There is strife where there is similarity. And when there is obvious difference, perhaps in beauty, the thought of disputing seems funny. Friends are both like and unlike, and can reflect on the ways in which they are so. And their reflection can take the form of disputing and even laughing. Not in spite of their differences but because of their reaction to their differences, especially their laughter, they are friends. Socrates' first use of the dual in this dialogue – the Greek form that designates a pair – occurs when he reports of the boys that "they laughed."

When Menexenus is called away, rather than continue questioning Lysis about the relative merits of himself and his friend, Socrates turns to another manifestation of friendship, the love (*philia*) of parents for children. Specifically, he asks Lysis whether his parents love (*philein*) him, using the verb for love from which friendship (*philia*) is derived.[19] Although commissioned to demonstrate how a lover should speak to a

---

[18] Bolotin, *Plato's Dialogue on Friendship*, 80.

[19] Both *philein*, which is related to friendship (*philia*), and *eran*, which is related to erotic love (*erōs*), can be translated as "to love." The latter we have seen is the focus of the *Symposium*'s encomia and at issue in the speeches in the first half of the *Phaedrus*. Given its sexual connotations, *eran* would be inappropriate to use for the affection between parents and their children (see *Symposium* 199d). My use of the verb "to love" henceforth in this chapter refers to *philein*, unless the context indicates otherwise. See Bolotin, *Plato's Dialogue on Friendship*, 53 n. 10, and 55 n. 22. Once inside the palaestra, Socrates and his companions use the verb *eran* only at 221e–222a, where Socrates applies his definition of friends as kindred to lover and beloved.

beloved, Socrates turns the conversation toward other kinds of love, first toward the friendship between Lysis and Menexenus, and then toward Lysis' parents' love for him. Lovers should turn their thoughts to friends. Only near the end of the dialogue, when Socrates includes *erōs* in an inference he draws about friendship (221e–222a), is there any further mention of *erōs*. The discussion of love in the *Lysis* focuses on *philia*.

Prodded by Socrates' questioning, Lysis reveals that while his parents love him and desire him to be happy, they prevent him from doing many things he desires to do. In fact, he has a great many masters and rulers – his parents and teachers, and even some of his parents' slaves. The cause is not simply his youth, Socrates points out, for his parents do entrust certain things to him in spite of his age – namely, those things that he understands (209c). Once he has become wise, moreover, his neighbor as well will let him manage his household, and the Athenians will entrust their affairs to him, and finally the Great King of Asia himself will entrust him with everything in regard to which he thinks Lysis the wiser (209c–210a). The wise, Socrates continues, will have not only power and freedom – for he will be able to do whatever he wishes – but friendship as well: since one is loved to the extent that he is of use to others, "if you become wise," Socrates tells Lysis, "all will be your friends and your kindred (*oikeioi*) – for you will be useful and good" (210d).

The word translated as "kindred" is derived from the Greek for "home," and is used of relatives. But if relatives are relatives because of natural ties of birth, they cannot be chosen on the basis of their wisdom or utility. Socrates calls attention to the way in which he stretches the word "kindred" beyond its ordinary meaning when he juxtaposes his use of it with its ordinary sense: "if you become wise, my boy, all will be your friends and your kindred. . . . But, if you don't, no one else will be your friend, and neither will your mother, father, nor your own kindred" (210d). Socrates might have reached this conclusion without appeal to kindred: that all will become kindred of the wise is not an obviously necessary step toward the conclusion that all love the wise for his use to them. When Socrates turns from Lysis' parents, whom Lysis admits will entrust themselves and all that is their own to him when he becomes wise, to his neighbor, Socrates asks Lysis whether his neighbor has the same "standard" as his parents (209c–d). Lysis supposes he does, but Socrates' use of *horos*, the word translated as standard, calls attention to the problem with Lysis' answer. *Horos* in Greek means boundary, or definition, and specifically refers to the boundary stone separating one piece of property from another. Lysis' father and his neighbor do have the same *horos*, but as a boundary it both connects their properties and distinguishes them. Their common standard is a boundary that keeps them separate. Lysis ignores his neighbor's sense of his own boundary that will prevent him from turning over his affairs to Lysis, even if he considers him wise.[20] Socrates thus highlights the danger of wisdom's rule: as a result of his wisdom, everyone becomes the wise person's "own." His wisdom in effect dissolves any distinction between his own and another's (see *Republic* 344a).

Moreover, while Socrates' argument seems to give the knower absolute power, it also understands him as useful to those whom he rules. It is because of his utility that all entrust themselves to him, and that everyone loves him. He is loved not because he is "beautiful and good" but because he is "useful and good" (210d). He is only a means to others' good. Not for himself is he loved by others, even by his parents, but for his wisdom, not for his own sake, but for theirs. The world ruler becomes the servant of all (see *Republic* 341c–342e). When Socrates reports that he has "humbled" Lysis by means of this argument, he has not shown simply that Lysis should not expect to rule unless he must become wise. He has also shown that ruling implies subjection to the ruled. The name of the dialogue's title character "Lysis" is the Greek word meaning "releasing," as when someone is released from chains or bondage. The dialogue's title, scholars have argued, therefore refers not only to the boy bearing the name but to the effect of Socrates' questioning him, for Socrates "dissolves" the bonds that connect Lysis to his family.[21] But Lysis' "release" from his family by being shown the way to universal love and rule through his becoming wise and useful to others only binds him again. This model of friends that arises from discussion of the love of parents for their children early in the *Lysis* merges the wise beloved's total rule with his complete subordination to the ruled. Should a friend of the ruler, whether it be parents, neighbor, or the whole world, sing the praises of the wise individual he loves,

[20] As Benardete comments on this prospect that "Lysis's wisdom be accepted world-wide": "Not even in the *Republic* does Socrates imagine that the philosopher-king could put an end to evils in more than one cave." *The Argument of the Action*, Benardete, *The Argument of the Action: Essays on Greek Poetry and Philosophy*, ed. Ronna Burger and Michael Davis (Chicago: University of Chicago Press, 2000), 207.

[21] Mooney, "Plato's Theory of Love," 140; Bolotin, *Plato's Dialogue on Friendship*, 65–66; Umphrey, "Eros and Thumos," 380; Tessitore, "Plato's *Lysis*," 118, 119, and 126; Gonzalez, "Plato's *Lysis*," 73 and 76; and Scott, *Plato's Socrates as Educator*, 53.

he would, like Hippothales, end up singing his own praises – the great good that was his from his dear one's wisdom.

Socrates' exchange with Lysis concerning his parents' love is Vlastos' starting point for his argument that Plato fails to have any understanding that love might be directed at the whole person, rather than at the good – and in this case useful – qualities of one's beloved.[22] His case, however, requires abstracting from any defects Plato suggests in the argument, and from Socrates' stated intention of humbling Lysis.[23] Even Hippothales, who is interested in capturing his beloved, is as a result of his beloved's humiliation, Socrates' observes, "in agony and disturbed by what had been said" (210e). Although Socrates does not speculate further on Hippothales' reaction, Bolotin's suggestion that it may provide "evidence of his love of the boy" seems plausible.[24] The effect of Socrates' argument on him would then reveal more about love than the argument itself. Hippothales may love Lysis, and not simply love the use he might be to him once captured.

As Menexenus returns, the humbled Lysis whispers to Socrates a request that he "chasten" or "punish" his friend by repeating to him the argument that he has just heard from Socrates. Menexenus, Lysis believes, is "contentious" (211a–c). Socrates agrees to oblige Lysis in undertaking a conversation with Menexenus, just as he agreed to oblige Hippothales in undertaking a conversation with Lysis. Socrates' talents help friends as well as lovers. Instead of repeating the line of questioning that culminates in a vision of world dominion enjoyed by the wise, and his absolute servitude that follows from it, however, Socrates turns the discussion to friends. Socrates contrives a ruse to speak with Menexenus: Lysis doesn't understand something Socrates said, supposes that Menexenus does, and urges Socrates to ask Menexenus about it. Socrates thus humbles Lysis even further, attributing to him an admission that Menexenus is better able than he to engage in a conversation with Socrates. At the same time, however, Socrates presents Lysis as a better friend of Menexenus' than he has shown himself to be.

---

[22] Vlastos observes that this exchange lacks any hint that one could wish another's good for his own sake. He finds a view of "utility love" as well in arguments later in the dialogue that "the doctor, the rich, the wise are loved by one who needs them for what *he* can get out of them" (emphasis Vlastos') and that the person lacking in nothing would not love. "The Individual as an Object of Love in Plato," 7–8.

[23] See Rhodes' excellent discussion of this point, "Platonic *Philia* and Political Order," 27–32.

[24] Bolotin, *Plato's Dialogue on Friendship*, 104.

Socrates again asks Lysis, in effect, to look at his relationship to his friend. For the moment, Lysis listens in silence.

For the third time, Socrates turns the discussion to friends, having first asked Menexenus to compare himself with Lysis, and then asking Lysis whether his parents love him. These questions are what we might call conversational. Socrates is getting acquainted with the boys. Now Socrates approaches the issue of friendship with Menexenus in abstraction from any particular friendships, even though it arises from his own experience. He explains that he has desired to acquire a good friend since youth, but he is so far from having done so that he does not know even how one becomes a friend of another. That is why he is amazed when looking at Menexenus and Lysis, for they have been able "to acquire this possession quickly and easily." He is therefore asking Menexenus about the friend, "inasmuch as he is experienced" (211d–212a).

The language of acquiring and possessing figures heavily in Socrates' description of his situation. Because one who has acquired something then possesses it, the perfect tense of acquire (*ktasthai*) in Greek means to possess (*kektēsthai*).[25] What one possesses is, literally, one's property (*ktēmata*). But what does it mean to "possess" a friend, as opposed to other possessions that Socrates mentions, such as horses, dogs, or gold (212d–e)? While Socrates desired from childhood a certain possession (*ktēma*), he says, it is toward the "acquisition" (*ktēsis*) of friends that he claims to be erotically inclined. In speaking of his goal, he substitutes a word that can mean an activity as well as the object produced by the activity, using a noun formed from the verb, just as "releasing" (*lusis*), the title of the dialogue, is formed from *luein*. When Socrates speaks of the act of acquisition (*ktēsis*) rather than the possession (*ktēma*) as the object of his desire, he suggests that in the case of friends the verb cannot have its perfect sense of possessing, that the act of acquiring a friend cannot be completed.

What is acquired becomes one's possession, or property, an extension of oneself, and in the case of a human being a slave (see Aristotle, *Politics* 1253b32). If possession were perfect, as it is grammatically, there could be no strife, no dispute between possession and its possessor (see 207c). An individual does not yet possess a friend while he is still acquiring

---

[25] Forms of *ktasthai*, or the nouns derived from it, occur eight times between 211d and 212a.

him, but once acquired the other becomes a possession rather than a friend. A middle ground on which friends could stand, so that attaining what is desired does not mean losing it, would require that "releasing" be as essential to friendship as "acquiring."[26] Just as Lysis' name literally means "releasing," Menexenus' name literally means "remains a stranger."[27] Should the names of these friends be significant, as a result of Plato's art, their names suggest their qualifications as friends rather than their disqualifications. Friends are always becoming friends. Of them we should use the imperfect tense.

When Socrates describes himself as a "lover of companions" (211e), he uses the word in an uncommon sense.[28] A "lover of companions" (*philhetairos*) usually refers to one who is fond of his companions or one who delights in his companions, just as "a lover of listening" (*philēkoos*), as Hippothales calls Lysis (206c), is one fond of listening. But Socrates uses *philhetairos* as *philosophos* (philosopher) is often used, as one who seeks and therefore does not possess the wisdom he loves (218a). Wisdom does not replace philosophy because the philosopher knows enough to ask questions about his answers. His experience of knowing is that of simultaneously acquiring and releasing. Every answer about the friend that comes up in this dialogue, as we shall see, Socrates proceeds to call into question. Socrates does not know any answer he cannot question, but he also knows that he doesn't know and why he doesn't know. That is, he knows what questions to ask. That question is now that of the friend. Socrates and

[26] The *Lysis*, according to its subtitle, to say nothing about its discussion, is "On Friendship." If we understand its title to refer to "releasing," as well as to the name of one of its characters, the *Lysis* points to the connection between releasing and friendship.

[27] There is some ambiguity even in "stranger" (*xenos*). Although the Greek word means "stranger" in a general sense, it is also used of a foreigner who has special ties with a citizen. Bolotin points out that the word "refers to foreigners who give and receive kindly treatment to each other – both 'hosts' and 'guests.' In particular, it refers to those inhabitants of other cities with whom a man or a family would maintain a relation of reciprocal hospitality." *Plato's Dialogue on Friendship*, 56 n. 41. To support the view that there are objects that are dear (*phila*) regardless of whether they love in return, Socrates quotes Solon: "Blessed is he for whom children, or single-hoofed horses, hunting dogs, and a guest-friend in a foreign land are *philoi*" (212e). The word translated as "guest-friend in a foreign land" is *xenos*. Solon uses *xenos* as an example of one we love or hold dear and hence of a friend. A *xenos* is a distant friend. See Benardete, *The Argument of the Action*, 213.

[28] Bolotin, *Plato's Dialogue on Friendship*, 56 n. 34. For the common usage, see Thucydides, 3.82.4; Xenophon, *Cyropaedia* 8.3.49; and Aristotle, *Rhetoric* 1389a35, and *Virtues and Vices* 1251b35.

Menexenus – and Lysis as well – discuss five possible explanations of the friend: (1) whether the ones loving, the ones loved, or both are friends; (2) whether friends are those like each other; (3) whether friends are those unlike each other; (4) whether "the neither good nor bad" is friend to the good; and (5) whether the kindred are friends.

ARE FRIENDS THE ONES LOVING, THE ONES LOVED, OR BOTH?

Socrates asks Menexenus whether when someone loves, the one who loves or the one whom he loves becomes the friend. Menexenus answers that they both do. As a noun derived from the verb *philein*, to love or befriend, the Greek *philos* (friend) refers in the active sense to the one who loves, while derived from the adjective it means one who is dear or loved. Socrates' discussion with Menexenus is plagued by this ambiguity. If someone who loves is a friend, then someone who hates is an enemy. But inasmuch as we sometimes love those who do not love us in return, or who even hate us, our friend (in the passive sense, one whom we love) could also be our enemy (in the active sense), one who hates us. Similarly, one who is hated, our enemy (in the passive sense), might love us and be our friend (in the active sense). Since the active and passive senses are not clearly distinguished in the discussion, it happens, time after time, that Menexenus' suggestions fall because the friend turns out to be the enemy.

Menexenus momentarily escapes this dilemma when he suggests that friends are those who love and are loved. If friendship is reciprocal, we could not love (or be a friend to) someone who hates us. But as Socrates points out, we often hold someone or something dear that does not love us in return. If friendship must be reciprocal, Socrates observes, we could not explain how parents could be friends to their children even when their children hate them, or how anyone could be friends to what neither loves nor hates, as wine lovers are friends of wine, or philosophers are friends to wisdom (212b–213c).[29]

---

[29] David B. Robinson argues that Plato's "difficulties" in the dialogue involve his "not realizing the dangers in ambiguity in his *definiendum*" – inasmuch as *philon* refers to "two distinct topics" – friendship and what human beings pursue. "Plato's *Lysis*: The Structural Problem," *Illinois Classical Studies* 11 (1986): 73–74, 77, and 82. Of course, if friends are among those things that human beings pursue, as at least Socrates claims is true in his case, the ambiguity in the Greek word points to a deeper difficulty. See Bolotin, *Plato's Dialogue on Love and Friendship*, 114.

Although the argument might justify his doing so, Socrates does not conclude that our friend need not love in return to be a friend, or that only the relation between the philosopher and the wisdom he loves remains as the true exemplar of friendship. Rather, he states that he is "at a loss" as to "who become friends to each other," and that he and Menexenus may be seeking in an altogether wrong way. He asks whether "there are still some others, aside from these, who become friends to each other" (213c). There is more to be said and discussed, he suggests, and his statement prompts Lysis to burst into the discussion to agree that the pursuit is on the wrong track.

ARE LIKES FRIENDS?

When Lysis' outburst brings him back into the discussion, Socrates suggests that they seek help from the poets, "our fathers and guides in wisdom." He quotes a line of Homer's verse from the *Odyssey* that "a god always leads like to like" (214a–b). The words are spoken contemptuously by the goatherd Melantheus when he sees the swineherd Eumaeus guiding a disreputable looking beggar (*Odyssey* 17.218). Melantheus is deceived, however, for the pair are not alike in the way he supposes. The beggar, in fact, is Odysseus disguised as an ugly old man, so that he can return to Ithaca undetected by his enemies. The goddess Athena has "withered" his "beautiful" flesh, ruined his brown hair, and "dimmed [his] eyes once so beautiful" (*Odyssey* 13.398–403; 430–438). Eumaeus, for his part, may have as poor an appearance as the transformed Odysseus, but the enslaved swineherd is the son of a king (*Odyssey* 15. 455 ff.). Athena leads these "likes" together in order to give Odysseus access to his enemies for the sake of revenge, not in order to bring them together as friends, as Socrates suggests. Indeed, the Homeric verse does not even refer to the likes brought together by the god as friends.

Even more remarkable is Socrates' addition of a phrase to Homer's verse. He attributes to Homer the thought that the god leads like to like and "makes them acquainted" (214a–b). Not only is the last phrase not in Homer, but it contradicts Homer's story, for the god hides Odysseus' identity from Eumaeus. Athena and Odysseus believe that making Eumaeus acquainted with their plan might impede its execution. Even though Athena herself admits to Odysseus that "[Eumaeus'] thoughts are always kindly," and that he "is a friend to your son and circumspect Penelope," she and Odysseus do not appear to trust him (*Odyssey* 13.405–06).

Socrates' addition to the Homeric text corrects it and thereby suggests his disagreement with the poets, who give insufficient scope both to the capacity of human beings to know one another and also to the place of trust in human life.[30] It is only by becoming "acquainted," or known to each other, that trust becomes possible. Although we treat the poets as our "fathers and guides," their wisdom about friends, as indicated by Socrates' revision of Homeric verse, is inadequate. Socrates calls them "guides" for us, using a word related to the one Homer uses for Eumaeus' guiding Odysseus (*Odyssey* 17.218), but Eumaeus knows neither whom he guides nor the purpose of his guiding. He supposes that he is leading a beggar into the city so that he can obtain food, and not the beautiful Odysseus disguised as a beggar so that he can obtain revenge.

After mentioning the poets, Socrates appeals to a second authority: those who "converse and write about nature and the whole" also say that "like is by necessity always a friend to like" (214a–b). While these nat-uralists may agree with the poets that like goes with like, however, they disagree about how they come together. Socrates' authorities are not exactly alike. While the poets hold the god responsible for leading like to like, "the wisest," as Socrates calls them, hold that likes are friends by "necessity." If they are wisest, they are wiser than the poets. Their superiority lies in their recourse to nature. If we are friends by necessity, we belong or fit together with what we love, and thus there is a sense in which nature is good to us. No external force, no god, is needed to bring likes together.

In contrast to the account of the "wisest," the poets' recourse to the divine suggests an arbitrariness in nature. If it takes a god to bring likes together, there is no reason to suppose that they belong together. It is the god who makes friendship possible. In a similar vein, Socrates suggests in the *Euthyphro* that the poets suppose that the holy is holy because the gods love it (*Euthyphro* 10a). If love is arbitrary, however, and therefore not evoked by the objects of our love, nothing in them would prevent us from using them for our own purposes. Indeed, that we can so use them may account for why we love them. Odysseus uses Eumaeus to gain access to the suitors, just as Lysis uses Menexenus to gain access to Socrates, and perhaps even Socrates uses Hippothales to

---

[30] Bolotin understands Socrates' addition to the Homeric text to reveal the poetic view rather than to criticize the poetic view for what it lacks. He consequently offers a different interpretation of Socrates' "core" opposition to Homer. *Plato's Dialogue on Friendship*, 124–27.

gain access to Lysis. But if we love those we love only for our own sakes, we have little reason to become acquainted with them, for they serve as extensions of ourselves. And what we control, we have no need to trust. The poets do not see sufficiently that the holy exists apart from our love of it, and draws us to itself. It is not surprising that Homer does not call Odysseus and Eumaeus friends in the passage that Socrates quotes, nor that Athena and Odysseus distrust him. The poets do not understand that if matchmaking is all there is, matchmaking would be impossible. To bring Odysseus to Eumaeus, Athena must use her divine power to make him appear like what he is not. This match is a deception, supported only by divine power to transform, in this instance the beautiful into the ugly.

Socrates, however, does not explicitly criticize the poets as our guides in wisdom. He appeals to them along with the wisest. The poets have something to contribute. In referring to necessity, those who study nature and the whole see no need for matchmaking. Whereas in the world of poets there is no choice or art that is not despotic, in the world of the naturalists there is no choice or art at all. And just as we do not have to trust what we control, no trust is required for what is necessary. In leaving no room for art, or for choice, the naturalists allow no distinct place for the human within the nature they study. Socrates mentions that they converse and write about the whole, but he does not say that they also investigate its parts. The naturalists speak of "like" in the neuter (214b). But neuters cannot become acquainted with or know each other. Those who study the whole understand even less than the poets that acquaintance or knowledge is necessary for friends. They may be wiser than the poets for they favor the view that the gods love the holy because it is holy (see *Euthyphro* 10a), but Socrates says of them no more than the Delphic oracle said of him – that they are the wisest, not that they are wise (214b, see *Apology* 21a–b). Socrates says that they converse, but their view of the world allows no place for conversation.[31] To understand how one becomes the friend of another, one cannot take either the poets or the naturalists as one's sole guide. They both have something to contribute,

[31] Bolotin notes the superiority of the naturalists to the poets, and traces it in part to their greater "comprehensiveness," for their view "is not limited to that part of the whole of immediate concern to men," and in part to "their willingness to converse about the reasons for their opinions." *Plato's Dialogue on Friendship*, 123. He does not explore how their view of necessity is consistent with their propensity for conversation.

and must somehow be made friends. Socrates refers in the *Symposium* to the proverb that the good go uninvited to the feast of the good in order to invite Aristodemus to accompany him to Agathon's house.

Socrates quickly refutes the opinion of poets and naturalists that likes are friends. Can the bad be friends with each other, Socrates asks. Since the bad do injustice to whomever they go near, they become hated. If the bad are "like" each other, then the like cannot in all instances be friend to like, and what is said about friends can be only half-true – it must apply only to the good. Perhaps these sayings mean that the bad "are never alike, not even themselves to themselves," Socrates says, but are "at variance with [or different from] themselves." Their variability makes it impossible for them to be like anyone whatever, even like themselves. The good, by implication, who do not suffer from such variability, are like themselves. They can therefore be like each other. The saying that likes are friends must mean, Socrates reasons, only that the good is a friend to good (214b–d). One must be something to be something to someone.

On the other hand, Socrates continues, someone cannot be useful to another, insofar as he is like him. There is nothing that one's like can do for one that one cannot also do for oneself. Not being able to benefit, or to be of help to one's like, one would not be treasured and hence be a friend to him (214e–215a). Moreover, the good are self-sufficient, in want of nothing, and therefore would not treasure anything or love. But someone who does not love is not a friend. Just as Socrates concluded with Menexenus that neither the ones who love nor the ones who are loved, nor the ones who love and are loved could be friends, he now concludes with Lysis that neither the bad with the bad, nor the bad with the good, nor the good with the good could be friends. And, when asked, Lysis can think of no "device" (*mēchanē*) by which those who "neither long for each other when absent – for even apart they are sufficient for themselves – nor do they have any use for each other when they are present" might be friends (215a–c).

Thus it seems to Socrates that they have been "deceived in some manner entirely" by the argument that likes are friends (215c). Not only is half of the position that likes are friends incorrect – for it cannot apply, to the bad – but also the whole, for it cannot apply even to the good. Socrates' "in some manner," however, suggests a hesitancy about his conclusion. To recognize that he has been deceived only "in some manner" is to not be simply deceived. It may be incorrect to reject entirely the argument that likes are friends. After all, as Socrates says in the palinode, "it is fated that neither the bad is a friend to the bad, nor the good not a friend to the good" (*Phaedrus* 255b). "Fate" rules out one possibility, but leaves open another – that the good might become friends to each other. It does not determine it. If the good are "like themselves," as Socrates' contrary description of the bad implies, moreover, they too may need another to help them becomes friends with themselves, to make them acquainted with or know themselves.[32] The good, then, would have need of each other for the sake of self-knowledge. The palinode's account of how lover and beloved see themselves in each other is not sufficient, if only because when lover and beloved see themselves in the other they do not know it (*Phaedrus* 251b and 255d). The mirroring of love described there gives only an illusion of otherness, just as the palinode's account of love is simplified by virtue of the lover's seeking one of the same soul type as himself. Socrates now turns to the possibility that unlikes are friends.

ARE UNLIKES FRIENDS?

Socrates offers an argument he once heard that unlikes are friends: whereas those who are alike have no need of each other, the argument goes, the unlike can be friends, such as the poor person, who befriends the wealthy, the weak the strong, the ill the doctor, and the one who doesn't know the one who does know (215c–e). Socrates had heard something like this from Diotima, who taught him that love was neither beautiful nor good but the desire for those things which itself lacks, although in that case the subject is love rather than friendship. In the *Lysis*, Socrates even uses the example of the poor person who befriends the wealthy, just as Poverty in Diotima's story sought out Resource. In Diotima's account, however, it is because Poverty is resourceful that she overcomes her poverty, which suggests that those who are absolutely different will not prove capable of becoming friends.

The one from whom he heard this argument about unlikes, Socrates says, pushed it still further, applying it to the natural world: the dry desires what is wet, the cold the hot, the bitter the sweet, and the sharp the blunt. By the same argument, the wet would desire the dry, the hot the cold, and so on. When Socrates moves to the natural world, it

---

[32] The word Socrates uses for "acquainted" is from the same verb (*gignōskein*) as in the command "know thyself" on the Delphic temple (*Phaedrus* 229e; see also *Charmides* 164d–e).

appears at first that he has found the reciprocity that has been proving so difficult to find among human beings. The "empty desires filling and what is full emptying," Socrates continues, "for what is opposite is nourishment to its opposite" (215e). What each desires is not the other, but the nourishment that the other provides. And so the dry does not desire the moist, but moistening; the cold does not desire the hot, but warming, just as the sick does not desire the doctor, but healing. Those unlike, or even opposite, are really alike – selfish beings who seek their own nourishment and use others in order to obtain it. They are alike in a way that calls into question their becoming friends.[33] It is paradoxical to say that opposites attract, almost as if one were to say that enemies were friends. The very thing that has been the downfall of so many of the attempts in this dialogue to define the friend easily becomes the downfall of this argument as well: Socrates points to the many unlikes that have already been revealed to be incapable of friendship: the unjust and the just, and bad and the good, and of course the enemy and the friend (216a–b).

In light of Socrates' revelation that a desire for their own nourishment underlies the attraction between unlikes, Bolotin speculates that Socrates supposes that human beings are deceived by friendship: what we think of as a single friendship, or as a whole, in which desires are "truly shared" and "truly reciprocal," "in fact consists of different friendships." Specifically, while appearing to be friends of each other, each desires only what is useful to himself. What seems like a whole – friendship – deceives us, and is in fact two friendships. Each is a friend to himself. Accordingly, "when Socrates makes his own first suggestion about what a friend is," Bolotin notes, "he will disregard reciprocal loving and will hardly use the word 'friendship.'"[34]

What applies to the wet and the dry, which seeks the other only as a means to its own fulfillment, however, does not necessarily apply to human beings. Socrates' list of the needy reveals a complexity not found in the natural world. The weak may befriend the strong, who will protect him if he is in danger. But the strong cannot necessarily help the weak overcome his weakness. That would take a trainer. In

---

[33] It is therefore appropriate that the discussion of unlikes become one of opposites. The word "opposite," *enantion*, is literally something that exists "in" (*en*) a condition of being "against" (*anti*). Just as the English "opposition," *enantion* suggests conflict or hostility. The word may be used to refer to enemies. See, for example, Herodotus, 7.225 and Thucydides, 4. 64.

[34] Bolotin, *Plato's Dialogue on Friendship*, 139.

Socrates' lists of examples, the sick person does not seek his opposite, a healthy one, but a doctor, the individual who can help him become healthy. Unlike the wet, the moist, and the other "natural" opposites that Socrates mentions, human beings become aware of their own deficiencies and seek help in overcoming them. Whereas a doctor may show us how to become healthy, as he prescribes drugs and other procedures, however, only a healthy person manifests to us what health is. Socrates' final example of the needy – an ignorant person who befriends the one who knows – befriends someone who both could become his teacher and also manifests the condition to which he aspires. Our very desire to become good, then, might lead us to love another because of his goodness – which is useful to be sure as a model of what we would like to become – and not merely (or even) because of his skill in making us good.

It is therefore appropriate that Socrates at this point calls attention to what the discussion has left out. His search for a friend reminds him of the beautiful, for the friend is eluding them, just as the beautiful, which is "soft, smooth, and sleek," "easily slides past us and gives us the slip." He therefore fears that the old saying that "the beautiful is dear [or a friend]" may be true (216c–d). The beautiful is appreciated, not possessed; it is loved, but not mastered. When Socrates speaks "through divination" about the next view of the friend that he will examine, he states that "whatever is neither good nor bad is a friend of the beautiful and good" (216d). The beautiful appears in the argument again, if only in passing. Although Socrates soon restates the position he is examining without reference to the beautiful (see 216d ff.), he has nevertheless reminded us of the beautiful, which may be useful in understanding the friend precisely because it is not useful in any ordinary sense.

Bolotin argues that Socrates disagrees in part with the old saying about the friend. The old saying implies that we could love something that is beautiful but that is not simply good for us, inasmuch as it speaks only of the beautiful as dear. By coupling the beautiful and the good, according to Bolotin, Socrates implies "that the beautiful, to the extent that it is not also good, will not be truly loved," and refuses to separate our love of the beautiful "from that good which the friend has need of for himself." Thus, Bolotin argues, Socrates' use of the old saying that the beautiful is dear "suggests a selfish aspect to [Socrates'] notion of what a friend is."[35]

---

[35] Bolotin, *Plato's Dialogue on Friendship*, 144–45. See also Rhodes, "Platonic *Philia* and Political Order," 38–39.

Coupling the beautiful and the good as Socrates does, however, does not qualify our love of the beautiful in light of our love of the good any more than it qualifies our love of the good in light of our love of the beautiful. Inasmuch as the discussion has been about an individual's desire for his own good (for example, the desire of the sick for healing), for Socrates to interject a reminder of the beautiful has the effect of qualifying the selfish component of loving. What is good for us, to the extent that it is not also beautiful, will not be truly loved. Whereas the dry desires moistening, human beings are aroused by the beautiful as well as the good, possible models of which their own needy condition falls short, and which they experience as unlike themselves. We are deceived into thinking we have discovered a whole, not by seeing one friendship when there are in fact two, but by seeing only ourselves, and the other only insofar as he is subordinate to ourselves. We are deceived in thinking that we are wholes, and in assuming self-sufficiency.

Socrates foreshadowed the fall of the argument that unlikes or opposites are friends when he introduced it as the "very opposite" of the argument that likes are friends (215e; see also Aristotle, *NE* 1155a33–b8). If opposites are friends, these arguments, which are the "very opposite" to each other, could be friends. The argument for unlikes in that case would not stand alone, but find a place in company with the argument for likes. Socrates' next step brings these opposite arguments together, for it seems to answer the arguments against likes and unlikes. Having recourse to Diotima's teaching that what is not good is not necessarily bad (*Symposium* 201e), Socrates states another position for examination, that it is the "neither good nor bad" that is a friend to the good (216c).

ARE THOSE WHO ARE NEITHER GOOD NOR BAD FRIENDS TO THE GOOD?

Socrates tells his listener(s) that with this new conception of the friend, he "rejoiced greatly, as if he were a hunter and had found, in a way that [he] cherished, what [he] had been hunting for [him]self" (218c). Just as friends "cherish" each other (215a and b), Socrates "cherishes" his understanding of a friend. Socrates claims that he has captured "for himself" what he has been hunting. He uses the Greek middle voice, which indicates that the speaker is both the actor and the beneficiary of his action. If Socrates' satisfaction were complete, he would have found a way – by means of a concept that he claims to have through "divination" (216d) – to escape the dilemmas of reciprocal friendship, such as the possibility that the one whom one loves does not love in return, or even hates. Socrates, however, is trying to understand the friend because he is seeking a friend. Since he cherishes the knowledge he gains, he experiences how he might love something both for itself and as a means to something else for which he is searching.

Like Diotima, Socrates explains how someone neither good nor bad is a friend to the good by appealing to the example of the philosopher, literally one who is a friend to wisdom. While the philosopher is not wise, his ignorance does not make him so stupid and senseless that he thinks that he knows what he does not know. He has "this evil, ignorance," but it has not made him ignorant. There are two ways in which something can be present to something else, Socrates explains, using whiteness as an example: while hair can become white through aging, hair that has white dye rubbed onto it is not yet white. So too an evil, ignorance, may be present to the philosopher, without making him evil (218a–b). In such a case, the one for whom the evil is present still desires the good. Taking the "philosopher" or "the friend of wisdom" as the model of the friend, however, does not yield reciprocal human friends. Indeed, it threatens the reduction of friendship to one's own good.

Socrates' next move makes this result even clearer, as he dramatically claims that it is only a dream that the inquiry has been successful (218c). A friend is friend to someone because of some other good, just as the sick becomes a friend to the doctor for the sake of health. Since health in this case is dear, and hence a friend, Socrates says moving back to the passive sense of friend, a friend is a friend for the sake of another good or friend. We have what would be an infinite regress of friends unless we stop at a "first friend," in relation to which all the instrumental friends are only phantom friends that deceive us (219c–d). Only the "first friend" is truly a friend, who is not a friend for the sake of another friend. And "all those we assert to be friends" are friends "in name only." "What is really a friend is that in which all these things spoken about as friendships terminate" (220a–b).

Menexenus is understandably "afraid" that Socrates' argument is correct (220b), for those he considers his friends would be friends in name only. Even if they are necessary means to that further good that is the true friend, they deceive us into thinking that they are more than they are. As Bolotin says, the phantom friends "include all those human beings whom we ordinarily call our 'friends'" whom we "don't truly love . . . at all. What we love instead . . . is that further good which we need and which we use them for." Thus "no human being . . . , however good, is truly a friend to another."[36] Socrates' "matchmaking," then, would attenuate human relationships as it turns listeners to philosophy. Bolotin thus concurs with Vlastos' position that for Plato "it would be a mistake to love [another] 'for his own sake,' to treat him, in Kant's phrase 'as an end in himself,'" and that Socratic dialectic is a "cure . . . to break the illusion, and make us see that what we 'really' love is something else."[37] Less willing to reject Plato's position on love as a flawed understanding than is Vlastos, Bolotin concludes that "the love of the good is ultimately inconsistent with our deepest hopes for friendship," and "the *Lysis* brings this truth to light."[38] His remark about the illusory character of friendship that we have seen in his discussion of unlikes thus applies more broadly: what we think of as a single friendship, in which individuals "[appear] to desire or even to love each other," is in fact two friendships, between each individual and his own good.

If the truest exemplar of friendship is the philosopher's love of wisdom, and philosophy replaces reciprocal friendship between human beings as the true human fulfillment, what character would philosophy have? If one pursues the truth because it is one's good, one's good would become the measure of the truth rather than the truth the measure of one's good. Whatever truth is not good would be irrelevant to one's search. The initial exchange between Socrates and Lysis, which demonstrates that knowledge alone justifies Lysis' ruling his parents, his neighbors, fellow Athenians and foreigners alike, does not foreshadow the notion that the deepest friendship is between the philosopher and his own good. To the contrary, it suggests the dangers of that very conception: insofar as the philosopher loves the truth because he loves his own good, he runs the risk of confounding the object of his search with what is good for him, or the true with the useful. He would be like Hippothales, who supposes that he praises his beloved when he praises only himself, in as much as he praises the good that would be his if he captures his beloved (205d–e). Philosophy in such a case would not be a refuge from the illusion of phantom friends but would fall prey to a version of that same illusion. Philosophy cannot be a means of escaping

---

[36] Bolotin, *Plato's Dialogue on Friendship*, 169. See also David K. Glidden, "The *Lysis* on Loving One's Own," *Classical Quarterly*, 31 (1981), 57.

[37] Vlastos, "The Individual as an Object of Love in Plato," 10.

[38] Bolotin, "Response to Umphrey," 424.

illusion unless the philosopher's understanding of the world were informed by an experience of another that resists being reduced to his own desires and needs, and therefore cannot be understood simply as a means to his own ends.

Love alone cannot serve as this experience. To be sure, a lover needs and loves someone other than himself. As Hippothales' case illustrates, the lover can long for his beloved from a distance (see 207b), but he is also eager to capture him. His beloved might remain other or become his own. Unlike love, friendship is reciprocal. Of course, a potential friend might not have loved in return, but if he did not do so, he would not become a friend. One cannot become a friend unless another does so as well. As one's friend he is one's own, but he is also other, for one's friendship depends on his loving in return. Because friends do not therefore merge into one, they can be considered a pair. This is how Menexenus understands his relationship with Lysis. When Socrates first asks Menexenus which one of them is the older, he does not use Lysis' name (207b–c). Menexenus assumes that when Socrates refers to him and another, Lysis is the other. And Socrates knows, or at least suspects, that he can speak in that way to him and be understood. The boys do not hesitate to acknowledge they are friends when Socrates asks (207c). Yet Lysis finds his friend contentious, and Menexenus admits to Socrates that he and Lysis dispute (211a–b and 207c). The rivalry between friends, as Plato portrays existing between Lysis and Menexenus, results from and at the same time preserves their experience of their own as other, which is necessary for their being friends. Lysis is annoyed by Menexenus' contentiousness, but he would not find it so disconcerting if Menexenus were not his friend (see also 213d–e).

It is not, then, that philosophy serves as the true experience that friends seek, free of the illusions of friendship. Rather, philosophy must turn to the experience of friends – an experience of one's own as another who cannot be assimilated or subordinated. The experience of friends offers us access to a world that must be known rather than mastered, one that is not so radically different from ourselves that it must remain unknown. As we have seen, Socrates calls a friend a "possession," but then claims "to be erotically disposed to acquiring [or possessing] friends" (211e–212a). "Possessing" a friend is an ongoing activity. The argument that Socrates gives at this point in the *Lysis* – that our friends are phantom friends in light of the first friend in which all our friendships terminate – is therefore not the dialogue's deepest teaching about friendship.

Socrates uses a father's love for his son to illustrate the person who loves his friend for the sake of some further "first friend," who alone is truly a friend: like that person, the loving father cares for other things only for the sake of his son whom he "values more highly than all of his other possessions." Indeed, Socrates explains, if his son drank hemlock, he would value the wine that is its antidote, and even the vessel that contains the wine (219d–e). In Socrates' analogy, the father's love for the wine stands to love of his son as would love for a particular person to one's love for the first friend. On the other hand, the son also stands in Socrates' analogy to the "first friend," and thus the father loves him, in Vlastos' Kantian language, as an end in himself. Vlastos supposes that this merely highlights the mistake of loving a particular person for his own sake,[39] but the analogy, which appeals to the father's love of his son rather than criticizes it, also cautions against treating one's friends merely as vessels that bring one other goods. As Socrates elaborates this position concerning the "first friend," he argues that we love our friends on account of (*dia*) the bad for the sake (*heneka*) of the good. But when presenting the argument, Socrates strangely slips in the phrase that we love our friends "for the sake of" an enemy (220e).[40] Perhaps the good for whose sake we love our friends is an enemy, if in its pursuit we understand our friends as only means, thereby undermining the good we can obtain through friendship.

In order to produce the result that those whom we call our friends are only phantom friends, Socrates asks Menexenus whether the friend is a friend to someone "for the sake of nothing" or "for the sake of something" (218d). Given the alternatives, Menexenus of course says that a friend is a friend for the sake of something, and as Socrates leads the discussion to a further good for whose sake friends are loved, friends soon become only phantom friends, since we love them for the sake of some further good, or friend. But when Socrates poses his question, Menexenus admits that he "does not quite follow" Socrates (218e). Plato is issuing a warning. A third option is suppressed – the one that Vlastos looks for in Plato in vain – that we love our friend for his own sake.

---

[39] Vlastos, "The Individual as an Object of Love in Plato," 10 n. 23.
[40] Paul Shorey argues that Socrates slips away from the usage he has established in his argument for these prepositions (*dia* and *heneka*) and returns to ordinary Greek usage, where they are interchangeable, "The Alleged Fallacy in Plato's Lysis 220e, *Classical Philosophy* 25 (1930), 382. See discussion by Bolotin, *Plato's Dialogue on Friendship*, 175–76, Umphrey, "Eros and Thumos," 363–68; Bolotin, "Response to Umphrey," 424–28; and Pangle, *Aristotle and the Philosophy of Friendship*, 26–28.

Parents love their children when their children are not good, when they are stupid enough, for example, to drink poison. At the same time, children are not as good as their parents would like them to be. That is why parents punish their children (212a–213e), and why Lysis' parents set over him "a great many masters," among whom are teachers who rule over him (208c–d). Parents both love their children when they are not good, and also want their children to become good. Their love cannot be separated from their love of a good that those whom they love are yet to manifest and that they wish for them. They would like their children to be better than they are, and even help them by means of punishment and teaching to become so. Even parents, whose love of their children is most obviously a love of their own, love what is in part elusive and must be pursued. If we take parents as models of friends, as Socrates' examples encourage us to do, our love of another is of someone more or less on the way to becoming good, a process to which we attempt to contribute.

In his earlier discussion with Menexenus about whether the friend is the one who loves or is loved, Socrates nevertheless dismissed the parent–child relationship as a model for friendship, for parents love their children even when their children hate them (212a–213e). Whereas a beloved is not sufficiently his lover's own for their relationship to serve as a model for philosophy, a child is not sufficiently other from his parents for their relationship to do so. Children are extensions of their parents, through whom the parents preserve themselves (*Symposium* 206c–207a; Aristotle, *NE* 1161b22–24). Parents educate their children, but their memories are better served the better their children are. Just as the drama of the dialogue moves from the lover's inquiry about how to speak to his beloved to a discussion of friends, so too does Socrates drop the discussion about parents and children that Lysis asks him to repeat with Menexenus. He asks instead how one becomes the friend of another (212a).[41] Socrates is interested in those who become friends, rather than in those who are born friends, as children are born dear to their parents. One's own is more obviously other if it has not always been one's own, and if it might not always be one's own.

----

[41] In reference to Socrates' example of parents' love for their children, Benardete comments that of Socrates' examples of friends, this relation is "the simplest to understand," but on this model "the philosopher seems in danger of mistaking . . . the extension of himself in the beings for the disclosure of the beings themselves," *The Argument of the Action*, 213.

In introducing this prospect that our friends are only phantom friends, Socrates addresses both boys by name, "Woe is me, Lysis and Menexenus, I'm afraid that . . . we have come across some false arguments about the friend" (218c–d). Socrates thus reminds them of their friendship. He does so as well by now addressing them in the dual (218b), as he had not done since his earlier questions of them about their friendship (207c).[42] That is, Socrates highlights the contradiction between the argument that turns them into phantom friends and their own experience of each other. Again, he encourages them to think about their friendship, and how they might make sense of it.

ARE THE KINDRED FRIENDS?

If the one who is neither good nor bad loves the good, even if that good is the first friend in which all other friendships terminate, Socrates goes on to argue, we love the good on account of the bad. Therefore if the bad were out of the way, we would not love the good at all. The good is loved only as a remedy for the bad, as the sick person seeks the doctor and the medical art only because he is sick. "If that which is an enemy would go away," Socrates concludes, "[the good], as it seems, is no longer a friend to us" (220a). Even the good, in light of which all our friends are phantom friends, loses its status in this argument as anything more than a drug or remedy for our ills. Love of the good collapses into self-love.

In the absence of the bad, Socrates maintains, there will still be hunger and thirst and other desires that are neither good nor bad. Then we would desire what we are in want of, what we are deprived of. We are deprived of that which is our own, or of that to which we are akin (221e). But if one is kin to another, that other is kin to him. Friendship is reciprocal. The dialogue has circled back to Menexenus' initial answer that when one loves both are friends (212b). Insofar as the friend is one to whom one is akin, that answer is not as mistaken as it first appears.

Socrates does not forget about Hippothales, who still lurks in the background, for he generalizes his account of friends as one's "kin" to all desire and love. The beloved, akin to the lover, with respect to his soul, or to some character or aspect of his soul, will become his lover's

---

[42] In his narration, Socrates also speaks of them in the dual, reminding his listener(s) as well of the boys' friendship (218b–c).

friend (222a). Socrates captures friendship for the lover. If Hippothales loves Lysis, the two are soulmates and Lysis will become his friend in return. When Socrates draws this conclusion, he reports, the boys "barely nod," and Hippothales "radiates all sorts of colors" (222b). Unlike the boys' previous responses throughout the dialogue, this one is not verbal. They are both literally silent, as was Lysis when a moment before, Socrates brought his argument about friends to bear on lover and beloved (222a). At that point, Menexenus had agreed with Socrates, perhaps not immediately seeing the implications for those pursued by lovers. Now they are equally hesitant, for they "barely" nod. Perhaps they have become more reflective, more aware that they do not know what to say about friendship, even though they think that they are friends. Their hesitation is a sign to us to hesitate as well.

Socrates presents this argument in abstraction from good and bad, but if love is love of one's own of which one is deprived and in need, one's relief from need is good.[43] The good is what satisfies desire. The cause of affection does not lie in the friend whom we love, or in the object of desire. Rather, as Socrates says when discussing this possibility, "desire is the cause of friendship" (221d). The good is good because it is our own, because it is what we desire (see *Euthyphro* 10a). This move concedes much to the speech Plato attributes to Aristophanes in the *Symposium*, where love is love of one's own, one's other half, of the one of whom one has been deprived.[44] Although Socrates does not trace our deprivation to the gods, and thus removes Aristophanes' inference that the gods are hostile to our pursuing our desires (*Symposium* 190d and 193a), Socrates has recourse in his final attempt to explain friends in the *Lysis* to Aristophanes' explanation of the need underlying love (*erōs*). Although Diotima objects to that understanding, as we have seen, Socrates' return to that possibility here indicates that we cannot understand an individual merely in terms of the good qualities that he shares with others. While Plato does not give Aristophanes an opportunity to defend his speech in an exchange with Socrates due to Alcibiades' abrupt entrance, he gives some credence to Aristophanes' position by bringing Alcibiades into the dialogue and sitting him by

---

[43] See discussions by Gonzalez, "Plato's *Lysis*," 81–83; Pangle, *Aristotle and the Philosophy of Friendship*, 34; Rhodes, "Platonic *Philia* and Political Order," 41–42; and "Versenyi, "Plato's *Lysis*," 196.

[44] Benardete, *The Argument of the Action*, 227–28; Bolotin, *Plato's Dialogue on Friendship*, 183; Friedlander, *Plato: The Dialogues, First Period*, 103; Ludwig, *Eros and Polis*, 212–14; and Price, *Love and Friendship in Plato and Aristotle*, 12.

Socrates' side. Alcibiades seems as unique as Socrates. There is weight on Martha Nussbaum's side in her argument against Vlastos and her understanding of "the individual as the object of love in Plato."

The boys' discomfort with the argument should make us wary of a confusion that throws a young boy into his lover's arms. Socrates does not rest with the argument that friends are simply those who are our own, an argument that reduces the good to what we desire. Socrates claims that it is "ridiculous" to ask what would be the case if the bad ceases to be (221a), and in short order demolishes the argument that the kindred are friends. Who are the kindred? he asks. If we go beyond our initial connection to our parents and our homes for an understanding of our own, we must find some way, in other words, to explain why what is our own is our own. We must have recourse to the good. We desire our own to be good, whether it be our own limbs that we are ready to sacrifice if we think they are harmful, to use Diotima's example (*Symposium* 205e), or parents who punish and educate their children out of love for them, to use examples from the *Lysis* (208c–e and 213a). There is also weight in Vlastos' position on Plato.

Hippothales' triumph, as we might expect, is therefore short-lived. Like the embracing half-beings of Aristophanes' speech (*Symposium* 191a–c), the discussion must move on. And while Socrates says to the gathering that if the kin are not friends, he "no longer know[s] what to say," he intends to question one of the others present, as he reveals in the narration of the event (222e). And he no longer tells his hearer(s) what effect the argument has on Hippothales. In fact, Socrates does not mention him again as he recounts the end of the dialogue. The conclusion of the investigation leaves Hippothales as distant from his beloved as when Socrates first met him.

WHO MIGHT FRIENDS BE?

Near the end of the dialogue, Socrates summarizes the arguments discussed and rejected, including those who are loved, those who love, those alike, those unlike, the good, and the kindred (222e). Bolotin nevertheless deduces a teaching on friendship from the *Lysis* by combining what he regards as the two most weighty arguments – the good are friends and the kindred are friends. He argues that "beings who are sufficient or good for themselves might be considered akin to their own good – and this means primarily the virtue of their own souls." While he admits that this "seems to leave no room for reciprocity," he also suggests that the good is "in 'need' of a needy being in order for it to be useful or good."[45] There is a reciprocity of sorts between an individual who loves his own good, say his own virtue, and the good that he loves. Bolotin thus explains even Socrates' move to reciprocity at the end of the dialogue in a way that is consistent with the view he attributes to Plato, that one is primarily a friend to oneself. The kindred are friends, for an individual and his own good are kindred.

Bolotin does acknowledge that those who have become good, "whose more or less lasting self-sufficiency includes the perfection of wisdom," might "being kindred, desire and enjoy one another's company," even "without needing one another, and longing for one another in order to become whole." Theirs might be "among the purest, if not the deepest, of 'friendships.'"[46] Their friendship is pure because it is not selfish, for these friends do not need each other. And while each may delight in the company of the other, they can take it or leave it. Bolotin admits this is friendship "only in a limited sense."[47] The relation of these "friends" is less deep, presumably, than a human being's love of the good for himself. In the end, self-love characterizes even the deepest recesses of the soul, including that of the philosopher, who is less deceived by "phantom" friends than others. The philosopher most of all, then, is a true friend to himself, as he more clear-mindedly than others seeks his own good.[48]

---

[45] Bolotin, *Plato's Dialogue on Friendship*, 192–93. He thus follows Friedlander, who refers to "the love of *sophia* that is returned by *sophia*," and "the reciprocal relation" between the soul and the good. *Plato: The Dialogues, First Period*, 96 and 101.

[46] Since conjoining these two types of friendship is, as Bolotin admits, "accidental," Umphrey argues that "Bolotin's conjunctive account" "puts one and one together and gets two when he wants one" and thus fails to save "the whole phenomenon of friendship." Umphrey does not think it can be saved, and argues that the two conceptions of friendship are at variance with each other, "Eros and Thumos," 369–70. See also Gonzalez, "Plato's *Lysis*," 83.

[47] Bolotin, *Plato's Dialogue on Friendship*, 194–95. For further comment on whether Plato thought that two non-needy beings could be friends, see Pangle, *Aristotle and the Philosophy of Friendship*, 33; Hadon, "Friendship in Plato's *Lysis*," 352–55; and the "Pohlenz-von Arnim Controversy," summarized by Bolotin, *Plato's Dialogue on Friendship*, 201–25.

[48] For another understanding of the relation between love of the good and love of one's own in the *Lysis*, see Geier, *Plato's Erotic Thought*, esp. 115–35. In his analysis, as in Bolotin's, friendship between a human being and his good that he lacks and pursues is prior to that between human beings and is essentially different from and superior to it (see, e.g., 130–34 and 142). So too Gonzalez, who finds reciprocity in the relation between Socrates and the boys insofar as they "[seek] together the good that belongs to all of them but of which all of them are deprived," understands this to mean that non-reciprocal love is prior to reciprocal love, "Plato's *Lysis*," 86.

The *Lysis* fails to produce an acceptable definition of the friend time after time in the dialogue, however, because Socrates refuses to abandon friendship as a reciprocal human relationship, rooted in need. The need friends have for each other, for example, disqualified the argument that friends are likes. Nor does Socrates give up his search for reciprocity when the argument that the friend is one who loves such things as wine, gymnastics, or wisdom avoids the contradiction that one's friend might hate in return and therefore be one's enemy. Rather, he suggests that the discussion is "on the wrong track." And when Lysis jumps in to agree, Socrates expresses his approval (212d–213e). Moreover, it is because Socrates counts himself with Lysis and Menexenus as friends that he is so perplexed when they cannot say what a friend is (223a). Any understanding of friend that does not give its due to this perplexity is inadequate.

When Socrates first turns to the "neither good nor bad," he mentions the possibility that those who are neither good nor bad might be friends with others who are also neither good nor bad. He dismisses this possibility without discussion, since he has already shown that like could not be a friend to its like (216e; see also 222c). One who is neither good nor bad is, strictly speaking, identical to any other who is neither good nor bad since each is defined only by what it is not. When Socrates speaks of those who are neither good nor bad, he speaks in the neuter. But when he speaks of "us," who love the good, he says that we "are in the middle of the bad and the good" (220d). If we are in the middle of the bad and good, both are present to us, and we cannot be understood apart from them. The bad is present to someone "in the middle" without making him bad; if it did, he would not desire the good. After all, Socrates explains, something can be present to something else without determining its character, just as white dye rubbed onto his interlocutor's blond hair would not make it white. His example is revealing: his blond hair would be neither black nor white (217d), not because it has white lead rubbed on it, but because it is blond. We are not as undefined as Socrates' language of the "neither/nor" suggests, even if one day our blond hair will become white.

Socrates earlier asked Menexenus to compare himself with Lysis in point of age, birth, beauty, and property, and intended to ask him about their respective virtues as well. When we look at Menexenus and Lysis, we see those who are neither simply good nor simply bad. Rather they are mixed beings, who are more or less nobly born, and just, and wise, as assumed by Socrates' questions. Their being friends, as these comparisons indicate, cannot be understood apart from their attributes, including their virtues. We cannot know them by some unchanging identity or form, underlying their changing attributes, something neither good nor bad, for it is their attributes that identify and form them.[49] When Socrates at the beginning of the *Lysis* does not recognize Lysis' name, one of those present claims that Socrates cannot be "ignorant of his form (*eidos*), for this alone is enough to know him by." Form is used here to mean his appearance, what can be seen of him. Socrates wants to know other things about him as well, for he immediately asks, "whose son [is he]?" (204e). When *eidos* is used again in the *Lysis*, it is in connection with the soul rather than the body, and Socrates associates it with the soul's character (*ethos*) and ways (*tropoi*) (222a).

Socrates' other model for how something can be present to something else – hair that has become white through aging – is also an inadequate model for understanding ourselves. Blond hair will inevitably become white, in the normal process of aging, whereas we do not become better in time through necessity. We cannot be reduced to our attributes. On the basis of the *Lysis*, at least, Plato was not a Platonist, Vlastos to the contrary. Plato shows us who Lysis and Menexenus are not simply from their attributes, which they compare, but also from their activity of comparing. We have seen their relation not simply in their relative ages and nobility, for example, but also in what they say about themselves – in their disputing, and in their laughing together, and in their admission that they are friends. It is self-awareness, according to Socrates, that makes one unlike someone so "stupid and senseless" that he doesn't know his own ignorance, but also unlike someone, perhaps a god, already wise (218a–b). We know that we can know more than we do, and that we can become better – and worse – than we are. It is our self-awareness that puts us in the middle. It is a sign of our freedom.[50] And although our freedom makes friendship contingent – for friends must admit that they are friends, they must be willing – it also makes it possible.

Moreover, if friends are present to each other as white dye is present to hair on which it is rubbed, they would never truly touch each other;

---

[49] For a good analysis of the differences between Lysis and Menexenus as they are revealed in the action of the dialogue, see Tessitore, "Plato's *Lysis*," 119–20. Benardete notes the differences between the friends Hippothales and Ctesippus. *The Argument of the Action*, 201. See also Geier, *Plato's Erotic Thought*, 87–90, and Robert G. Hoerber, "Character Portrayal in Plato's *Lysis*," *Classical Journal*, 41 (1945–46): 272–73.

[50] See also Davis' analysis of the problems with understanding a human being solely in terms of his attributes. *The Autobiography of Philosophy*, 75–76.

their union would be only superficial. Because they would be merely rubbed onto the other, they could rub each other off. If friends, on the other hand, are present to each other as white is present to hair due to aging, there would be no space between them, no separation, and no freedom. This is why both the naturalists and the poets mentioned earlier fail to capture the truth about friends. For the naturalists, white dye is sufficient to make hair white, for nothing eludes the material causation of necessity. For the poets, in contrast, not even aging can make hair white, for it could always be otherwise, as Athena's transformation of Odysseus indicates. Friends must be able to go away, as Lysis and Menexenus do at the end of the dialogue, while able to come back, as Menexenus does earlier. The *Lysis* is the only Platonic dialogue in which one of the discussants goes away and comes back to take part in the conversation. And it is the only dialogue explicitly about friends.

It is appropriate that Socrates' initial conversation with Menexenus about him and Lysis be left in the middle. Of course, this may seem accidental, as many things about friendships are, for Menexenus is called away. But when Menexenus returns, Socrates does not return to the conversation that had been interrupted. If Menexenus' discussion about Lysis and himself is to continue, it must be with Lysis himself (see 211a–b). Socrates of course could push his questions further, but at some point reflecting on their friendship must become something they do without Socrates. Only if friends incorporate into their own friendship the matchmaking in which Socrates engages, only if their friendship survives Socrates' going away, is friendship possible. One must ultimately become one's own matchmaker in order to be matched. To acquire a good friend requires becoming a good friend. Socrates thus asks not how one captures a beloved, as a lover might, but how one becomes the friend of another (212a).

Lysis and Menexenus, it is believed, are the youngest interlocutors in the Platonic corpus. It would not be correct to assume that their youth casts doubt on their experience of friendship on the ground that being so young they could not have had extensive experience of anything. Rather, their youth shows that the experience of friendship, even of boys so young, manifests in a simple way what friends are and what Socrates himself seeks.[51] Friendship at its best is not experienced by two more or

---

[51] See discussions in Bolotin, *Plato's Dialogue on Friendship*, 67; Hans-Georg Gadamer, *Dialogue and Dialectic*, trans. P. Christopher Smith (New Haven: Yale University Press, 1980), 6; Gonzalez, "Plato's *Lysis*," 84; and Scott, *Plato's Socrates as Educator*, 52. It is

less self-sufficient beings who enjoy each other's company in a pure but not very deep relationship because it is free of self-interest. The satisfaction of such beings lies elsewhere than in each other, and they are similar in their self-sufficiency. Such "friends" are therefore neither sufficiently each other's own nor sufficiently other to give each other an experience of his own as other, or of another as his own. It is this experience that supports the pursuit of truth, suggesting both the necessity and possibility of that pursuit, necessary because one's own is experienced as other, possible because another is experienced as one's own. Friendship itself cultivates both awareness of lack and belonging. It therefore offers support for our complex identities as human beings and citizens.

FRIENDLY COMMUNITIES

Even if the *Lysis'* inconclusiveness is appropriate to its subject matter, the dialogue seems to end on an ominous note. Although Socrates has in mind to continue the discussion with one of the older fellows there, his plans are interrupted when Lysis' and Menexenus' pedagogues arrive to take them home. Pedagogues, literally "ones who lead boys," were typically slaves entrusted with bringing boys to and from school and watching over them. Socrates and the others, he recounts, try to drive the pedagogues away. He may intend to talk to someone else, but he appears to want the two boys to remain to hear what is said. When their confrontation with the pedagogues is unsuccessful, Socrates reports, "we dissolved the gathering" (223b). Since "dissolved" is *dielusamen* in Greek, the *Lysis* ends as its name foreshadows, in *lusis*, a dissolution. The shuffle at the end appears as a confrontation between Socrates and the city, at least as represented by the fathers or their representatives, the pedagogues.[52] That is, the fathers reassert their authority over their children, and Socrates' pursuit of the question of the friend is at least for the moment thwarted.

The break-up of the gathering, however, does not necessarily suggest a threat to philosophy. The pedagogues do not intend to break up the

---

also the case that being so young, Lysis would be less likely to have had contact with his lover. Plato can use Hippothales' love of him to indicate more clearly the alienating character of love (*erōs*), as opposed to friendship. At the same time, a young beloved seems more vulnerable, easier to "capture." Plato thus can use Lysis' youth to suggest as well the potentially despotic character of love.

[52] For a version of this interpretation, see Bolotin, *Plato's Dialogue on Friendship*, 198.

meeting, or even to take the boys away from a conversation with Socrates; they intend only to take the boys home. They are merely doing their job – one that Lysis alluded to earlier (211b). The boys' going away does not preclude their coming back for further discussion, as Menexenus did earlier. Going away and coming back is in fact characteristic of friends, for they are not as inseparable as Aristophanes' lovers wish they could be. Going away and coming back reflects the releasing/acquiring character of friendship discussed in this chapter. Socrates earlier imagined another conversation with Lysis at a future date (211b), and readers of the Platonic corpus know that Menexenus returns on at least two occasions – in the dialogue bearing his name and on the day of Socrates' death (*Phaedo* 59b).[53]

Socrates says to the boys as they are leaving that the three of them – "I an old man and you" – have become ridiculous, for the others "will go away and say that we believe ourselves to be friends – for I place myself among you – but have not been able to discover what a friend is" (223b). Just when the representatives of the boys' fathers effect the end of the gathering, Socrates envisions another larger community becoming aware of the dilemmas of friendship they have been unable to resolve. Those who have been listening to their conversation at the palaestra, Socrates imagines, will speak about Socrates' and his interlocutors' comic state: the contradiction between their belief about themselves and their inability to articulate exactly what it means. Aristophanes had some years earlier in his play the *Clouds* prompted Athens to laugh at Socrates for his pretensions to wisdom, although Aristophanes' criticism found its way to the Athenian law court, where it was no longer a laughing matter (*Apology* 19c; see *Euthyphro* 3c; cf. *Gorgias* 486a–b and 511a–b).

That the relation between the philosopher and the political community remain a friendly one depends on the success of the very view of friendship that arises from the *Lysis*. Inasmuch as friendship does not disappear into philosophy, and philosophy maintains itself by taking friendship as its standard, philosophy defines itself in terms of ordinary human experience. There can be no radical separation between

---

[53] The contentious Menexenus (211b), who we know from this dialogue is willing to converse, appears to become like Lysis, "fond of listening" (206d), at least to Socrates. In the *Phaedo*, he is among those present for Socrates' last conversation but who do not speak. In the *Menexenus*, he listens to a long speech delivered by Socrates – a version of a funeral oration. For speculation that as a result of this dialogue, Menexenus becomes a friend of Socrates, see Bolotin, *Plato's Dialogue on Friendship*, 186.

philosophers and others. In contrast to love, which can remain alienated from its object or lead to its conquest, friendship is a model for a political community in which some things are held in common, while others remain private (Aristotle, *Politics* 1260b36–61a9). If members of political communities in the manner of friends say "not mine" as well as "mine" of one another, and philosophers say "mine" as well as "not mine" of their fellow citizens, political communities would allow philosophers space to philosophize, and philosophers would understand what they had in common with others. Such friendly relations might be fostered by publicizing such demonstrations as the *Lysis*, whether we understand that demonstration as Socrates' attempt to rescue a boy from the pursuit of a lover or as a demonstration that the fulfillment of love lies not in capture but in friendship. Only then might laughter remain a friendly reminder of ignorance – for both Socrates and his interlocutors – rather than a prelude to inevitable or tragic conflict. The *Lysis* does not conclude simply with the dissolution of the gathering, for Socrates proceeds to tell the story after it happens. He does not simply rely on others in the palaestra to deliver his message to the city; he will help out as well, and he knows the whole story of the conversation.

It is to his anonymous listener(s), as we have seen, that Socrates reveals what those at the palaestra would not know – what Lysis whispers to Socrates, for example, or that Socrates sees the effect of the discussion on Hippothales. Being there in this instance does not yield as full an understanding of events as hearing about them from Socrates (see *Euthydemus* 271a ff.). It is only in his narration, moreover, that Socrates mentions his intention to question someone else just before the discussion ends. Because the gathering breaks up before Socrates turns to another interlocutor, only the one(s) listening to Socrates' story of his conversation – and of course the readers of Plato's dialogue – learn that Socrates has further discussion in mind. We see a middle, whereas those present see only an end.

On the other hand, Socrates does not tell his listener everything that those present would know. In narrating several parts of his discussion, Socrates neglects to identify whether his interlocutor is Lysis or Menexenus, although he refers to his blond hair (e.g., 217a–218b and 219c–221e). Had we been there, we could have seen which of the two had blond hair. Of course, had we been there, or even if the dialogue were written as a drama rather than a narration, we would know which of the two boys answered Socrates' questions. As narrator, Socrates makes the conversation accessible to his listener(s), but he also separates him (or them) from it. He (or they) know only what Socrates tells. But even if a dialogue is dramatic rather than narrated, so that there is no middle man who reports it, the dialogue reveals only what Plato tells us. Narration thus makes clear the truth about all Platonic dialogues – that they conceal as well as reveal. Consequently, they can never become ours by a process as automatic as hair becomes white through aging.

Plato requires in his reader one who is, as Hippothales says of Lysis, "fond of listening" (206d). If someone merely listened, however, what he heard might go in one ear and out the other, or he might absorb it without understanding. Apollodorus, who memorizes and repeats Socratic conversations (*Symposium* 173c), and Phaedrus, who delights in hearing speeches and is trying to memorize Lysias' (*Phaedrus* 242b; 243b; and 228b), might serve as examples. Lysis, Socrates indicates, must be more than fond of listening, for he asks whether Lysis can be made to converse with him (206c). Because Platonic dialogues require interpretation, they require a reader who is not merely fond of listening but who can be made to converse. When interpreted, Platonic writing is neither merely rubbed on nor perfectly rubbed in.[54] Platonic dialogues can be present to such a reader only in the manner of a friend, for they become his own through his act of interpreting, and yet they can never be simply his own inasmuch as they depend on the author's text for its "meaning" or "intent" (*Phaedrus* 228d). Not every interpretation is as valid as another.

At the end of the *Symposium*, Plato acknowledges this dependence by leaving the report of Socrates' discussion with the two poets to a narrator too sleepy at the time to catch more than its drift. And Plato has his Socrates concur with his decision by not volunteering to report the particulars of the conversation to Apollodorus when the latter checked with him about other details of the evening (*Symposium* 173b). By calling attention to the incompleteness of what his narrator reports, Plato also calls attention to the artfulness of his own poetry. If Alcibiades' speech about Socrates is incomplete, inasmuch as he fails to understand Socratic wisdom, as I have argued, Plato's report is incomplete precisely because he does understand. Socratic wisdom knows that wisdom does not simply flow from the fuller to the emptier, but can be only acquired by one who plays a part in the inquiry. Because Plato does not reproduce the dialogue between Socrates and the poets for us, he allows us to

[54] Davis notes that when Socrates' interlocutor does not understand, Socrates "seems to rub him with an argument that he does not absorb." *The Autobiography of Philosophy*, 75.

do so for ourselves. That is, he reproduces the dialogue for us in the only way possible.

We can suspect from Plato's portrayal of Apollodorus that he does not draw the anonymous listeners of the *Symposium* into any conversation about the erotic speeches he recounts (see, e.g., *Symposium* 173d). We have no evidence that Phaedrus delivered his message to Lysias, or Socrates his to Isocrates. And we can only wonder if Socrates draws his anonymous listener(s) of his narration of the *Lysis* into conversation. We have no way of knowing. But this is as it should be, just as it is fitting that Socrates leaves Menexenus' exploration of his friendship with Lysis to the friends themselves. Friendship as it emerges in the *Lysis* requires experience, whether it be of a friend or of a Platonic dialogue.[55] In his relation to his readers, Plato demonstrates how friendship can be translated into a larger community, one that transcends any given pair of friends and therewith the limits of any particular time and place. The community formed by Plato and his readers through his writing, mediated by Socrates, gives readers through their activity of interpreting the experience of another as their own and of their own as other that is essential to friendship. Such a community therefore serves not as an alternative or substitute for political communities but as their standard.

[55] Christopher W. Tindale argues that the inconclusive character of the *Lysis* points to the inadequacy of any definition of the friend to capture "living reality [of friendship]," and finds support in Plato's Seventh Letter, where Plato refers to "the weakness of speech" (*logos*) (342e–343a). "Plato's *Lysis*: A Reconsideration," *Apeiron* 18 (1984): 107. See also Mooney's conclusion, "Plato's Theory of Love," 155. Although I also emphasize the importance of the experience of friends in any understanding of friendship, this experience requires talking about and reflecting on friends. Moreover, Socrates intends to continue speaking to others present when they are interrupted. The *Lysis* does not reject speech in favor of experience. Rather, it suggests their inseparability for human beings.

5

Socratic Philosophizing

If the community expressed through friendship serves for Plato as a model for both philosophy and politics, as I have argued, why does he often present the philosopher as transcending political life, or even human life altogether? Perhaps the most striking of such presentations involves Socrates' description in the *Phaedo* of philosophy as "the practice of dying and being dead" (64a).[1] At the beginning of that dialogue, set on the last day of Socrates' life and concluding with his death, Socrates explains to his companions why he does not fear death: since the soul's bondage to the body – and to the senses – prevents clear understanding of the truth, only with the separation of his soul from his body might a philosopher find the knowledge that he seeks. Thus it is by dying, if at all, that a human being could become wise (64a–68b). Socrates even claims that anyone serious about philosophy should desire to follow him by dying as quickly as he can (61b–c). Philosophy, by this account, requires removing oneself from embodied, human life,

---

[1] Socrates' insistence in the *Republic* that the philosopher must leave the cave in order to know the truth (*Republic* 514a ff.), and his contrast in the *Theaetetus* between the philosophic way of life and that of the law courts (*Theaetetus* 172c–176a), also come readily to mind. On the former, see my discussions in "The *Republic*'s Two Alternatives: Philosopher-Kings and Socrates," *Political Theory* 12 (May 1984): 252–74, and *Socrates and the Political Community*, 118–19. For a good discussion of the ways in which the drama of the *Theaetetus* qualifies this description of philosophy, see Paul Stern, "The Philosophic Importance of Political Life: On the Digression in Plato's *Theaetetus*," *American Political Science Review* 96, no. 2 (June 2002): 275–89. As Jacob Howland comments, Socrates' "ability to describe both philosophers and clever orators suggests that he is a member of neither of the choruses he describes." *The Paradox of Political Philosophy* (Lanham, MD: Rowman and Littlefield, 1998), 60. References in parentheses in this chapter, unless otherwise noted, are to Plato's *Phaedo*. Translations from the Greek are my own, although I have relied on the translation of Brann, Kalkavage, and Salem.

not only from one's political community, but also from one's friends – a point with which Simmias and Cebes reproach Socrates (63a). The *Phaedo* thus seems to contradict the view of friendship and philosophy that I have developed in this book.

Try as he might, however, Socrates cannot remove the sting of death, which Plato captures in the tears of Socrates' companions at the end of the dialogue. And the poignant words that Plato gives to Socrates' wife, Xanthippe, at the beginning of the dialogue echo throughout: "Now's the last time your companions will speak to you, and you to them" (60a). Moreover, when Socrates has the opportunity to hasten his death, he refuses to do so. A guard sends the warning that he should converse as little as possible, since discussion produces heat that slows down the action of the poison. Indeed, the guard says, some have had to drink several additional drafts. Socrates ignores his advice, however, and continues the conversation (63d–e). Socrates, in fact, is more concerned in the *Phaedo* with "keeping the argument alive" than with hurrying to death, and it is here that he argues against "the hatred of speeches," or misology, for the death of the argument is the greatest cause for mourning. Keeping the argument alive – not death – is the condition for philosophy. Socrates withdraws the phrase "being dead" when for a second time he refers to philosophy as "the practice of dying" (67e). Philosophy may be the practice of dying in the sense of distancing oneself from what is one's own in order to question it, or as Socrates says "withdrawing" or "standing back" from the body (64e), but Diotima describes philosophic Love as at the same time "dying" and "flourishing and living," for it is "in-between" due to its dual origins. Poverty connects Love to death, and Resource connects Love to life (*Symposium* 203e).

In the *Phaedo*, when Socrates is about to die, he attempts to leave something of his own experience of philosophy behind with his companions, for he tells them of his search as a young man for answers to his questions, and his recognition of the need to undertake a new way of philosophizing. It is this philosophic turn to which Strauss refers when he credits Socrates with being the founder of political philosophy.[2] As Cicero says, whereas previous philosophers investigated the things in the heavens, Socrates brings philosophy into the cities and the homes, and inquires into good and bad (*Tusculan Disputations* v.10; see also

---

[2] Leo Strauss, *Natural Right and History* (Chicago: University of Chicago Press, 1953), 120. See Catherine H. Zuckert's excellent discussion of the stages of "The Socratic Turn," *History of Political Thought* 25, no. 2 (Summer 2004): 189–219.

Xenophon, *Memorabilia* I. I. 11–16 and Aristotle, *Metaphysics* 987b1–4). In this final chapter, I shall examine Socrates' turn from the way of previous philosophy to his own distinctive way of inquiry. Socrates reminds his companions on the day of his death, I shall argue, not of the alienation of philosophy, but of its inseparability from human and political life. It is fitting to conclude our exploration of Plato's dialogues on love and friendship with consideration of the *Phaedo* because it, more than any other Platonic dialogue, portrays Socrates together with his friends (see 58c).[3]

SOCRATES' YOUTHFUL SEARCH FOR CAUSE

Having given a number of arguments for the immortality of the soul, and now facing yet one more objection from Cebes, Socrates "paused for a long time, examining something within himself" (95e).[4] Instead of directly addressing Cebes' concerns about the soul's perishing at the time of death, Socrates tells his companions about his own experiences in seeking "the cause of generation and destruction." As a young man, he recounts, he "was wondrously desirous of that wisdom they call inquiry into nature" – "to know the causes of each thing, why each thing comes to be, and why it perishes, and why it is." He raises such questions as: Is it by some action of heat or cold that life is generated? Is it by blood, or air, or fire, that we think (96a–b)? Socrates' initial questions are not simply about nature, but about the human soul, insofar as they seek the cause of life and the cause of thinking.[5] The Delphic "know thyself" remains in Socrates' account the beginning of his philosophic inquiry.

Becoming confused as he pursues these questions, Socrates admits, he loses the knowledge he thought he had before, knowledge in fact that seems clear to everyone – for example, that by eating we grow, that a tall man is taller by a head than a short one, that ten is more than eight by two, and that a two-foot length is greater than a one-foot length by half of itself. He no longer thinks that he understands, he recounts, what

---

[3] This is so much the case that the narrator Phaedo notes the absence of Plato when he describes the group who were present for the dialogue: "Plato, I think was sick" (59b).

[4] My reading of the *Phaedo* has been guided by Ronna Burger, *The Phaedo: A Platonic Labyrinth* (New Haven: Yale University Press, 1984), and Paul Stern, *Socratic Rationalism and Political Philosophy* (Albany: State University of New York Press, 1993).

[5] Burger, *The Phaedo*, 136; Stern, *Socratic Rationalism*, 109; and Davis, "Socrates' Pre-Socratism," 560.

happens when one is added to one; whether it is the one added that
becomes two or the one to which it is added that becomes two, or
whether each of them together become two. He wonders how it is that
each when separate is one and not two, but when brought together they
become two (96a–97b).

Socrates' questions about number can be asked of the body and soul,
whose relation Socrates and his companions discuss in the *Phaedo*. When
a human being comes into being, does a body become two – that is, itself
and something else, a body that is ensouled or animated? Or does the
thing added become two – that is, itself and something else, a soul that is
embodied? Or is it each of them together that becomes two? Socrates'
third possibility highlights the emergence, indeed generation, of something new, which cannot be reduced to the parts that compose it. Socrates
proceeds to report his wonder that division can produce the same result
as addition: when ones are brought together, or added to each other,
they become two, but when two are divided, or one subtracted from the
other, they also become two (97a–b). By implication, birth is no more
explicable than death. In this light, one can hear in Socrates' initial
questions of Phaedrus – where do you come from, and where are you
going – an expression of this mystery. They are questions to which we,
like Phaedrus, can provide only limited answers. And although Socrates
is eager to follow Phaedrus in order to hear Lysias' speech, it is the one
who sees naturally into the dialectical processes of collection and division,
he later tells Phaedrus, whose tracks he would follow as if they were a
god's (*Phaedrus* 266b–c).

As a youth, however, searching for answers, Socrates hears someone
reading from a book of Anaxagoras that Mind arranges and causes all
things. He supposes that this means that things are arranged for the
best, and that he has found a teacher "to his taste," literally, "after his
own mind." He expects Anaxagoras, he recounts, to explain the cause
and necessity of everything being as it is, in terms of "what is best for
each thing and the good common to all" (97c–98b). If there is a good
for each, and a good for all, and if Mind arranges all things for the
best, there would be no conflict between the good for each and the
good for all. "Teleology cannot treat a part," as Burger says, "except as
part of a whole."[6] The young Socrates, who places "wondrous hope" in
Anaxagoras (98b), is content to read the philosopher's writing: if there
is a good in common for all, there is one speech appropriate to

---

[6] Burger, *The Phaedo*, 140.

everyone. But then we have seen him admit in the *Symposium* that as a young man he, like Agathon, supposed that Love is both beautiful and good.

Socrates discovers upon reading Anaxagoras that rather than explaining how all things are arranged for the best, Anaxagoras makes no use of Mind or intelligence at all, but understands material things, such as air, ether, and water, as causes. He gives, it turns out, not an account of things in terms of what is best, but an account in terms of material causation. Like Aristophanes in his *Symposium* speech, Anaxagoras offers no wholeness that satisfies human longing. After promising a world without Poverty, Anaxagoras allows no room for Resource. He is in need of Diotima. Whereas Socrates seeks from Anaxagoras an explanation of how "the good binds together and holds together all things" (99c), and finds in his books nothing that binds, Diotima explains that it is the daemonic, such as Love, that lying between human and god "binds together the whole itself" (*Symposium* 202e). Although the daemon Love is neither beautiful nor good, he desires what he lacks. That is why he can be a binder.

Anaxagoras' account of cause, Socrates continues, implies that Socrates' bones and sinews are the causes of his sitting in prison, and voice and air are the causes of their conversing. This view ignores what in fact are the causes – that it seemed better to the Athenians that they condemn him, Socrates says, and that it seemed better to him to stay and pay the penalty (98c–99a). Human beings are the ones who act according to what seems to them good, or at least better than other alternatives.

Whereas a theory that Mind arranges all things understands human beings (who have intentions and purposes) to be the model for the whole, the account that Anaxagoras actually gives reduces human beings to the material causation of non-human nature. Non-human nature becomes a model for what is human.[7] Both materialism and teleology seek a non-contradictory account of the whole, or one principle or cause that explains both the human and the non-human. The former sees merely an animated body, and finds no good apart from the necessary. The other sees merely an embodied soul, and the good becomes necessary. Both see the unsatisfactory character of leaving things at two, and consequently make them into one, while closing off the possibility that there might be two that form a whole. Socrates thus comes to understand what

---

[7] Burger, *The Phaedo*, 142.

is wrong with both the teleological account of the world that Anaxagoras promises and the material account that Anaxagoras gives. Whereas "mind" disappears in Anaxagoras' account of the world, it is Socrates' "mind" that is pleased when he first hears about Anaxagoras' teaching. The whole must include the human. At the end of the *Phaedrus*, Socrates prays to Pan, a half-goat, half-human being, who serves as a visible image of a whole whose disparate parts cannot be reduced to each other. The teleologists as well as the materialists "rationalize" the tales of such monsters. It is appropriate that Socrates' perplexity about himself prevents him from doing so (*Phaedrus* 229c), for rationalization would require Socrates to understand himself wholly as a beast with no share in community, or as a gentler being sharing in a divine lot.

When Socrates presents the human pursuit of the good, he gives the example of his sitting in prison. Although he insists on the difference between the necessary conditions and the true causes, he gives two causes, not one. He is there because of what seems better to the Athenians – that he be executed – and because of what seems better to himself – accepting the punishment they have imposed on him. In this case, both causes contribute to the same result – Socrates is about to die. His example points not merely to this agreement between himself and the Athenians, but also to the conflict between them: the Athenians are executing Socrates. Socrates' philosophic life, which has led to his trial and execution, makes visible the fact that the city too is divided against itself. It is not simply that the city is at odds with Socrates, but that the city is almost equally divided for and against his execution, as Socrates emphasizes in court when he expresses his wonder that the number of votes in his favor was so close to the number against him (*Apology* 36a). The presence of Socrates within the city, and the city's need to respond to him, make visible its "Pan-like" character, for it has parts that are not in harmony. Although Socrates delivers his defense speech to the city as a whole, he addresses his final speech, once he has heard the verdict and penalty, first to those who voted for his execution and then to those who voted for his acquittal (*Apology* 39e–41c and 41c–42a).

It is therefore not the case that one simply finds among human beings the ends or purposes that Socrates sought in nature as a whole, or that human life is directed toward the good as the rest of nature is not. It is rather that the difference between human life and the rest of nature is reflected in human life itself. By investigating human concerns, Socrates inquires into nature. We can know that human beings seek the good, but we do not know the good. Socrates highlights our lack of knowledge by his use of "seeming" and emphasizing it by repetition: only what "seems" better to the Athenians and what "seems" better to him are "truly" causes of why he is there (98e). And while it may seem better to him to stay and accept the city's penalty once the city has pronounced it, it remains unclear to him, he says to the jurors at the end of the *Apology*, whether their continuing to live or his dying is "better" (*Apology* 42a). While Socrates uses "best" several times to refer to what Anaxagoras' theory of mind promises (97c, 97d, 98a, 98b), he uses "better" to describe what he and the Athenians seek (98e). For us, there is only better and worse.

If all things were ordered toward the good, however, we would have no need for choice. It is by "choosing" (*hairesis*), Socrates says, that we "act from intelligence (or "mind")" (99b). Socrates connects choice with our "distinguishing" (*dihairein*) what is "really a cause" from those things such as bones and sinews, without which causes could not be causes but which are not causes themselves (99b). Mind – and choice – are good, without being necessary, whereas these material conditions are necessary without necessarily being good, just as dying is necessary while its goodness remains a question. We must understand human life in terms of both the necessary and the good, although they remain two. It is the turn to political life that makes this clear. Socrates illustrates the inadequacy of Anaxagoras' account of cause with reference to the decision of an Athenian law court and his own acceptance of his obligation to obey the judgment. As Stern observes, "the very existence of political life and its characteristic distinctions – that humans are free to order their existence in a variety of ways – must belie the notion that nature orders all as it is best for each and for all."[8] Nature does not order all things for the best, but human beings do what seems to them good, or at least the better of their options. We gain from nature's imperfection.

Moreover, when Socrates refers to what he is doing at the moment in the *Phaedo*, he mentions not only that he is sitting in prison but also that he is conversing with his companions (98d). It is only what seems better to Socrates – and to his companions – and not what seems better to the city that explains the latter. Earlier in the *Phaedo*, as we see have seen, Socrates chooses to converse even though he is informed by the guard that conversing makes it more difficult for the poison to work (63d–e). Nevertheless, the Athenians allow Socrates to converse, for "the rulers did [not] forbid his companions to be present" at his death (58c). The

[8] Stern, *Socratic Rationalism*, 117.

Athenians are not a cause of Socrates' conversing, but they allow Socrates and his companions to choose what seems better to themselves. The city itself thereby recognizes that however much Socrates is a part of the city, he also remains separate from the city. Socrates' turn from Anaxagoras to his own inquiry into cause will treat "parts" as if they are more than merely parts of the whole.

The Athenians, including Socrates, come together to form a city. The existence of the city offers an answer to the problem that Socrates poses as a young man (97a–b): at least in political life, addition and division do not have the same result. They are as different as founding and dissolution. The first results in a whole, the latter in a plurality. The city is both at the same time. Because it is the former, Socrates has reason to stay and accept the city's penalty, and to consider the "Laws" his father as he does in the *Crito* (*Crito* 50d–e), and the city can justify its prosecution of those who break its laws. Because it is the latter, the good common to all is not necessarily the good for each, as Socrates' sentence reminds us. Socrates is able to say "not mine" as well as "mine" of his city, as can the city of Socrates. That Socrates sits in prison awaiting execution calls into question Anaxagoras' promised teleology as well as his materialism. If Anaxagoras were right about Mind, Socrates would not have been charged and sentenced to death. If Anaxagoras were right that the only causes at work are material, Socrates would escape rather than accept the penalty. In neither case would Socrates be awaiting execution. It is perfectly appropriate that Socrates' companions on his last day are both Athenians and foreigners (59b–c), that the Athenians do not forbid but cannot require the presence of his friends so that Socrates does not die alone, and that Plato has the Athenian Phaedo narrate the words and deeds of that day to a foreigner in a foreign land (57a–b).

SOCRATES' SECOND SAILING AND THE IDEAS

When Socrates is unable to learn from anyone how Mind is the cause of all things, and unable to discover it himself, he makes "a second sailing," he reports, in search of cause (99c–d). The phrase means taking to the oars when the wind fails. It requires human effort. Socrates explains that his situation was like those who look at the sun during an eclipse, not directly, lest they be blinded, but at an image or likeness of the sun in water or some such thing. Therefore fearing that he would be "blinded with respect to his soul if he looked at things directly with his eyes" or "attempted to touch them by means of the senses," Socrates "takes refuge in speeches" (99d–e). He "hypothesizes" (literally, "places down," from *hupotithēmi*) the speech he judges to be the strongest, and whatever appears to agree with this, he accepts as true, and whatever does not he rejects as untrue.[9] Specifically, he "hypothesizes those things he never ceases talking about, the beautiful itself, the good itself, the great itself, and all other such things" (100b).

If anything is beautiful, Socrates continues, it is beautiful for no other cause than it "shares in" the beautiful. But what does "sharing in" mean? Throughout this section, Socrates calls attention to this question: he first refers to what "participates in" (*metechei*) the beautiful itself (100c), and then observes that "nothing makes a thing beautiful but the presence of (*parousia*) or communion with (*koinōnia*) the beautiful, or however one calls it" (100d).[10] But of course one wishes to call it what it is. If Socrates does not know what to call it, he may not know precisely what it is. The connection between the beautiful itself and those things that are beautiful by "sharing" in it defies reason as much as does the divine itself. As Burger points out, Socrates' expression for his ignorance of how to speak of "participation" is like that used in public prayers to the gods, which acknowledges human ignorance of the correct way to speak of the gods.[11] Socrates in effect confesses near the very end of his life that he still does not understand the way in which temporal beings are related to the eternal.[12] Claiming that beautiful things are made beautiful by the beautiful, he says is the "safest" answer, although he admits that this way of speaking about cause, although the safest, is also "simple, artless, and perhaps naive" (100d).

Scholars are impressed that this formulation does not tell us everything we want to know about cause, even in the words of Stern, "purchas[ing]

---

[9] It is not clear whether Socrates' reference to "agreement" between the hypothesis and what follows from it means what is consistent with it or what is deducible from it. See, for example, Richard Robinson, *Plato's Earlier Dialectic* (Oxford: Clarendon Press, 1953), 126–29, and David Gallop, *Phaedo*, trans. with notes (Oxford: Clarendon Press, 1983), 180. As Stern observes, "Neither interpretation offers a solid ground for thinking a proposition true or false." *Socratic Rationalism*, 125. Socrates' statement about his procedure in the *Phaedo* recalls that of his first speech in the *Phaedrus*, when its speaker proposes that there is only "one beginning" for those deliberating – placing down (*tithēmi*) a definition of what is at issue and so ending up in agreement with himself and with his addressee (*Phaedrus* 237b-d). But Socrates did not as a result arrive at the truth about love.

[10] In giving an account to Echecrates, Phaedo uses even a fourth verb, *metalambanein*, "to partake of," to describe the relation (102b).

[11] Burger, *The Phaedo*, 150.

[12] Stern, *Socratic Rationalism*, 23 and Zuckert, "The Socratic Turn," 196.

irrefutablity at the cost of being uninformative."[13] But the account does not simply provide a safe and therefore consoling doctrine, for it captures a problem that has been plaguing Socrates in this and other dialogues. By this account, the beautiful itself, the good itself, and other such things are not simple. Like the self-moving soul of the *Phaedrus* that also cares for all that is soulless, the ideas do double duty: the beautiful and such things, as Socrates describes them now, both are themselves by themselves, and also are the causes that other things are what they are.[14] Even the "safest" answer is not simply "safe." Kierkegaard identifies a radical version of this question as Christianity's – how a perfect being comes into relation to something else, how the god reveals himself to man and thus comes into being in time.

Earlier in the *Phaedo*, as we have seen, Socrates argues that the soul desires to be free from body, to be itself by itself because as long as it is connected to body it will never know anything clearly, and yet it is its very connection to body that gives the soul its greatest perplexity.[15] We experience ourselves as both one and many, or self-moving and erotic, in terms of the *Phaedrus*, or like and unlike ourselves, in terms of the *Lysis*. Death, which seems to be the separation of elements whose union is as perplexing to us as is their separation, assures us that exploring these issues is no "idle chatter" about what does not concern us. This may be the deepest meaning of the *Phaedo*: as we face our own deaths and the deaths of those we love, the inadequacy of accounts of ourselves as merely body or merely soul – or our own lack of self-knowledge – keeps philosophy alive for us. Life, and the soul's union with the body, is therefore the condition for philosophizing: it assures us that the questions about ourselves can never be completely or finally answered.

Participation has to preserve both the difference and the similarity between the things that participate and those things in which they participate. Without the similarity there would be so much difference that

---

[13] Stern, *Socratic Rationalism*, 125.

[14] See Burger's excellent discussion of this point, *The Phaedo*, 149. As Stern observes, "not only the soul [in the *Phaedo*] but also the beings themselves are complex," *Socratic Rationalism*, 132–33.

[15] Socrates uses the same expression of the beautiful, which is itself by itself (*auto kath' hauto*) (100b), and of the soul. In seeking knowledge, the soul seeks to be itself by itself (*autē kath' hautēn*), not "sharing in" or "constituting a community with" (*koinōnousa*) body (65c). Since this is possible, if at all, only with death, the soul does share in or constitute a community with body.

there could be no participation. Socrates' use of the word community (*koinōnia*) – the word used in the phrase "political community" – to refer to the relation between the beautiful and that which shares in it (100d) illustrates the need for similarity. But without any difference, those things in which others participate lose their status as other, and then we need something to explain them too. This is the dilemma into which Parmenides keeps driving Socrates when as a young man he offers the older philosopher his theory of the ideas: either they are like what participates in them, and then something else is needed to explain what they have in common, or inasmuch as they are separate or other they have no relation to the world they are trying to explain (*Parmenides* 132d–134c). In other words, an idea must be present in the world, but if wholly present it cannot be an idea. This is why Christianity resembles Platonism, although not in the way in which Nietzsche presents it.[16] It is not that Christianity posits another world in the way that Plato posits separate ideas. Rather Christianity understands that human wisdom founders on the paradox of participation, or that the Incarnation is the deepest mystery, the mystery that Being, which is what it is, and is explicable in no terms other than itself, also creates a world, speaks to human beings within it, and finally becomes one of them.

Moving from his example of the beautiful back to his original question of number, Socrates illustrates the safe answer: "When one is added to one, and when one is divided, neither addition nor division is the cause of two, . . . for something can come into existence only by participating in the proper being of each thing in which it participates, and there is no other cause of two coming into being than twoness, and things that are to be two must participate in twoness." It is an answer that Socrates says Cebes should "shout loudly" while "leav[ing] divisions and additions and other such subtleties to those who are wiser" (101b–c). The cause of generation and destruction has become identical with the cause of being, although Socrates recounted how as a young man he sought "the cause of each thing, why each thing comes into being, and why it perishes, and why it is" (96a–b). Our births, understood as the coming together of soul and body, and our deaths, understood as their separation, would both by this conclusion have no other cause than twoness. The same cause will produce opposite results, or, in other words, result in the sort of contradiction that Socrates describes to his companions as "a monster" to

[16] See Friedrich Nietzsche, *Beyond Good and Evil*, trans. Walter Kaufmann (New York: Random House, 1966), 3.

be "feared" (101b–c). Apparently, one can be too safe, and as a result come face to face with the monster one seeks to avoid.

Socrates does not rest, however, with "safety first." He calls into question the "hypothesis" of the ideas as causes by returning to the status of the "hypotheses" that constitute his second sailing. When he first gave an account of his second sailing, he spoke of laying down the argument that he judges strongest, and considering as true whatever agrees with it, and as false whatever does not (100a). Now Socrates reveals that one's hypotheses themselves are open to challenge, and that the various things that follow from a hypothesis may or may not agree with one another. If someone attacks one's "hypothesis," he says, one "should dismiss him and not answer *until* one examines the consequences [of the hypothesis] to see whether they agree with one another or not" (101d, emphasis mine). And "whenever it is necessary to give an account (*logos*) of the [hypothesis] itself, one would give it in the same way by laying down another hypothesis, which appears best from among higher ones, until one comes to something sufficient" (101d–e).

Socrates' account recalls his description of the divided line in the *Republic*, where mathematicians begin from "hypotheses" and "don't give any further account of them to themselves and others," but go ahead and "end consistently at the object toward which their inquiry is directed" (*Republic* 510d–e). At the highest section of the intelligible, in contrast, hypotheses are "not beginnings" but stepping stones "in order to reach what is free from hypothesis at the beginning of the whole" (*Republic* 511b). In his discussion in the *Phaedo*, however, Socrates is more cautious.[17] As in the *Republic*, he does not rest with hypotheses as beginnings, but he does not suggest that one must or can reach what is free from hypotheses, or arrive at "the beginning of the whole." He speaks only of a "sufficient" hypothesis, but he gives no indication of how one decides what is "sufficient"; apparently, every hypothesis is open to further challenge.[18]

Socrates' statement is perplexing, inasmuch as he has presented the ideas as the hypothesis that he supposes the strongest. Thus he appears to be questioning the ideas. Gallop observes that Socrates' arguments

---

[17] As Glaucon says in the *Republic* in another context, Socrates indulges in "daemonic excess" (*Republic* 509b).

[18] Burger comments on this passage: "Every step forward would actually be a step backward in recognizing an apparently self-evident starting point to be in fact derivative," *The Phaedo*, 156.

"seem to have cut loose from their moorings."[19] And Stern asks, "To what more comprehensive hypothesis should one refer in order to substantiate their existence?"[20] Intending to save Socrates from Nietzsche's criticism of the "dogmatic rationalism" of Socrates' Ideas, Stern suggests that Socrates' return to the issue of hypotheses indicates that the hypotheses with which he begins cannot be "separate Ideas," but "the speeches we express in our everyday existence."[21] Those speeches, as they appear in the *Phaedo*, include the many even contradictory things we say about the soul that imply both its difference and inseparability from body, just as the ideas require their difference and inseparability from those things that participate in them. This is why Socrates must return to the hypothesis of the Ideas. It is his refusal to dismiss the problem of "separate" ideas that preserves Socrates from dogmatic rationalism.

Stern provides a good formulation of Socrates' position: "A being is not only itself – this individual – but also possesses characteristics that make it akin to other beings."[22] Because this is true of human beings, as we have seen, friendship is possible. That human beings are both themselves by themselves and akin to other beings, moreover, creates tensions that animate political life. Human beings are both separate from their cities and parts of them. The tension between human being and citizen holds the threat of fatal conflict, as between Socrates and Athens, even if it also means that political communities can approach friendship as their standard.

PIETY, POETRY, AND FRIENDSHIP

As we have seen, Kierkegaard presents a challenge – and an alternative – to Socrates in the name of faith, as does Nietzsche in the name of art. Yet both discern in Socrates a more complex representation of Western rationalism than at first appears. Kierkegaard's Climacus refers us to Socrates' perplexity about himself, and Nietzsche refers us to Socrates' turn in his last days to art in recognition of the limits of reason. And yet, as the preceding readings of the Platonic dialogues have shown, Plato's Socrates remains less a confirmation of their positions than a challenge to

---

[19] Gallop, *Phaedo*, 190.
[20] Stern, *Socratic Rationalism*, 127.
[21] Stern, *Socratic Rationalism*, 128.
[22] Stern, *Socratic Rationalism*, 133.

them. This is because both Socrates' piety and his appreciation of poetry turn on his view of friendship as essential to his philosophic life, an aspect neglected by both Kierkegaard and Nietzsche in their presentations of Socrates.

Climacus initially attributes to Socrates the view that self-knowledge is God-knowledge. It is Agathon, however, not Socrates, who identifies himself with the god. Climacus' interpretation of Socrates, at least in his description of Socrates' understanding of recollection, assimilates him to Agathon, or rather to Socrates in his youth, who like Agathon mistakenly thought that love is beautiful and good. If self-knowledge were God-knowledge, there would be no need for the daemonic to connect human and divine. Socrates' response to Agathon also in effect replies to Climacus. Piety cannot lie in divine wisdom, whether it comes to a god-inspired poet, as Agathon suggests, or is found by a philosopher whose self-knowledge is God-knowledge. As Socrates says more than once, only the gods are wise (e.g., *Symposium* 204a and *Phaedrus* 278d).

When Climacus claims that Socrates' speech in the *Symposium* is about "the relation of the autodidact to the beautiful" (*PF* 31), he conflates Diotima and Socrates. But Socrates chooses to attribute to another the source of his understanding about love. He does not present himself as an autodidact. He even admits to Diotima, as he recounts the story, that he "is in need of teachers" (*Symposium* 207c). He presents himself as returning to her several times for further instruction (*Symposium* 207a and c). In effect he returns to her again when he recounts her lessons in his own speech at the symposium. Climacus to the contrary, Socrates does not act as if enthusiasm for one's teacher, as Plato had for Socrates himself, is merely "a muddiness of mind" that arises from an "illusion" that one's learning owes something to another (*PF* 12).

Diotima, as Socrates recounts, corrects his view about Love by questioning – and illustrating for him a way of teaching that he himself adopted and made famous, a way of teaching that Climacus associates with reminding one's interlocutor of what he already knows, and of what in fact every human being already knows (*PF* 9–11). It is true that Diotima claims that Socrates already knows the truth about Love – namely, that Love cannot be a god inasmuch as he desires and hence lacks beautiful and good things (*Symposium* 202d). When she draws out the implication of this understanding of love for philosophy, she tells Socrates that "even a child" could say that philosophers desire but lack wisdom (204a–b). This is the "wisdom" available to everyone, of which she reminds Socrates. It is not that our self-knowledge is

God-knowledge, but that we seek a truth outside ourselves that as a consequence can never be perfectly accessible to the human mind. This in fact is the position that Climacus himself later attributes to Socrates (*PF* 37).

According to Climacus' revised view of Socrates, Socrates' piety lies not in his identity with the divine but in his awareness of need. Although he is needy, there is no God in the machine who descends to him, to relieve his confusion, and his longing. Curiously enough, Climacus' Socrates, as the philosopher who confronts the unknown, resembles the needy half-beings of Aristophanes' speech in the *Symposium* who long for and are aware of their own incompleteness. They are aware of their need, but they have no knowledge of what alone would satisfy them – their original wholeness that they lost through their own transgression. What it is that they want, they "are unable to say"; Zeus's plan fails: their navels do not remind them of their ancient suffering (see *Symposium* 191a). They lack consciousness of sin, as Climacus claims of Socrates (*PF* 47). In Aristophanes' story, it would require a god, in this case the smithy Hephaestos, to reveal to them what will make them happy and offer to bring it about through his mediation. Like Climacus, Aristophanes presents the view that happiness is inaccessible to human beings as a result of their own transgression, and that only a god can bring them understanding and redemption. But Hephaestos does not come to them, nor does the god descend to Climacus' Socrates. Divine pity for human beings, in Aristophanes' story, leads Zeus to give them only sex, not the wholeness they long for (192b–e). This expedient that Aristophanes attributes to Zeus provides neither truth nor happiness: Aristophanes' half-beings still have no understanding of their condition, and happiness the poet concludes is another divine gift for which we can only hope (193d). While the piety that collapses into divine wisdom alienates us from human life, the piety that is derived from unrelieved need leaves us alienated from what we long for. There is no happiness within our reach.

Socrates' speech in the *Symposium*, however, responds not only to Agathon but also to Aristophanes. In responding to Agathon, Socrates denies that self-knowledge is equivalent to God-knowledge, the position that Climacus attributed to him. In responding to Aristophanes, he denies that we have become so alienated from ourselves that we can only hope for a savior to perform a miracle. To the contrary, love directs us to the beautiful and that experience leads to generation and nurture. And it also leads (or can lead) to friendship with the one whom we love (*Symposium* 209c), a position in which Socrates' tale of the lover and beloved in the *Phaedrus* culminates, and which the *Lysis* explores and develops. Whereas Socrates' response to Agathon corrects Climacus' initial view of his piety, his response to Aristophanes corrects Climacus' revised view.

From time to time during his narration of his conversation with Diotima, Socrates reports wondering at something she says. He wonders at Diotima's account of how all mortal things preserve themselves, both their bodies and their souls, by a constant process of replication. A mortal being is preserved, she explains, "not by being always the same like the divine, but because what departs and grows old leaves behind a different, new thing, such as it was" (208a–b). He wonders, in other words, that over time one is only like oneself, not the same. So too he wonders when Diotima describes all human beings as lovers (205b). Here his wonder arises out of his awareness that love of beauty cannot be reduced to a desire to possess good things for oneself, as would be the case if all were lovers. He is aware that love includes an element that brings one outside oneself, and even leads one to sacrifice oneself for another. Therefore he wonders as well at Diotima's description of our sacrifice of ourselves for our offspring, who are other than ourselves however much we may be preserved in them (206b ff). Diotima admits that such deeds cannot be explained from "calculation" or "reasoning" (207b). Wonder comes when we understand the strange in what is most familiar, or in these cases for Socrates when he becomes aware that "otherness" penetrates our most intimate experiences such as loving and giving birth and even our very identities.

This teacher who arouses wonder is a prophetess, whose profession connects her to what is beyond herself. Socrates emphasizes her foreignness by calling her "stranger" (201e, 204c, and 211d), and yet she is his own, his own creation. Like love itself, as she describes it, prophecy is not a matter of reasoning, and yet her piety is expressed in her commanding pious speech (*euphēmein*) when Socrates asks whether because love is not beautiful or good, it is ugly and bad (201c).[23] Pious speech protects what Diotima describes as the daemonic, and is illustrated by Socratic poetry, whether it be Socrates' creation of Diotima, his palinode in the *Phaedrus*, or his fable in the *Phaedo* about the connection between pleasure and pain, to mention examples we have had occasion to refer to.

---

[23] The word *euphēmein*, from which our word "euphemism" is derived, contains *phēmi*, to say.

Pious speech must steer between the "piety" that understands love as simply beautiful and good and thereby collapses human and divine, on the one hand, and the "piety" that makes divinity inaccessible to human beings, on the other. It must steer, in other words, between the Heavenly and Popular Loves of Pausanias' speech, and thereby avoid the collapse of poetry into either the tragedy or comedy represented by the poets at Agathon's party. God and mortal do not mix so much that daemons are not needed to link them, nor so little that daemons cannot serve that role. This is consistent with Socrates' palinode in the *Phaedrus*, which distinguishes divine souls from those that will come to inhabit bodies and that can nevertheless through friendship regain a place in the heavens. For Socrates, self-knowledge is not God-knowledge, nor is divine descent necessary to make the truth accessible to human beings. In the *Phaedrus*, Socrates becomes aware of his error, his transgression against the divine, and moves to correct the mistake before blindness sets in. For Socrates, philosophy is possible, and friends capture for us that wonder that moves philosophers, who experience their own as other and the other as their own. Only because the truth is "absolutely other" (*PF* 44–46) does Climacus need recourse to a god in the machine. When the structure of reality is miraculous, one does not need miracles. As Diotima teaches Socrates, the daemonic "fills up the interval" between humans and gods and so "binds together the whole itself" (203a). When Socrates denies in the *Apology* that he is an atheist and insists that one who believes in daemons must believe in gods (*Apology* 27a–e), he is not lying.

To find the strange in the familiar might seem to resemble Nietzsche's view of art, especially tragedy, in which the tragic hero becomes aware of the strange Dionysian world underlying the familiar Apollonian boundaries in which human beings live. That Socrates' hymn to a god near the end of his life is directed to Apollo could hardly be from this perspective a true recantation of his rejection of poetry, certainly not of the Dionysian character of the recantation Nietzsche found in Euripides' *Bacchae*. But Socrates did not really leave to his dying days a recantation of his "views" of poetry. In the *Republic*, Socrates calls for poets or lovers of poetry to offer a defense (*Republic* 607a), but just such a defense is implicit in Socrates' own speech on love in the *Symposium*. Only a comedy in which the low is open to the high, and a tragedy in which the high finds its limits in the low, preserves comedy and tragedy from the decline Plato depicts in the *Symposium*. Because of the "marriage" of Poverty and Resource, which serves as an exemplar of Socratic poetry long before

Socrates made his reinterpretation of his dream in prison, comedy is as appropriate a lens to human life as is tragedy. Had Socrates written a poetics, the birth of comedy would have occupied as important a place as that of tragedy. For Nietzsche, tragic art reveals the terrifying and strange world of the Dionysian underlying the comfortable and familiar world of the Apollonian. For Socrates, the strange is just not as strange as Nietzsche would have it, nor is the familiar quite so familiar.

When Socrates in the *Phaedo* refers to his new way of philosophizing as "taking refuge in speeches," he echoes an earlier remark of Simmias, who sought "to take refuge in the beautiful" (76e–77a). Socrates agrees with Nietzsche that the beautiful deceives with its appearance of self-sufficiency. But instead of dissolving the appearances and effecting his own destruction, as Nietzsche's tragic hero does, Socrates proposes that questioning and answering move back and forth between the wholeness implied in a hypothesis insofar as it serves as a starting point for inquiry and the problems questioning brings to light. The wholeness that beauty conveys is not simply a deception: it is a reflection of the self-motion of the soul and makes possible thinking and speaking just as much as the processes of collection and division Socrates describes in the *Phaedrus* (*Phaedrus* 265d). This "dialectical art" is not self-sufficient, but must direct itself to a fitting soul, in which it plants seeds that come to fruition and from which spring others in other souls, "capable of continuing this forever" (*Phaedrus* 277a). As I have argued in my analysis of Socrates' criticisms of writing in the *Phaedrus*, the Platonic dialogue is the best way to keep Socrates' argument alive – inasmuch as it shows his speaking only in response to others. In this way, Platonic dialogue recognizes the marriage of Resource and Poverty that Socrates' *Symposium* speech celebrates. Thus it might fall to the same person to write Socratic poetry and to philosophize. Such a poetry is not what Nietzsche meant by art, which revels in the hero's divinity, although a suffering divinity. Nor does the pious speech of such poetry reflect Kierkegaard's view of faith, which requires a god's revealing himself in time. Socrates' reply to Nietzsche and Kierkegaard would be the same as his reply to Agathon and Aristophanes: the former sees no need for the daemonic to link human and divine; the latter gives no reason to believe that such a link is possible. For Plato's Socrates, friends constitute evidence both of the need for such a link and of its possibility.

If there were no essential difference between human and divine – if, for example, self-knowledge were God-knowledge – neither faith nor philosophy would be necessary. Recollection of the truth would remove any role for faith, as Climacus makes clear in *Philosophical Fragments*.[24] And while questions might help us to recollect what we know, they are in principle unnecessary. We have the truth within ourselves. We would have no need of a friend, nor of a teacher, only at most a midwife who could – and should – disappear, as Climacus indicates. This would also be true if Anaxagoras had succeeded in accounting for the world in the way that he proposed, for if all were arranged for the best, we would have no cause to question it. There is irony in Socrates' looking for a teacher who could explain what Anaxagoras promises to explain. But then Socrates was "young," and did not know that the god himself commands that we know ourselves (*Phaedrus* 229e), and that this paradox means that our fulfilling the command remains forever beyond our reach. The distance between self-knowledge and God-knowledge keeps philosophy as well as faith alive.

On the other hand, if there were no link between human and divine, if we shared no vision of anything eternal, neither faith nor philosophy would be possible. Everything and everyone would be "itself by itself," separate and without relation to anything else. If the divine existed, it would be inaccessible (see *Parmenides* 134d–e), and questions would be futile because nothing could be understood in terms of anything else. Philosophers might suppose they have discovered the truth when they would have discovered only themselves and their own creations. Our friends would be at best phantom friends, and our friendships conceal our use of our friend for our own purposes. The human condition would be one of essential alienation.

There is much in Nietzsche's thought that leads us in this direction. When Zarathustra preaches about friends, he warns that our friend is our "best enemy," to whom we become closest only by resisting. "Our longing for a friend is our betrayer," Zarathustra says, for it betrays our lack of faith in ourselves (*TSZ* 168). Nietzsche gives no reason to trust anyone but oneself.[25] From such a perspective, speech becomes merely playful. According to Nietzsche's Zarathustra, words and sounds are only "illusive bridges between things which are eternally apart." To every soul, he insists, "every other soul is another world," and he

---

[24] Or, to use the words of Kierkegaard's John the Silent, "Faith has never existed in the world precisely because it always existed". *Fear and Trembling*, 55.

[25] See also Peter Berkowitz's discussion of the treatment of friendship in *Thus Spoke Zarathustra*, in *Nietzsche: The Ethics of an Immoralist* (Cambridge: Harvard University Press, 1995), 171–74. According to Berkowitz, "Zarathustra's radically instrumental doctrine of friendship is another inexorable and fearful consequence of his effort to invest the creative will with absolute sovereignty," 171.

understands other worlds, we have seen in Chapter 1, as creations born of suffering and incapacity. Zarathustra therefore proclaims, "For me – how should there be an outside myself? There is no outside. But all sounds make us forget this . . . . Speaking is beautiful folly" (*TSZ*, 329; see 145). Whereas Socrates and Phaedrus resist the humming of the cicadas in order to converse (*Phaedrus* 259a; see Aristotle, *Politics* 1253a8–15), Zarathustra takes delight in the "chattering" of animals (*TSZ* 329).

If this gap between human and divine were bridged by a god's revelation of himself to man, as described in *Philosophical Fragments*, the paradox of this "communication" would make it incommunicable to human beings. In *Fear and Trembling*, Kierkegaard's pseudonym John the Silent contrasts the sectarians with the knights of faith. The former "deafen one another with their noise and clatter," and think that "going arm and arm with one another," they can "assault heaven." The knight of faith, in contrast, belonging to neither Church nor state, is "always in absolute isolation" and "feels the pain of being unable to make himself understandable to anyone" (*FT* 79–80). Thus he must live with terror even though or precisely because he "becomes God's confidant" (*FT* 77). Kierkegaard's knight of faith, who becomes God's confidant in fear and trembling, paradoxically resembles Nietzsche's Zarathustra, who "wanders alone," climbing "mountains and ridges and peaks," and to reach the greatest heights must in "[his] ultimate loneliness" descend into the deepest pain (*TSZ* 264–66). Whether these images are Kierkegaard's and Nietzsche's deepest understandings of the human condition, I do not know. To be sure, Kierkegaard has an interlocutor appear at the end of several chapters of the *Fragments* to engage Climacus in dialogue, as if the truth itself might emerge from the exchange, in contrast to the positions that learning the truth is being reminded of what one already knows and that learning occurs when one receives from another what can be possessed only miraculously. And in *The Gay Science*, Nietzsche makes statements about friendship that point us back to a more classical understanding, contrary to Zarathustra's musings.[26]

Both Kierkegaard and Nietzsche understood themselves to be presenting challenging tasks to arouse humanity out of the complacency of

---

[26] Friedrich Nietzsche, *The Gay Science*, trans. Walter Kaufmann (New York: Random House, 1974) – for example, sections 14, 16, and 61. See Denise Schaeffer's challenging and thoughtful argument in "Nietzsche's Woman as Friend: The Paradox of Distance and Proximity," in *Nature, Woman, and the Art of Politics*, ed. Eduardo A. Velasquez (Lanham, MD: Lexington Books, 2000).

modernity, even if it took fear and trembling, or the terrors of the Dionysian, in order to do so. Plato's Socrates, in contrast, spends his time engaging others in conversations, including those whom he considers friends. Even when he thinks they will not be able to understand, he offers images that serve as a bridge for them (see *Republic* 506e–507a). It is not that he reaches no heights or depths, but he does it only indirectly: he himself, he says, must look at the sun only in its reflections in water and other such things (*Phaedo* 99d–e). Socrates' pursuit of friends is an image of a good life that reflects a richer understanding of the human experience than the images of "absolute isolation" that we find in Kierkegaard and Nietzsche. Such a Socratic pursuit saves us from alienation while preserving our identity. Inasmuch as friendship involves finding one's own in another, and serving as another's own, it is not without fear, and even grief. Because it requires for our happiness another whom we neither control nor perfectly understand, trust is necessary. Misanthropy, like misology, remains a danger. But because we experience goodness in another, trust is possible. Friendship is a source of joy for us. It is no less of a challenge than we find in Kierkegaard and Nietzsche, and perhaps an even greater one.

Works Cited

Anderson, Daniel E. *The Masks of Dionysus*. Albany: State University of New York Press, 1993.

Anton, John P. "Some Dionysian References in the Platonic Dialogues." *Classical Journal* **58** (1962–63): 49–55.

Arieti, James. *Interpreting Plato: The Dialogues as Drama*. Lanham, MD: Rowman and Littlefield, 1991.

Bacon, Helen. "Socrates Crowned." *Virginia Quarterly Review* **35** (1959): 415–30.

Benardete, Seth. "Symposium." In *Plato's "Symposium."* Trans. Seth Benardete, with commentaries by Allan Bloom and Seth Benardete. Chicago: University of Chicago Press, 2001.

The Argument of the Action: Essays on Greek Poetry and Philosophy. Eds. Ronna Burger and Michael Davis. Chicago: University of Chicago Press, 2000.

The Rhetoric of Morality and Philosophy: Plato's Gorgias and Phaedrus. Chicago: University of Chicago Press, 1991.

"Sophocles' *Oedipus Tyrannus*." In *Ancients and Moderns*. Ed. Joseph Cropsey. New York: Basic Books, 1964.

Berkowitz, Peter. *Nietzsche: The Ethics of an Immoralist*. Cambridge: Harvard University Press, 1995.

Bloom, Allan. "The Ladder of Love." In *Plato's "Symposium."* Trans. Seth Benardete, with commentaries by Allan Bloom and Seth Benardete. Chicago: University of Chicago Press, 2001.

Love and Friendship. New York: Simon and Schuster, 1993.

Bolotin, David. "Response to Umphrey." *Interpretation* **10**, no. 2 and 3 (May and September, 1982): 423–429.

Plato's Dialogue on Friendship: An Interpretation of the Lysis, with a New Translation. Ithaca, NY: Cornell University Press, 1979.

Brann, Eva, Peter Kalkavage, and Eric Salem. *Plato's Phaedo*. Translation, introduction, and glossary. Newburyport, MA: Focus Classical Library, 1998.

Brown, Malcolm, and James Coulter. "The Middle Speech of Plato's *Phaedrus*." *Journal of the History of Philosophy* **9** (1971): 405–23.

Burger, Ronna. *The Phaedo: A Platonic Labyrinth*. New Haven: Yale University Press, 1984.

Burger, Ronna. *Plato's Phaedrus: A Defense of a Philosophic Art of Writing.* Tuscaloosa, AL: University of Alabama Press, 1980.

Bury, R. G. *The Symposium of Plato.* Ed., with introduction, critical notes and commentary, 2nd ed. Cambridge: W. Heffer and Sons, Ltd., 1969.

Cobb, William S. *The Symposium and the Phaedrus: Plato's Erotic Dialogues.* Trans. with introduction and commentary. Albany: State University of New York Press, 1993.

Cropsey, Joseph. *Political Philosophy and the Issues of Politics.* Chicago: University of Chicago Press, 1977.

Dannhauser, Werner. *Nietzsche's View of Socrates.* Ithaca, NY: Cornell University Press, 1974.

Davis, Michael. *The Autobiography of Philosophy.* Lanham, MD: Rowman and Littlefield, 1999.

    "Socrates' Pre-Socratism: Some Remarks on the Structure of Plato's *Phaedo*," *Ancient Philosophy* (1980): 69–80.

De Vries, G. J. *A Commentary on the Phaedrus of Plato.* Amsterdam: Adolf M. Hakkert, 1969.

Dobbs, Darrell. "Communism." *The Journal of Politics* **62** (2000): 491–510.

Dover, K. J. *Greek Homosexuality, Updated and with a New Postscript.* Cambridge: Harvard University Press, 1989.

Ferrari, G. R. F. *Listening to the Cicadas.* Cambridge, UK: Cambridge University Press, 1987.

Forde, Steven. *The Ambition to Rule: Alcibiades and the Politics of Imperialism in Thucydides.* Ithaca: NY: Cornell University Press, 1989.

Freeman, Kathleen. Trans. *Ancilla to the Pre-Socratic Philosophers: A Complete Translation of the Fragments in Diels, Fragmente der Vorsokratiker.* Cambridge: Harvard University Press, 1948.

Friedlander, Paul. *Plato: The Dialogues, Second and Third Periods.* Vol. 3. Trans. Hans Meyerhoff. Princeton: Princeton University Press, 1969.

    Plato: The Dialogues, First Period. Vol. 2. Trans. Hans Meyerhoff. New York: Random House, 1964.

    Plato: An Introduction. Vol. 1. Trans. Hans Meyerhoff. Princeton: Princeton University Press, 1958.

Frutiger, Percival. *"Les Mythes de Platon: Etude philosophique et litteraire.* Paris: Librairie Felix Alcan, 1930.

Gadamer, Hans-Georg. *Dialogue and Dialectic.* Trans. P. Christopher Smith. New Haven: Yale University Press, 1980.

Gagarin, Michael. "Socrates' *Hybris* and Alcibiades' Failure." *Phoenix* **31** (1977): 22–37.

Gallop, David. *Phaedo.* Trans. with notes. Oxford: Clarendon Press, 1983.

Geier, Alfred. *Plato's Erotic Thought: The Tree of the Unknown.* Rochester, NY: University of Rochester Press, 2002.

Glidden, David K. "The *Lysis* on Loving One's Own." *Classical Quarterly* **31** (1981): 39–59.

Gonzalez, Francisco J. "Plato's *Lysis*: An Enactment of Philosophical Kinship." *Ancient Philosophy* **12** (1995): 69–90.

Griswold, Charles L. Jr. *Self-Knowledge in Plato's Phaedrus.* University Park, PA: Pennsylvania State University Press, 1996.

"The Politics of Self-Knowledge: Liberal Variations on the *Phaedrus.*" In *Understanding the Phaedrus.* Ed. Livio Rossetti. Sankt Augustin: Academia Verlag, 1992.

Guthrie, W. K. C. *History of Greek Philosophy.* Vol. IV. Cambridge, UK: Cambridge University Press, 1975.

Hackforth, R. *Plato's Phaedrus.* Translated with an introduction and commentary. Cambridge, UK: Cambridge University Press, 1952.

Hadon, James. "Friendship in Plato's *Lysis.*" *Review of Metaphysics* **37** (December, 1983): 327–56.

Halperin, David M. "Plato and Erotic Reciprocity." *Classical Antiquity* **5** (1989): 60–90.

Hobbes, Thomas. *Leviathan.* Ed. Michael Oakeshott. New York: Collier Macmillan, 1962.

Hoerber, Robert G. "Thrasylus' Platonic Canon and the Double Titles." *Phronesis* **2** (1957): 10–20.

"Character Portrayal in Plato's *Lysis.*" *Classical Journal* **41** (1945–46): 271–273.

Howland, Jacob. *Kierkegaard and Socrates A Study in Faith and Philosophy.* Cambridge, UK: Cambridge University Press, 2006.

Howland, Jacob. *The Paradox of Political Philosophy.* Lanham, MD: Rowman and Littlefield, 1998.

Kass, Leon. *Toward a More Natural Science.* New York: The Free Press, 1985.

Kaufmann, Walter. *Nietzsche: Philosopher, Psychiatrist, Antichrist.* 3d. ed. Princeton: Princeton University Press, 1968.

Kierkegaard, Søren. *The Concept of Irony.* Ed. and trans. Howard V. and Edna H. Hong. Princeton: Princeton University Press, 1989.

Stages on Life's Way. Ed. and trans. Howard V. Hong and Edna H. Hong. Princeton: Princeton University Press, 1988.

Either/Or. Ed. and trans. Howard V. Hong and Edna H. Hong. Princeton: Princeton University Press, 1987.

Philosophical Fragments. Ed. and trans. Howard V. and Edna H. Hong. Princeton: Princeton University Press, 1985.

Fear and Trembling. Ed. and trans. Howard V. and Edna H. Hong. Princeton: Princeton University Press, 1983.

Concluding Unscientific Postscript. Ed. and trans. Howard V. Hong and Edna H. Hong. Princeton: Princeton University Press, 1982.

Soren Kierkegaard's Journal and Papers. Ed. and trans. Howard V. Hong and Edna H. Hong. Bloomington: Indiana University Press, 1967–68.

Klein, Jacob. *A Commentary on Plato's Meno.* Chapel Hill, NC: The University of North Carolina Press, 1965.

Lamb, W. R. M. "Introduction to the *Lysis.*" In *Lysis, Symposium, Gorgias.* Trans. and introduction. Cambridge: Harvard University Press, 1930.

Lawrence, Joseph P. "Socrates and Alcibiades." *Southern Humanities Review* **37** (Fall 2003): 301–27.

Lebeck, Anne. "The Central Myth of Plato's *Phaedrus.*" *Greek, Roman, and Byzantine Studies* **13** (1972): 267–90.

Ludwig, Paul W. *Eros and Polis: Desire and Community in Greek Political Theory.* Cambridge, UK: Cambridge University Press, 2002.

Lutz, Mark J. *Socrates' Education to Virtue: Learning the Love of the Noble.* Albany: State University of New York Press, 1998.

Monoson, S. Sara. *Plato's Democratic Entanglements: Athenian Politics and the Practice of Philosophy.* Princeton: Princeton University Press, 2000.

Mooney, T. Brian. "Plato's Theory of Love in the *Lysis*: A Defence." *Irish Philosophical Journal* **7** (1990): 131–59.

Neumann, Harry. "Diotima's Concept of Love." *American Journal of Philology* **86** (1965): 33–59.

Newell, Waller R. *Ruling Passion: The Erotics of Statecraft in Platonic Political Philosophy.* Lanham, MD: Rowman and Littlefield, 2000.

Nichols, James H. *Plato Phaedrus.* Translated, with introduction, notes, and interpretative essay. Ithaca: Cornell University Press, 1998.

Nichols, Mary P. "Philosophy and Empire: On Socrates and Alcibiades in Plato's *Symposium.*" *Polity* **39**, no. 4 (October 2007): 502–21.

    "Friendship and Community in Plato's *Lysis.*" *Review of Politics* **68**, no. 1 (Winter 2006): 1–19.

    "Socrates' Contest with the Poets in Plato's *Symposium.*" *Political Theory* **32**, no. 2 (April 2004): 186–206.

    Socrates and the Political Community: An Ancient Debate. Albany, NY: State University of New York Press, 1987.

    "The *Republic's* Two Alternatives: Philosopher-Kings and Socrates." *Political Theory* **12** (May 1984): 252–74.

Nietzsche, Friedrich. *The Gay Science.* Trans. Walter Kaufmann. New York: Random House, 1974.

    The Birth of Tragedy and The Case of Wagner. Trans. with commentary by Walter Kaufmann. New York: Random House, 1967.

    Beyond Good and Evil. Trans. Walter Kaufmann. New York: Random House, 1966.

    Thus Spoke Zarathustra. In *The Portable Nietzsche* Ed. and trans. Walter Kaufmann. New York: Viking Penguin, 1954.

    Twilight of the Idols. In *The Portable Nietzsche*. Ed. and trans. Walter Kaufmann. New York: Viking Penguin, 1954.

Nussbaum, Martha. *The Fragility of Goodness.* Cambridge: Cambridge University Press, 1986.

Pangle, Lorraine Smith. *Aristotle and the Philosophy of Friendship.* Cambridge: Cambridge University Press, 2003.

Plato, *Platonis Opera.* Ed. John Burnet. Vol. I–V. Oxford: Oxford University Press, 1900–07.

Plochmann, George Kimball. "Hiccups and Hangovers in *The Symposium.*" *Bucknell Review* **11**, no. 3 (May 1963): 1–18.

Price, A. W. *Love and Friendship in Plato and Aristotle.* Oxford: Clarendon Press, 1989.

Rhodes, James M. "Platonic *Philia* and Political Order." In *Friendship and Politics: Essays in Political Thought.* Eds. John von Heyking and Richard Avramenko. Notre Dame, IN: Notre Dame University Press, 2008.

Eros, Wisdom, and Silence. Columbia, MO: University of Missouri Press, 2003.

Robinson, David B. "Plato's *Lysis*: The Structural Problem." *Illinois Classical Studies* **11** (1986): 63–83.

Robinson, Richard. *Plato's Earlier Dialectic.* Oxford: Clarendon Press, 1953.

Rosen, Stanley, *Plato's Symposium.* 2nd ed. New Haven: Yale University Press, 1968.

Rowe, C. J. "The Argument and Structure of Plato's *Phaedrus*." *Proceedings of the Cambridge Philological Society* **32** (1986): 106–25.

Plato: Phaedrus. With trans. and commentary. Warminster: Aris and Phillips, 1986.

Santas, Gerasimos. "Passionate Platonic Love in the *Phaedrus*." *Ancient Philosophy* **2**, no. 2 (Fall 1982): 105–14.

Saxonhouse, Arlene. *Fear of Diversity: The Birth of Political Science in Ancient Greek Thought.* Chicago: University of Chicago Press, 1992.

Schaeffer, Denise. "Nietzsche's Woman as Friend: The Paradox of Distance and Proximity." In *Nature, Woman, and the Art of Politics.* Ed. Eduardo A. Velasquez. Lanham, MD: Lexington Books, 2000.

Schaeffer, Denise and Mary P. Nichols. "Platonic Entanglements." *Polity* **35**, no. 3 (April, 2003): 459–77.

Schein, Seth L. "Alcibiades and the Politics of Misguided Love." *Theta Pi* **3** (1974): 158–67.

Scott, Gary Alan. *Plato's Socrates as Educator.* Albany: State University of New York Press, 2000.

"Irony and Inebriation in Plato's *Symposium*: The Disagreement between Socrates and Alcibiades over Truth-telling." *Journal of Neoplatonic Studies* **3**, no. 2 (Spring 1995): 25–60.

Scott, Gary Alan, and William A. Welton. "An Overlooked Motive in Alcibiades' *Symposium* Speech." *Interpretation* **24**, no. 1 (Fall 1996): 67–84.

Shorey, Paul. "The Alleged Fallacy in Plato's Lysis 220e." *Classical Philosophy* **25** (1930): 380–83.

Sinaiko, Herman L. *Love, Knowledge, and Discourse in Plato: Dialogue and Dialectic in Phaedrus, Republic, Parmenides.* Chicago: University of Chicago Press, 1965.

Stern, Paul. "The Philosophic Importance of Political life: On the Digression in Plato's *Theaetetus*." *American Political Science Review* **96**, no. 2 (June 2002): 275–89.

Socratic Rationalism and Political Philosophy. Albany: State University of New York Press, 1993.

Strauss, Leo. *Plato's Symposium.* Chicago: University of Chicago Press, 2001.

Natural Right and History. Chicago: University of Chicago Press, 1953.

Tejera, Victorino. *Plato's Dialogues One by One: A Dialogic Interpretation.* Lanham, MD: University Press of America, 1999.

Tessitore, Aristide. "Plato's *Lysis*: An Introduction to Philosophic Friendship." *The Southern Journal of Philosophy* **28**, no. 1 (1990): 115–32.

Thompson, W. H. *The Phaedrus of Plato, with English Notes and Dissertations*. London: Whittaker and Co., 1868.

Tindale, Christopher W. "Plato's *Lysis*: A Reconsideration." *Apeiron* **18** (1984): 102–09.

Umphrey, Stewart. "Eros and Thumos." *Interpretation* **10**, no. 2 and 3 (May and September 1982): 355–422.

Versenyi, Laszlo. "Plato's *Lysis*." *Phronesis* (1975) **18**: 185–98.

Vlastos, Gregory. "The Individual as Object of Love in Plato's Dialogues." In *Platonic Studies*. Princeton: Princeton University Press, 1973, 1–34.

Waterfield, Robin, "Introduction to the *Euthydemus*." In *Early Socratic Dialogues*, trans. Trevor J. Saunders, Iain Lane, Donald Watt, and Robin Waterfield. London: The Penguin Group, 1987.

White, F. C. "Love and the Individual in Plato's *Phaedrus*." *Classical Quarterly* **40** (1990): 396–406.

Zuckert, Catherine H. *Plato's Philosophers* (forthcoming University of Chicago Press, 2009).

    Postmodern Platos. University of Chicago Press, 1996.

Index

Achilles 38–39, 66, 79, 87
Admetus; *see* Alcestis
Aesop, 19
Agathon (*see also* Diotima; tragedy), 85n99
 as character in *Symposium*, 23, 34–35, 52–59, 63, 66, 73, 82–86, 208, 210, 212
 meaning of his name, 33–34
Alcestis, 38–39, 64, 66
Alcibiades (*see also* impiety), 27n4
 as character in *Symposium*, 23, 56–57, 61, 70–86, 98, 102, 103, 140, 184–185
 his relationship to Athens, 26–28, 66n64, 71, 84
 Pericles and, 135–136
 his relationship to Socrates, 4, 26, 28–30, 87, 184–185
alienation, 5, 154
 and modern thought, 1–2
 Socratic remedy for, 2–6, 24, 155, 190n51, 192, 197, 209–210, 213–215
Alcibiades I, 28, 71, 73, 74, 75, 77n86, 78
Alcibiades II, 28n5, 73n77
Anaxagoras, 134–136, 141, 198–200, 201, 202, 213
Anderson, Daniel E., 75n83, 76n84, 79n90
Anton, John, 70n70, 71n73

Apollo, 23, 74n78
 in Agathon's speech in *Symposium*, 55
 in Aristophanes' speech in *Symposium*, 51, 52
 in *Birth of Tragedy*, 16–18
 Socrates' hymn to, in *Phaedo*, 19, 20, 211
Apology, 31, 140–142, 201, 211
 arts and artisans in, 30, 60n53, 94
 as addressed by *Symposium*, 30–31, 32, 34, 44–47, 57, 69
 charges against Socrates in, 25, 27, 146
 human wisdom in, 146
 poets in, 31, 91
 Socrates' accessibility in, 75
Arieti, James, 91, 147n70
Aristophanes (*see also* Clouds; comedy; Diotima; *Frogs*)
 as accuser of Socrates, 20, 25, 85, 191
 as comic poet, 85–86, 149
 role of in *Symposium*, 23, 47–52, 70n69, 84–86, 111, 129n54, 154, 184–185, 191, 209–210, 212
 hiccups of, 44, 47–48, 50, 51
Aristotle (*see also* comedy; justice; tragedy) 3
 as critic of Plato, 155

art (*technē*) (*see also* dialectic; erotic art)
   Eryximachus' appeal to power of,
      44–47, 59–60
   limits of, in Aristophanes'
      Symposium speech, 48, 50, 59–60
Asclepius, 19, 22, 55

Bacchae, 17, 18, 70, 72, 149, 211
Bacon, Helen, 70n70, 71n73
beautiful, the (*see also* ideas) 32–33,
      120, 121, 150, 212
   as standard for speeches, 57,
      122–123, 124, 126, 127, 140,
      142, 148–149
   Agathon's appeal to, 53–54, 58
   in Aristophanes' *Symposium* speech,
      52, 84
   in Diotima's speech, 59–60, 63, 67–68
   in Eryximachus' *Symposium* speech,
      44,
   in palinode, 100, 107, 108, 111,
      113–114, 118, 138
   in Phaedrus's *Symposium* speech,
      37–39
   poets and, 16, 31, 105
   relation to the good, 64–65, 68, 94,
      161–162, 176–177, 210
   in setting of *Phaedrus*, 97
   Socrates on, 23, 24
Benardete, Seth, 27, 49n36, 50n38,
      56n47, 86n100, 97n14, 101n17,
      113n31, 165n20, 168n27,
      182n41, 184n44, 188n49
Berkowitz, Peter, 213n25
Bloom, Allan, 3, 25, 29, 30, 56, 29n9,
      37n24, 50n37, 53n44, 56n47,
      58n50, 64n57, 65n63, 68n65,
      76n85, 82n95, 84n98
Bolotin, David, 152n2, 153–154, 161,
      162n17, 163n18, 163n19, 165n21,
      166, 168n27, 168n28, 169n29,
      171n30, 172n31, 175, 176,
      178–179, 181n40, 184n44,
      185–186, 189n51, 190n52, 191n53
Boreas, 92, 96, 103, 142n65
Brann, Eva, 21n13, 195n1
Brown, Malcolm, 147n70

Burger, Ronna, 21, 22, 96n13,
      101n17, 107n23, 108n25, 113,
      137n62, 146n69, 147n70,
      148n72, 197n4, 197n5, 198,
      199n7, 203, 204n14, 206n18
Bury, R. G., 27n4, 33n16, 41n29,
      61n55, 62n56

Calypso, 130, 131, 139
Cebes (character in *Phaedo*), 20–22,
      196, 197, 205
cicadas, 89, 93, 97, 124–125, 130,
      131, 143, 214
Charmides, 150, 156n11, 157n13, 159,
      160, 162
choice (*see also* freedom), 94, 110,
      111, 172, 201
Christianity, 1n2, 204, 205
Cicero, 196
Climacus, Johannes (*see also*
      Kierkegaard), pseudonymous
      author of *Philosophical Fragments*,
      8–14
Clouds (*see also* Aristophanes)
   deities in, 26, 48
   as quoted in Plato, 79
   Socrates' disciples in, 50
   Socrates in, 33n14, 57, 79, 134
   Unjust Speech in, 54–55, 57
Cobb, William S., 91–92, 92n6,
      93n10, 147n70, 150n73
Codrus, 66–67, 69
collection (*sunagogē*) (*see* dialectic)
comedy (*see also* tragedy)
   Aristophanic, 52, 106
   Aristotle on, 51
   connection to tragedy, 23, 56–57,
      84–86, 149
conventions; *see* law(s)
Coulter, James, 147n70
Cropsey, Joseph, 106n21, 126n46,
      138n63, 142n65, 148n71
Cratylus, 128n51, 149

daemonic, the (*see also* Diotima)
      59–63, 75n81, 97, 159, 199, 208,
      210

Dannhauser, Werner, 8n5
Davis, Michael, 20n12, 78n89, 153n4, 188n50, 193n54, 197n5
deus ex machina, 209, 211
  Diotima as, 59
  Nietzsche's criticism of, 18, 56
De Vries, G. J., 147n70
dialectic (or conversation), 22, 70, 76–79, 172, 199, 201–202
  absence in palinode, 118
  meanings of, 131
  principles (dividing and collecting) of, 128–131, 198, 212
Dionysus (*see also* Alcibiades; *Bacchae*)
  in *Birth of Tragedy*, 16–18
  as character in *Frogs*, 34, 48n35
  as connected with Aristophanes, 36
  as judge of Socrates, 23, 34
Diotima (*see also deus ex machina*; divination; generation; moderation; parents; poetry)
  addressing Aristophanes, 64, 70, 184
  as responding to Aristophanes and Agathon, 60–61, 67–69, 84, 85, 143–144, 209–210, 211
divination (prophecy)
  Aristophanes' half-beings', 49
  art of, for Eryximachus, 45–46
  as between mortal and god, 59
  calling of Diotima, 59, 66, 210
  madness and, 91, 106
  Socrates', 104, 147–148, 177–178
division (*diairesis*) (*see* dialectic), of madness, 128
Dobbs, Darrell, 155n10
Dover, K. J., 35n20, 96n12

erotic art, 46, 47, 55, 120–121, 158–159
Empedocles, 45n31, 50n37
Eryximachus (*see* art)
Euripides (*see also Bacchae*; *Helen*), on love 35
Euthydemus, 73n77, 152n1, 156n11, 157n13
Euthyphro, 109, 171, 172, 184

faith (*see also* piety), Kierkegaard's view of, 1–3, 7–15, 17, 213–214
Ferrari, G. R. F., 96n13, 122n41, 125n45, 144n68
Forde, Steven, 29n7
freedom (*see also* choice) 1, 30, 99, 112, 136, 164, 188–189
Friedlander, Paul, 28n6, 35, 93n10, 112n29, 153n3, 162n17, 184n44, 186n45
friendship (*see also* philosophy; politics)
  in palinode, 116–118
  possession and, 167–168, 180
  its relation to love, 3, 5, 24, 87, 183–185
  in speeches in *Symposium*, 38, 45, 86–87
Frogs (*see also* Dionysus), 34n18, 48n35
Frutiger, Percival, 93n10

Gadamer, Hans-Georg, 189n51
Gagarin, Michael, 29n8
Gallop, David, 203n9, 206
Geier, Alfred, 33n14, 70n72, 83n96, 122, 125n45, 134n58, 153n3, 162n17, 186n48, 188n49
generation (*see also* politics) 36, 70n69, 123–124
  absence of in palinode, 121
  Agathon's view of, 58, 84
  Diotima's view of, 63–70, 81, 87, 95, 114n31, 146
  in *Phaedo*, 197–198, 205–206
  rhetoric and, 94, 95, 122, 145
Glidden, David K., 179n36
Gonzalez, Francisco, 153n4, 165n21, 184n43, 186n46, 186n48, 189n51
Gorgias, 28, 53, 76, 132, 135, 136, 137
Griswold, Charles, 88n102, 88n101, 92, 93n10, 96n13, 97n14, 101n17, 103n18, 106n21, 107n22, 108, 112–113, 117, 117n35, 117n36, 122, 125n45, 128n50, 129n53, 130n55, 137n62, 134n58, 138n63, 141
Guthrie, W. K. C., 153n3

Hackforth, R., 91, 92, 93, 96n12, 134n58, 138n63, 147n70
Hadon, James, 153n4, 186n47
Halperin, David M., 75n83
Hegelians, 8, 14, 16
Helen, 80n93, 104, 105
  Euripides' play about, 105n20
Hermes, 128
  mutilation of statues of, 27, 83–84
Hesiod, 41n29
  quoted on love, 35, 37, 51
Hestia, 108, 109
Hobbes, Thomas, 52
Hoerber, Robert G., 33n15, 188n49
Homer (*see also* Achilles; Calypso; Odysseus) 26, 41n29, 77n86, 79, 104, 105, 146
  quoted in Plato, 33–34, 34n17, 80, 130, 170–171
homosexuality, 65–66
Howland, Jacob, 4n9, 4n10, 7n5, 10n7, 11n9, 195n1

ideas, 5–6, 21n13, 29, 30, 112, 203–207
  in doctrine of recollection, 21, 94
imperialism, 30, 83, 86, 135–136, 141
impiety (*see also* piety)
  charged against Alcibiades, 27, 72
  Phaedrus', 37, 95, 96, 140
  in *Symposium*, 26–27
Ion, 77n86
irony, 74–75
Isocrates, 147–148

John the Silent (*see also* Kierkegaard), pseudonymous author of *Fear and Trembling*, 8
justice (*see also* virtue), 18, 135–136, 137, 140
  Aristotle on, 82
  in palinode, 108, 111, 113, 115

Kalkavage, Peter, 21n13, 195n1
Kass, Leon, 49n36
Kierkegaard (*see also* faith) 4
  influence on Western thought, 2
  on the poet, 15

  on relation between human and divine, 54, 59, 204
  similarities to Nietzsche, 2, 16, 18–19, 214
  on Socrates, 1, 3, 4n10, 7–15, 207–209
  on *Symposium*, 208
Klein, Jacob, 111n27

Laches, 80
Lamb, W. R. M., 39n26
Lawrence, Joseph P., 29n8, 77n86
law(s) (or conventions) (*see also* writing) 140–141, 202
  Pausanias' revision of, 40–43, 44, 48
Lebeck, Anne, 96n13, 116n33, 138n63, 143n66
logographic necessity (*see* writing)
love (*see also* friendship), despotic character of, 75–76, 102, 162, 190n51
Lovers, 156n11, 157n13
Ludwig, Paul W., 43n30, 45n31, 48n33, 50n37, 52n41, 60n54, 68n67, 184n44
Lutz, Mark J., 28n7, 29, 48n33, 50n37, 52n41, 62n56, 64n58, 65n63, 68n65, 75n80
Lysis, meaning of his name, 165, 168, 190

madness (*see also* division), 23, 91–92, 102, 130
  in contrast to art, 94, 106–107, 120
  lover's fear of reputation for, 114, 119
Marsyas 74, 149
matchmaking, 158, 172, 189
  Socrates', 159, 160
Menexenus, 68n66, 191
Menexenus, meaning of his name, 161, 168
Meno (*see also* recollection) 12–14
midwife, 10, 65, 213
  Socrates as, 9, 70n68
misology, 22, 196, 215

moderation (*see also* virtue), 149
  in Alcibiades' understanding of
    Socrates, 73, 74, 79–82
  Diotima on, 114
  love and, 91, 102, 103, 105–106
  in palinode, 108, 113, 114
Monoson, S. Sara, 35n20
Mooney, T. Brian, 153n4, 165n21,
    194n55
Muses, 124–125
myth, 19–20, 92–93
  palinode as, 106n21, 112n29

necessity, 171, 172n31, 188, 189,
    198–202
Neumann, Harry, 65n60, 68n65, 70n68
Newell, Waller R., 52n41, 65n63,
    68n65, 68n67
Nichols, James H., 90n1, 108n24
Nicholson, Graeme, 92n8, 93n10,
    100n15, 109n26, 131n56,
    138n63, 150n73
Nicias (in *Laches*), 80
Nietzsche, Friedrich (*see also*
    Zarathustra)
  influence on Western thought of, 2
  on Platonism, 205
  on Socrates, 1–2, 3, 7–8, 7n5,
    17–19, 149, 207–208
  on tragedy, 3, 15–19, 85n99,
    149, 211–212
Nussbaum, Martha, 27n4, 29, 52n42,
    58n51, 73n76, 92, 93n10, 96n12,
    97n14, 112–113, 117, 185

oaths of lovers, 40, 112–113,
    117–118, 185
Odysseus, 80n93, 130, 131, 139,
    170–172, 189, 213
Oedipus, 17, 49
oracle at Delphi, 31, 140, 172
Oreithyia (*see* Boreas)
Orpheus, 38

Pan (*see also* prayer), 128, 130
Pangle, Lorraine Smith, 153n4,
    181n40, 184n43, 186n47

paradox (*see also* Kierkegaard),
    10–11, 14, 19, 94, 112–113,
    117n36, 120, 158–159, 175, 205,
    213, 214
parents, 38, 58, 163–166, 169, 181,
    182, 185
  in Diotima's speech, 65, 69
  Love's, 36–37, 61–62, 65–66
Parmenides, 32n13, 126n48, 134n59,
    213
Parmenides, 59, 126–127
  in Plato's dialogue, 54, 127n49,
    205
Pausanias (*see* law(s); Pausanias'
    revision of; philosophy)
Pentheus, 17, 72
Pericles (*see also* Alcibiades), 76,
    134–136
Phaedo (*see also* generation;
    recollection), 5, 19–23, 24,
    32n13, 134n59, 135, 191n53,
    195–207, 212, 215
Pharmakeia, 142n65
philosophy (*see also* political
    philosophy; politics; wonder)
  and faith, 14, 19, 207–214
  and friendship, 1, 3, 5, 154–155,
    169–170, 179–180, 190, 191–192
  lying between ignorance and wisdom,
    62–63, 74, 140, 142–143, 146, 168,
    178, 208–210
  in palinode, 110, 115, 116,
    118–119, 121
  in Pausanias' *Symposium* speech, 41,
    42, 43, 63
  as understood by Alcibiades, 80–81
piety (*see also* faith; impiety), 207–215
  self-knowledge and, 88, 213
  Socrates', 24, 26, 30, 96–97,
    103–104, 208, 211
Plochmann, G. K., 28, 43n30, 50n37
poison (or drug, *pharmakon*), 130,
    142, 196, 201
poetry (*see also* comedy; tragedy)
  Agathon and, 54
  Diotima's discussion of, 64
political community; *see* politics

political philosophy (*see also* second
    sailing), 6, 24, 154, 196–197
politics ((*see also* law(s)) 2, 6, 94,
    141–142, 201–202, 205
    friendship as a model for, 1, 5, 24,
        190, 192, 194, 207
    generation and, 4, 24, 68–69
    philosophy and, 4, 28–30, 190–192,
        197, 200
poverty; *see* resource
prayer, 59, 88, 96
    to Love, 120–122
    to Pan, 23–24, 149–150, 200
Price, A. W., 58n51, 64n57, 153n3,
    184n44
probabilities in rhetoric, 140, 141
prophecy (*see* divination)
Protagoras, 28, 34n17, 35n20, 76,
    76n85, 135, 156n11

reason (*see* madness; paradox)
reciprocity, 3, 75, 87, 88, 116, 153n7,
    154–155, 168n27, 169, 177–182,
    185–190
recollection (*see also* ideas)
    in *Meno*, 12–13, 14, 118, 111n27
    in *Phaedo*, 20–21, 111n27
    in *Phaedrus*, 111–115, 118–119
    as presented by Kierkegaard, 8–9,
        11, 111–112, 212–213
Republic, 14, 35, 110, 156n11, 195n1, 211
    arts in, 158
    divided line in, 206
    gods in, 109
    unity in, 155
resource (and poverty) (*see also*
    generation), 4, 24, 30, 62, 84–85,
    115, 120, 133, 174, 196, 199, 212
Rhodes, James M., 117n36, 122,
    150n73, 153n4, 166n23, 176n35,
    184n43
Robinson, David B., 169n29
Robinson, Richard, 203n9
Rosen, Stanley, 36, 29n8, 34n17,
    37n23, 37n24, 39n27, 43n30,
    52n41, 53n44, 55n45, 56n47,
    58n50, 65n61, 70n69, 70n71,

    71n73, 75n80, 75n83, 76n85, 78,
    79n90, 80n92, 81n94, 84n98
Rowe, C. J., 91n5, 138n63, 147n70

Salem, Eric, 21n13, 195n1
Santas, Gerasimos, 91n3, 117n36
Saxonhouse, Arlene, 29n8, 48n33,
    52, 59n52, 65n59, 65n61,
    68n65
Schaeffer, Denise, 214n26
Schein, Seth L., 72, 76n84
Scott, Gary Alan, 28n7, 72n74,
    74n79, 75n83, 76, 153n4,
    165n21, 189n51
second sailing, 5, 202–207
self-knowledge (*see also* paradox; piety)
    in friendship, 174, 187–189
    in love, 94, 115, 119
self-motion
    in logographic necessity, 128
    soul as, 94, 107–113, 114, 116–117,
        137, 212
self-sufficiency, 173, 177, 189–190
    in Alcibiades' view of Socrates,
        81–82
    in doctrine of recollection, 69
    in early *Symposium* speeches, 39, 48,
        55–56, 57, 66, 99
    non-lover's, 94, 99
Silenus statues, 72, 73, 74, 75, 84
Shorey, Paul, 181n40
Silent, John the (*see also* Kierkegaard),
    pseudonymous author of *Fear
    and Trembling*, 8
Simmias (character in *Phaedo*), 20–22,
    196, 212
Sinaiko, Herman L., 104n19, 117n36,
    129n53
Sirens, 71, 77, 137
Socrates (*see* Kierkegaard on;
    matchmaking; midwife; Nietzsche
    on; piety)
Sophocles, on love, 35
soul (*see also* self-motion) 197, 198,
    199, 204, 207
    in early *Symposium* speeches, 51, 55
    immortality of, 107–108

soul-leading, rhetoric as, 125–126, 137–139, 141, 147–148
Statesman, 129n54, 141
Stern, Paul, 195n1, 197n4, 197n5, 201, 203, 203n9, 203n12, 204n14, 207
Strauss, Leo, 34n18, 37n24, 50n37, 50n38, 51n39, 52n41, 53n44, 68n67, 71n73, 75, 79n91, 84n98, 196

Tehera, Victorino, 48n34, 122n41, 135n60
teleology, 198–202
Tessitore, Aristide, 153n4, 165n21, 188n49
Theaetetus, 69n68, 195n1
Thompson, W. H., 134n58
Tindale, Christoper W., 194n55
Tisias, 140, 141
tragedy (*see also* Agathon; comedy; Nietzsche), 29n9, 56–57, 59, 132–133
  Aristotle on, 56, 104
  the beautiful and, 56
  non-lover and, 103
  Plato and, 92, 149, 192, 211–212
trust, 5, 107, 119, 123, 142, 170–171, 172, 213, 215
Typhon, 11, 15, 24, 96–97, 139, 149

Umphrey, Stewart, 153n5, 165n21, 181n40, 186n46

Versenyi, Laszlo, 153n3, 184n43
Vlastos, Gregory, 29n8, 82n95, 91, 117, 117n35, 166, 179, 181, 185, 188
virtue (*see also* justice; moderation), 186
  Alcibiades on Socrates', 79–82
  as aim of rhetoric, 136–137
  as fostered by lover, 103

knowledge and, 12–15, 18
in *Symposium* speeches on love, 39, 41–43, 44, 50, 54–55, 63, 66–67, 69

Waterfield, Robin, 126n48
Welton, William A., 29n7
White, F. C., 117n36
wonder, 5, 36–37, 47, 64, 77n86, 97, 104, 122, 198, 200, 210, 211
writing (*see also* generation), 101, 148n72
  Anaxagoras', 198–202
  criticisms of, 91, 132, 142–146
  laws as, 124, 141–142, 145, 146
  Lysias', 93, 100, 142n65, 143n66
  logographic necessity of, 90, 127–129, 131, 133, 144
  Plato's, 76n85, 86, 90–91, 143–149, 192–194
  Socrates' tale about, 93, 142–143, 145–146, 148
  standards of, 90–91, 95, 143–145, 148–149

  statesmen's views of, 121, 123–124
  on temple of Delphi, 87, 96, 142

Xanthippe, 196
Xenophon, 26

Zarathustra (*see also* Nietzsche), 2, 2n5, 15, 16, 213–214
Zeus, 26, 96, 104
  role in Aristophanes' speech, 49, 51, 52, 60, 67, 209
  role in early *Symposium* speeches, 41
  role in palinode, 108, 109–110, 115
Zuckert, Catherine H., 4n9, 152n1, 153n4, 155n9, 196n2, 203n121